Guinevere

Guinevere

The True Story of
One Woman's Quest for
Her Past Life Identity
and the Healing
of Her Eternal Soul

Laurel Phelan

POCKET BOOKS
New York   London   Toronto   Sydney   Tokyo   Singapore

POCKET BOOKS, a division of Simon & Schuster Inc.
1230 Avenue of the Americas, New York, NY 10020

Library of Congress Cataloging-in-Publication Data

Phelan, Laurel.
   Guinevere : the true story of one woman's quest for her past life
identity and the healing of her eternal soul / Laurel Phelan.
      p.   cm.
   ISBN: 0-671-52611-1
   1. Phelan, Laurel. 2. Reincarnation—Biography. 3. Guinevere,
Queen (Legendary character) I. Title.
BL520.P48A3   1996
133.9'01'3092—dc20
[B]   95-38899
                                                                                          CIP

First Pocket Books hardcover printing February 1996

10 9 8 7 6 5 4 3 2 1

POCKET and colophon are registered trademarks of
Simon & Schuster Inc.

Printed in the U.S.A.

This book is dedicated to the memory and spirit of my father, Joseph B. Phelan, whose wisdom and unconditional love inspired and encouraged me.

I would like to thank Leslie and Emily for making things so easy for me. I would also like to thank my higher self and my husband Colm Weldon for his encouragement and support.

Contents

Contents

Contents

Author's Note
on Death and Reincarnation

REINCARNATION IS A SUBJECT THAT HAS BEEN HOTLY DE-
bated for hundreds of years. I wish to share with you
my understanding of the subject.

I have been a past life regression therapist for ten years
and have focused intensely on teaching past life regression and reincarnation for seven years now throughout
western Canada and England. I have been privileged to
help over two thousand people who have come to me
with intense emotional and physical pain or doubt about
their lives. As I taught them about reincarnation and
helped them to experience their past lives, I have seen
them transformed into happy, fulfilled, and loving people.

Past life regression enables you to move through
your previous lives with ease. It also enables you to
move through the death experience and into what is
known as the astral realm or the Bardo state, as it is
more commonly referred to by therapists today.

Author's Note

The Bardo state is a Tibetan term that means life between life. It is a dimensional realm where we exist as energy after we have left our bodies and before we enter another one. When I take people through their death experiences in past life regression sessions, it always amazes me that no one believes they are dead. Why? Because there is no such thing as "dead."

Science has proven that humans are made up of energy. Science has also proven that you cannot destroy energy. Therefore science, in spite of itself, has proven that we do not "die." Our energy merely leaves our physical body or "house" and moves into another dimension, namely the astral plane or Bardo state.

Our energy begins to lift easily out of the body well before our actual death, and the process of lifting is one of lightness and peace, not struggle. The lifting-out process is often considered the crescendo or ultimate experience that one can feel. Contrary to belief, it is not to be feared but rather welcomed. When I take people through their death experiences they almost always comment on how beautiful and peaceful it is, not in the least uncomfortable. They also most often want to linger in the experience rather than rush through it, as though taking off a too-tight boot that has been hurting for a long time. In other words, leaving your body feels like freedom.

As we feel our energy move through the Bardo state we are able to receive immediate understanding that helps us to examine the life we have just lived. We suddenly understand why we chose it (Yes, I said, "chose!") and what we learned from the experience.

What actually happens is that the right hemisphere of the brain awakens as we move into regression, and we are able to access memory and information not only from our many lives, but also from in between our lives. We also gain universal understanding, as in why we exist in the first place. It is there, in the astral realm or Bardo state, that people have continually told me that they *chose* the previous life to learn specific things. For instance, anger or fear. They have also told me that everything in their lives is chosen by them for the sole purpose of evolving.

While in the Bardo state, our spirit chooses the coming life with great detail. First by choosing the parents it wishes to connect with, then the sex, lessons to learn, etc. What has been made clear to me as well is that, although the spirit chooses a basic blueprint before birth, it allows itself the choice once in the body about how best to learn the lesson. When we leave the body of the previous life and look back to examine it, we soon realize that every minute detail was created as part of the learning. Nothing is accidental.

What often happens, unfortunately, is that once inside the body, we inhabit the personality and the ego. We then begin a process of learning about fear and separateness and we forget that we chose the life to begin with, so we often begin a path of powerlessness.

Through past life regression and understanding reincarnation, we can consciously change our patterns of behavior from fear to trust because we remember that we are spirit, not personality. Although we have a basic blueprint, we can learn our lessons in positive ways rather than negative ways.

I have often asked people why they chose to be a part of the human circle of lives in the first place. The answer is almost always the same. To find love. It often does not seem to exist on our planet. But through the lessons of life we can find it, and our energy grows a little larger and a little larger still until finally we come to a point called Enlightenment. Enlightenment means we have come full circle. We have experienced everything our lovely planet can offer and have found only love. Then there is no longer a need to reincarnate again. All lessons have been learned. Then we return from whence we came. Light.

People often ask me about religion and why religion does not accept reincarnation. Well to be truthful, most religions do. Christianity, for one, did in the beginning. It is well documented in the ancient Indian Vedic Scriptures about the two years Jesus spent in India studying reincarnation. In the Gnostic Gospel the quote still remains of Jesus saying, "the soul spills from one into another of bodies." In fact, it was only in the sixth century that Christianity decided to erase all mention of reincarnation from its religious documents. The Emperor Justinian in Rome in 546 was responsible for this, as he felt that people who believed in reincarnation were freethinkers and could not be controlled with the concepts of heaven and hell. There also began the persecution of any and all people who spoke of or believed in it. Religion felt the need to control by the use of fear, and those people who understood reincarnation knew that fear was a concept of the ego, that the concept of hell was created by the religious minds.

While in the Bardo state you understand that fear is an illusion created by ego. When you are beyond the body you are also beyond personality and therefore, ego. So, you are beyond fear. What you realize is that there is only love waiting beyond the doorway.

There are many wonderful benefits to past life regression. The obvious ones are healing emotional scars or blocks that stop you from receiving all that you desire in your life. When an emotional problem is left unresolved in a previous life it will be carried forward to be healed in a future time. This is why suppressed emotions or problems that have no known basis often resurface in people's lives.

Often situations of anger or depression, to name but a few, can easily be resolved by looking into past lives and reexperiencing the original cause. Only then can the blocked emotions be released and the problem solved.

Some of the common problems often solved with regression therapy are: guilt, fear, depression, anger or rage, unworthiness, lack of creativity or prosperity, eating disorders, weight problems, and difficulties with relationships.

There is also no need to be afraid of regression therapy. It is simply an act of remembering, not reliving. If you are not ready to deal with a suppressed emotion, you will not go into that lifetime. Only when you are ready to heal does a previous life's memory surface.

I would like to explain briefly the technique I use for past life regression. A light self-hypnosis state is obtained through relaxation of the body and mind. The awareness then moves from left brain to right brain—being memory. While in right brain, you are no longer limited by time and can move to any lifetime or back through the present lifetime and reexperience vivid memories.

To uncover Guinevere, I had to regress fully into her body and mind. By doing this, I was able to feel her emotions and think her thoughts as well as see great details around me. The extra gift of past life regression is that you are not limited to staying in the body and can lift from the body to follow those around you for a small distance.

I wish to note here that you can only follow those in your life whom you have a spiritual connection with, and even then only for a short distance. It was by doing this that I was able to gain information about the other people in Guinevere's life and their attitudes about her.

In this book I have chosen to use the original Celtic/Briton pronunciation of names rather than the English. Thus you will read the name Gwynnefwar, rather than Guinevere, and Lancirus, rather than Lancelot.

Author's Message

It is important for society as a whole to learn about reincarnation so that our planet may evolve to peace. If you experience past life regressions, you will soon realize that you have been both sexes and many races and have experienced all religions, for you exist in hundreds of lives.

When you have experienced being another race, religion, or sex, then you can no longer hate or carry prejudice or judgment within you. When you no longer hate or judge others, then and only then, can you love everyone. Then our planet will no longer need boundaries. Then our world will truly be a blissful place. This is my deepest wish.

1

How It All Began

I AWOKE SUDDENLY IN THE MIDDLE OF THE NIGHT. WAS IT real or was it a dream? Shaking and cold, I sat up in bed and gathered my thoughts. I looked around me. I was in Vancouver, in my bed. So why did I feel so different, so strange? I couldn't put my finger on it, but I felt as though I were two people. Then it came back to me—the dream. I started to remember. I closed my eyes and began to focus. Where was I? The first thing I realized was that this was no ordinary dream.

I was standing against an old wooden wall in a room that led to a hallway. It was dawn, and a smell of smoke filled my nostrils. I felt tense, almost fearful, but somehow powerful! As I stood there motionless, I heard footsteps. My body tightened and I looked down to see a long dagger in my hand. My breathing grew faster and I tried to hold myself still. The footsteps came closer, then they were passing my doorway. As I looked into the hallway, I saw a large unkempt man bend down to tend to another man of similar size on the floor. The man on the floor was not moving. Rage burned in me, and I jumped onto the man bending down and in one quick maneuver, I stabbed him in the back fiercely. He threw me off, yelling in some strange dialect as he fell to the floor. I crashed against the wooden wall, the breath knocked out of me.

Gasping, I lay there and watched as the vile-looking man lashed out at my leg with a knife, even as blood poured from the wound in his back. Suddenly, his body went limp with death and I pulled myself to a standing position and leaned against the wall. My heart raced and I felt a strange sense of power and fulfillment. I looked down at him with disgust and turned quickly at the sound of footsteps and the voice of a woman calling, "Gwynnefwar." Then I woke up.

"Gwynnefwar. What kind of name is that?" I said aloud to no one. I opened my eyes and again looked around my room. My body temperature was changing from cold to hot and back to cold again. I thought to myself, Laurel, it was just a dream, go back to sleep.

I closed my eyes and lay back down in bed. I tried to laugh at myself for having a great imagination, but instead lay there for hours, unable to sleep, still remembering. I could not stop seeing the dagger and the blood coming out of that man's back. Most of all I could not forget the feeling of fulfillment I had at killing him.

I sat up again. What is wrong with me, I thought? How could I possibly enjoy stabbing someone? I had always been so proud of being calm and stable, the one everyone depended on. The one who rarely got angry or judged another person. I finally went back to sleep, and when I awoke the next day I had a good laugh at myself and went back to work as a bookkeeper-secretary in a Vancouver oil and gas exploration firm.

I spent the next few days trying very hard to focus on my work and on opera. Opera was my dream. Ever since I could remember, I wanted to be an opera singer, and now it was finally happening. I had already begun voice lessons and my teacher was thrilled with my voice. I had also begun a quest for a greater understanding of reincarnation and past life regression therapy. My doctor had recommended hypnosis a year earlier as a remedy for my insomnia. I began working with a well-respected Vancouver hypnotherapist who taught me the fundamentals of hypnosis and regression. It was through my experiences with her that I was able to heal my insomnia.

I went into a self-hypnosis state to uncover the root of my insomnia and quite unexpectedly, found myself in a previous life in Ireland in the 1800s. I was a woman named Catherine Graham. In that life, I had watched my father die by burning to death in a fire that I had started. The pain I felt was overwhelming, and I realized that my father in that life was also my father in my present life.

When I came out of the regression, I came to understand how that lifetime in Ireland had been affecting my present life as Laurel. Since I was a small child I had always tried to protect my present father from fire. I would stay awake all night and tiptoe around his bed and pull all of the electrical plugs out of the wall. I would also trace my fingers around him to make sure there were no cigarettes left burning beside him.

This ritual went on for approximately fifteen years until my father passed away. After the regression, I realized that I had been protecting him from fire because I felt guilty that I had caused his death by burning in a past life in Ireland.

The night after that regression I slept for a full eight hours for the first time in my memory. Immediately thereafter, I realized that regression therapy was the most powerful healing tool that I had ever come across and began to research and read every book I could find on the subject.

A few days after my first dream of Gwynnefwar, I awoke again in the middle of the night, having just had the same frightening but exhilarating dream. Over the next weeks I experienced a number of similar dreams. I was in the body of a woman named Gwynnefwar. I decided enough was enough and felt it was time to try and regress myself and see what my subconscious memory would uncover.

I proceeded to use self-hypnosis and found myself again in the same scene as the first dream, but this time it was even more real. Everything was vivid. My senses were alert and I absorbed all the details around me. I was in an ancient fortification made of wood. My clothes were made of a rough linenlike fabric. The light was faint, coming from bronze pots filled with oil that hung from ceiling beams and stood on pedestals. As I moved through the same scene of myself using a dagger to kill a large, bearded man in the back, I again felt wonderfully powerful and fulfilled. I continued on. A woman dressed in drab-colored robes came running toward me calling, "Gwynnefwar, are you hurt?" I looked at her and answered, "No." I continued on and found myself interacting with various people. They mentioned the name Arthur to me. That name stirred something in me and I came out of the regression.

Arthur, Gwynnefwar—could it be, I thought to myself! No, it was just a coincidence. The Arthur and Guinevere that I had heard of lived in a castle where the men wore armor while the women wore beautiful clothes and jewelry. The Guinevere I had heard of was gentle and lovely.

I realized then that I needed to make a decision in my life. This woman I was remembering, Gwynnefwar, was someone I did not want to know more about. I was trying very hard to begin a path of meditation, peace, and transcending the ego. When I was in the body of Gwynnefwar I felt egotistical, angry, and completely self-absorbed.

After the regression, I started to feel nauseated and decided it was because I loathed people like Gwynnefwar. I found it very distasteful to think that I could have at one time been as she was. So I decided to forget about her and focus on my music and my meditation.

Five years went by. I was twenty-seven and the dreams began again. Dreams of myself stabbing men and watching a woman being beheaded in front of me. By this time I was quite involved with the technique of past life regression. It had become an important part of my life's work, although I spent most of my time regressing other people into past lives rather than exploring my own.

I felt my job was to help others understand their current problems by finding the root of them, often in a previous life. Since my own life was very fulfilling, I saw no reason to delve into the past. Nonetheless, I did experience a few of my own lifetimes over the years, one as a Minoan healer, one as a scribe in Europe, as well as many rather boring lives. I never looked at Gwynnefwar until the dreams began again.

The recurrence of these dreams was a sign to me that it was time to explore Gwynnefwar in more detail. I had a secure understanding of reincarnation and I wasn't concerned any longer that Gwynnefwar would pull me off of my path as a peaceful, gentle woman. I regressed again.

I found myself standing in a room, again in an old fort. There was a large, carved bed in front of me. Women were bustling around me excitedly, playing with my hair and my clothes. I felt nervous. As I looked down I saw a lovely cream and gold-colored dress, gold armlets on my arms and sandals on my feet. It was my wedding day, but I was not happy.

I realized very quickly that I hated being dressed in women's clothes, they felt uncomfortable and silly. I felt powerless. Suddenly a man came in the room; he was my father. A surge of love swept through me. Part of me wanted to throw my arms around him but a greater part of me wanted to make him proud of my strength. He looked at me with love in his eyes. Then he knelt before me. I was shocked. My father was kneeling before me and honoring me. I felt split inside, part of me was thrilled and my ego soared. I felt a rush of energy through me, as though I were a great leader, but the other part of me felt sad and I realized that I wanted to be daddy's little girl again. I was tormented but suddenly I was being ushered outside and helped onto a lovely little cart strewn with wildflowers. There were ladies walking ahead of me and two men pulling my cart. I was drawn through a large crowd of people. I was nervous. Then my cart came to a stop and I got out and stood beside a man. He was very tall with dark curly hair and beard and beautiful blue eyes. He looked at me with such love it almost overwhelmed me.

I felt myself try to hold my body tight, to remain rigid. I wouldn't allow myself to express that love in return. I turned and looked at an old man in front of us. He was dressed in religious garb like a bishop. He called me Gwynnefwar, he called Arthur, Arturius—the latin name for Arthur—duke of the Britons.

I then moved forward in time and found myself at my death. I started to sob uncontrollably, my body wrenching. I felt overwhelmed with love and pain all at once. Then I began to lift upward and peace consumed me. I was floating and looking down at my body. I opened my eyes and lay there stunned.

As I gathered myself together, a surge of sadness overtook me and I cried for a long time. Again I felt nauseated. From my years of understanding past life regression, I realized then that it had been important for me to reexperience my emotions in that life in order to balance the present. The nausea was a release of old emotions.

The next two weeks for me were difficult. A part of me felt very close to Gwynnefwar, whereas another part of me wanted to disown her. I felt weak and ill. Then it faded and I went back to work.

Life was changing dramatically for me. More and more people were coming to me for past life regressions and more and more I was realizing that a life of opera was not for me. I was not competitive enough to be a professional singer, and each day my desire moved toward spirituality and peace.

I became a full-time regression therapist by the age of twenty-eight and began teaching it as well. I also began teaching about creativity through awakening our inner power. Life was a joy and again Gwynnefwar became a part of my past.

Then in 1991, I was at a dinner party where I met a producer named Terence Hayes. As usual in my life, the topic turned to past lives. He asked me if I had been anyone famous. I said, "Yes, Guinevere." He laughed and said, "Sure, and I was Napoleon." Then he realized I was serious.

He asked me about her and I told him what little I knew. He asked me if I would consider writing a screenplay about her, and I told him that I had never written anything in my life, so I doubted that I could. He persisted and I decided to give it a try as I thought it might help me to purge her.

I realized that to write a screenplay I would have to regress through Gwynnefwar's life from birth to death. I was a little reluctant and put it off for six months. Terence called me again and encouraged me to delve into her. After much deliberation I felt that I was ready to fully understand this powerful woman who I was resisting so much.

I brought my tape recorder to my side and lay down on my couch. The next two days I regressed into Gwynnefwar for six hours. This is her life story.

I am going to relate events exactly as I experienced them in the regressions. All of the information in this book has been received solely through my past life regressions. I decided before writing this story not to read any books or information on Guinevere and Arthur, as I did not want it to influence my own experience in any way.

I still refuse to read any other material, as I feel it is not the truth but rather passed-on information that has become distorted and greatly embellished over the centuries.

2

❈

In the Beginning

THE YEAR IS A.D. 482, DARK AGE BRITAIN. THE ROMANS have left seventy years ago to return to their own land. They left behind their descendants, a powerful society committed to defending their land against the onslaught of invaders.

Tribes have begun to form throughout the land. Celtic tribes in the mid-North and Briton tribes of Roman descent in the middle and southern parts of Britain form alliances and together try to build a new society out of the Roman ruins, a society based on farming and communal living.

Celtic chiefs rule over their own lands and tribes. Their lives are filled with music, art, and a pagan lifestyle of worshipping the gods and goddesses of the earth and spirit. The Celts are very close-knit and passionate with a lust for pleasure and a pride in the land, which they feel is their mother. They spend their days farming and defending their lands as best they can while their evenings are spent in feasting and music making.

Their flowery Celtic language of symbols and their pagan beliefs are slowly being smothered by the southern Roman/Briton Christian influence. Although they often clash in their behavior and lifestyles, the Celts and Britons set aside their differences for the sole purpose of defending the Island.

The Briton Army in the south that has been watching over and protecting Britain since the exit of the Romans does the best it can, but the army is dwindling. Hungry Anglo-Saxon, Scot, and Pict invaders vie for this affluent land.

The Saxons and Angles from the eastern countries have entered Britain and begun the move westward, destroying communities and farms along the way. The Picts from the far north of the Island move south with precision along the eastern shore and inch their way into mideastern Britain.

What the invaders have underestimated is the determination and passion the Celts and Britons have for their land and their way of life.

3

⚜

The Birth

IN A LUSH GREEN VALLEY WITH ROLLING HILLS IN Northumbria, Britain, a heavy fog obscures the early morning. The fog clears and I notice a large timber fortification with outside walls rising to an impressive ten feet. I float through the main walls of the fort and notice a single wooden building rising from the center of a courtyard. All around this main building, small buildings of wood spew smoke out of holes in their straw roofs. A few people mill about their wooden huts, busy with their morning work of carrying food and wood to various other buildings. A few sheep and dogs wander around freely, searching for food.

I float into one of the larger timber buildings and find a room filled with simple but comfortable furnishings. Large wooden chairs softened with stuffed straw cushions have been handcrafted by the village women, and simplistic but sturdy square tables make up the rest of the room. There is little natural light in the room, a single window lets in more dampness than illumination. A large hanging bronze bowl filled with oil and lighted wicks lights up the room, as does a glowing fire in a crude stone hearth.

I notice a man, Lord Penryth, chieftain of this northern Celtic tribe, standing in front of the burning fire and rubbing his hand through his thick coarse beard. He is a tall, burly man of thirty-seven with long dark reddish hair and a ruddy complexion that spells of too much drink. Clad in a long brown leather and cloth tunic and breeches with leather boots laced up the side, he turns and walks absentmindedly to a table in the center of the room filled with bowls of half-eaten flat bread and fruit.

A worried look comes over his face. The look turns to fear as he hears a woman's scream. He races from the room and down a small damp corridor to the doorway of another room. I float behind him, aware of a strange pulling sensation coupled with excitement. Lord Penryth is stopped by a tiny, elderly woman clothed in layers of long tan-colored woollen robes who pushes her hand against his chest roughly.

"No . . . go back to your room. You are not needed here," she says firmly, not wanting a man in the room.

I find myself pulled inside the small room to find a fire glowing in one corner. In another corner sits a graceful young girl of ten, Merewyn. She wears long dark brown robes and has unruly brown hair. She focuses intently on the astrological charts on the table as her mother, a heavyset woman of forty, shows her how to chart the stars.

A wise woman and healer, Merewyn's mother is a gifted psychic who creates healing potions from the plants that grow around the fort. She emits an aura of all-knowing, as though she is here simply to help those who are ignorant find their way. She teaches her young daughter everything she knows, and many people in the village say Merewyn has the gift as well. I notice the table has a small bronze pyramid on it, which Merewyn tenderly caresses.

I find myself hovering in the center of the room, suddenly transfixed by the scene happening beneath me.

On a small bed lies a woman in pain. A lovely young woman with flaxen hair and delicate features, she seems almost out of place here. Iryanne, Lord Penryth's wife, writhes and moans as she begins to give birth to her first child. A strange feeling overwhelms me. I feel pulled toward this woman and suddenly find myself inside of her womb being pushed out. Her body feels weak, and I sense that it is not safe here, almost as though she wants to die.

Suddenly, I feel a great need to be born, to leave this woman. I feel uncomfortable inside her, as though I am not welcome. I don't feel loved by her. That man, Lord Penryth, he is who I want to be with.

Confused and powerless as Iryanne prepares to give birth, Lord Penryth tries to see what is going on, but is blocked by the old woman at the door. He sulks a moment and finally turns from her and wanders back to his room. He pulls a chair in front of the fire and waits.

Inside Iryanne's room, more screams erupt as I find myself moving in and out of her body, reluctant to connect fully with my own tiny body.

As Merewyn sits at her table with her mother calculating the exact placement of the planets, Iryanne screams out yet again.

The two other women in the room, a midwife and helper, hover about Iryanne, wiping her face with cool cloths and trying to ease her discomfort. Iryanne is pale and tired as she breathes hard and cries out, then shakes her head from side to side as the woman beside her strokes her face with a cloth. I decide to float back to Lord Penryth's room and notice him sitting with his head in his hands.

His right-hand man, Derwyn, a bearded, disheveled man of thirty, enters the room breathlessly, carrying a rolled-up map. He too is dressed in a brown tunic and breeches with tall boots. Over his shoulder is slung a long woollen cloak, which gives him warmth on a cold day like today. Derwyn speaks anxiously and holds out the map to Lord Penryth, but Lord Penryth ignores him.

"My lord, I have word," says Derwyn. "Many Picts come from the north along the river Lindinis. A boat has been seen. I have prepared a plan of attack, my lord," he says, then pauses and stares at Lord Penryth, hoping to get his attention.

"Will you look at it?" he continues.

Lord Penryth waves his hand and motions for Derwyn to leave. His mind is heavy with concern for his wife and unborn child.

"Not now ... it will wait. Do not disturb me with matters of battle now," he grumbles.

Derwyn frowns and presses on. "But, my lord, we must prepare ..."

Lord Penryth turns and stares at Derwyn impatiently. His eyes fill with annoyance and his breath becomes heavy.

"Later ... My wife gives birth to my first child. Return later ... ," he says, then pauses a moment and continues. "We will speak then of strategy."

Derwyn sighs in frustration, knowing that the Picts are moving closer all the time, endangering their very existence. War is at their doorstep and they must wait for a child to be born. He turns and leaves, determined to return soon.

Back inside Iryanne's room, the women busy themselves with the preparations for birth. Excitement and worry fill everyone as Iryanne becomes weaker and weaker. The midwife walks toward the fire, carrying a dish filled with liquid and herbs. She rests it on some embers for a moment then picks it up with a cloth and carries it over to the bed. She dips her hand into the bowl, then places it on Iryanne's stomach. She gently rubs the oil into Iryanne's skin and also onto her upper lip under her nose. Sighing softly, Iryanne inhales the oil deeply and begins to relax a little.

The midwife then moves toward Merewyn's mother, and the two check the astrological charts together. Iryanne cries out in pain again and the midwife rushes back to her and places her hands down between Iryanne's legs.

"The time is now, the child comes," she calls to the other women.

One woman climbs onto the bed and lifts Iryanne's body to a sitting position as she begins to bear down. I am suddenly pulled fully inside this tiny body. It's so dark and tight, I want out. Mother pushes hard then relaxes as the midwife begins to pull me from her womb. The women whisper words of encouragement and with one final push from Iryanne, I burst into the world, aware only of the sudden cold.

The midwife holds me in her hands, then lifts me high in the air and presents me to everyone. They all gather around, cooing at how tiny I am. I feel free and safe now in this woman's arms. Iryanne, weak and tired, strains to see me.

"She does not weep. Is she well?" she whispers.

The midwife looks at me and then back to Iryanne and smiles broadly. "She is well. Fear not."

I am then carried over to a table where there is an herb burning like incense. She lifts me through the smoke and I cough a little, then high in the air and calls out, "Spirit of wisdom, come, bless this child. Mother of our Earth, keep her safe."

She carries me over to Merewyn's mother, who is diligently gathering all her papers together. They smile at each other, proud of the role they played in my birth.

"There will be great power in this child," she says with confidence.

Wrapping me in blankets, the midwife places me in a basket and takes me to the bedside of my mother. Iryanne looks at me tenderly, then smiles weakly and closes her eyes to sleep. I feel strange somehow, as though I am not acknowledged. An emptiness worms its way through me.

Everything seems to move so quickly as I am whisked away in the arms of the midwife and down a cold hallway into a wonderfully warm room. Lord Penryth, tending to the fire, turns quickly as we enter the room. Excited, he comes over to us and looks tenderly down at me. His face fills with love as I am given to him. He looks up at the midwife with awe. She smiles knowingly at him, realizing that words cannot express this moment fully.

"Lord, I give you your daughter," she says softly.

He takes me over to a chair by the fire and sits with me in his lap. The midwife turns and walks quietly to the door, not wanting to disturb the moment. She leaves the room knowing that she has left me in good hands.

Father looks at me with so much love in his eyes it seems as though he will burst with joy. He ever so gently touches my tiny fingers with his, and we spend the first moments of my life together, touching and sharing, expressing pure love. His eyes fill with tears as he gently strokes my cheeks. I feel safe and loved. He is my protector, my savior, and I know I will always worship him and he will worship me. He whispers softly to me as he rocks me in his arms.

"My little girl . . . I will always protect you," he says and looks at me as though he is searching for something, then he smiles.

"Gwynnefwar . . . yes, that is your name," he says and looks tenderly at me. "It means powerful and wise one. I will raise you as I would raise a son. As a leader. To be strong and wise."

He holds me close to him and hums in a low soothing tone as I drift off to sleep, knowing he is watching me, guarding me.

4

※

Arthur

IN THE SOUTH OF BRITAIN LIE THE PLAINS OF SALISBURY IN Wessex, a beautiful sweep of rolling hills and swampy grasslands dotted with rivers and creeks. At the center of the plains there rises out of the ground an extraordinary hill. As though placed there to watch over the earth, it rises above the mist even on the foggiest night. Situated upon this vast expanse of land is Salisbury Fort.

It is a huge fort that is home to about three hundred people. It was built by a Briton/Roman duke by the name of Ambrosius Aurelianus. He is a magnificent tall man and a leader of the Briton Army. Well respected throughout Britain, he commands the largest mounted army in the land. He keeps a constant connection with Rome, trying to convince them to invest more men and equipment into the Briton fight against the invaders.

As a father to Arthur, he finds himself lacking in

many respects. Unable to give his son much time, he calls upon his friend and counselor, Merlin, to befriend Arthur and spend time with him as teacher and counselor.

Merlin is a tall, thin, and bearded man of thirty-six. Reserved and thoughtful, he spends most of his time analyzing Latin scrolls and writings of philosophy from early Christian civilizations. He feels more like a father to Arthur than a counselor.

A sunny fall day fills the air with crispness as Merlin stands by a wooden fence and watches two young riders racing ponies across an open field. He is contemplating the purpose of life.

Arthur, a tall six-year-old with dark wavy hair and bright blue eyes rides briskly through the many bushes and trees, relishing the wind in his face and the exhilaration of the pony beneath him. The ground is firm and the pony races with ease as Arthur skillfully maneuvers him around some trees and back toward Merlin.

Morgana, a gangly girl of twelve with straight light brown hair, tries to catch up to him. A skilled rider herself, she finds it frustrating that Arthur doesn't pay her much attention. She wants to show off for him but finds it difficult to keep up. A troubled and lonely child, Morgana focuses all of her days on pleasing Arthur.

Arthur's father accepted her into the family as an illegitimate child of his wife's but never gave her the love or attention of a real father. Arthur and Morgana's mother died in childbirth when Arthur was two, and since that time Morgana has taken it upon herself to be both mother and sister to him.

As Arthur turns his pony and rides toward Merlin, Morgana follows. Excited, Arthur comes to an abrupt halt in front of Merlin and yells, "Merlin! Did you see me! I won again!"

Merlin smiles, full of pride, and Morgana comes to a stop beside Arthur and dismounts. Arthur continues talking excitedly as he looks around for his father, wanting to impress him with his skill on the pony.

"Merlin, where is Father? Did he not come?"

Merlin shakes his head and takes hold of Arthur's horse. "No, Arthur. Your father was called to Rome this morning. He will be gone for a while."

Arthur sulks a little in obvious disappointment. "Again. He promised to show me how to jump today."

He pats his pony absently, trying not to show his sadness. Morgana comes quickly around and joins the two of them, taking the rope from Merlin's hands and smiling.

"I will show you, Arthur. I know how to jump ponies."

Arthur looks bored, his mind full of thoughts of his father. Although he understands that his father must often go to Rome and Gaul, it doesn't make his absence any easier. Merlin, sensing Arthur's disappointment, tries to change the subject.

"I have news for you, Arthur."

With hope in his eyes, Arthur's face lights up. "From Father?"

"No. From the village seer." He pauses a moment to think. "A girl child was born this day who will bear importance to your future."

Morgana freezes for a moment then turns to Merlin with glaring eyes, and Arthur's face squints at the thought of what little importance this could be to him.

"A girl? I have not time for girls! They are foolish and they do not like to fight!"

Morgana looks down a little, almost blushing as she listens, her body filling with emotion for this stepbrother who has no time for her. Meanwhile, Merlin smiles to himself, enjoying Arthur's desire to be like his father. Nonetheless, he chides him a little.

"Someday, Arthur, you will change your mind."

Arthur, unable to see any importance in girls and unwilling to stay and discuss it further, takes his rope from Morgana and starts to ride away.

Morgana looks up at Merlin with purpose. "Will this girl try to steal Arthur from me, Merlin?"

Merlin laughs a little at her childishness. "From you? Arthur is your half-brother, Morgana. He is not yours."

Suddenly feeling lost, Morgana can hardly breathe. "But I have always taken care of him. I promised Mother I would."

Merlin smiles and shakes his head, not really knowing what to say to her. Morgana, confused and upset, turns and watches Arthur as he rides faster and faster through the trees, his face intense as he burns off some of his disappointment. He races his pony down into the valley and toward a creek near the side of the fort as Merlin watches him with a careful eye.

Sitting by the creek in the glaring afternoon sun is a young lad of ten clad in a heavy green tunic and breeches with metal shoulder pieces and skirt attached to it in the Roman style. He is quite large for his age. He sits whittling away at a stick with his long knife as Arthur, seeing him in the distance, dismounts from his pony and sneaks up behind his friend.

Gulwain, fascinated with his knife, holds it up in the sun and turning it slightly, watches how its reflection lights up various rocks in the creek. Very quietly Arthur creeps up behind him and in one swift movement, jumps out at Gulwain and yells, "Ahhhhhhhh!"

Startled, Gulwain jumps up with lightning speed and turns, his body poised for a fight and his hand holding his knife tightly. Laughing, Arthur falls to the ground.

"Did I frighten you, my friend?"

Annoyed, but a little relieved, Gulwain breathes easier and sits down beside Arthur.

"You did not. I was hoping for a battle today."

They both look at each other seriously for a moment, then laugh at themselves. Although both Gulwain and Arthur spend much time being taught by their elders to fight in battle, they would much rather it stay in the form of play.

The two sit quietly by the creek, pondering their lives, not needing to speak but understanding each other anyway. Gulwain has taken on the role of big brother to Arthur. As a large boy, he enjoys a reputation in the community for strength as well as quick-wittedness, but Arthur, although younger, is the smarter of the two. They toss stones into the creek and speak idly, passing the time.

"What of your father, did you see him this day?" asks Gulwain.

"I did not. He has returned to Rome to ask for aid against the heathen invaders."

Gulwain nods in understanding. "So you will wait to jump your pony until he returns."

"If I must." He pauses and thinks a moment, throwing a stone into the glittering water, then asks hopefully, "Will *you* teach me Gulwain?"

Gulwain looks out at the creek and squints his eyes in the afternoon sun. "What of Merlin, will he not be angry?"

"He need not know, I will not tell him," Arthur replies with hope in his voice.

Gulwain stands up abruptly and salutes with exaggerated formality.

"Aye, my lord, it is my duty. I shall obey." He laughs excitedly and Arthur jumps up, ready to go.

"Let us go then. We have a duty to our people. If I am someday to lead our army, I must certainly learn to jump my horse."

Arthur races to grab his pony as Gulwain follows close behind.

5

The Learning Years

BACK IN NORTHUMBRIA, YEARS HAVE PASSED. I AM SIX NOW and a spirited girl with long, dark red curly hair and bright green eyes.

I am riding with Father through the nearby villages on this cold wintry day. I wave at everyone we pass and feel proud and excited to be with Father on his great big black horse. I love the way the wind whips my hair around my face and the warm safety of Father's arms around me.

As we pass through a busy village filled with women and children running about performing their daily chores of gathering and selling food and wares, I notice some of the women shaking their heads in disapproval at Father for taking me riding with him. Father tells me that the women have chided him for treating me like a boy and that he had better remember that I am a girl and start dressing me in female clothes rather than boys' tunics and boots.

We soon stop at a vendor's shop where Father notices some spears for sale. He calls out to the vendor and asks him if he has any smaller ones. The vendor soon comes out with a short spear of close to three feet, and my eyes light up with excitement. I look up at Father and he laughs as he sees my expression.

"Yes, my little one, you may have it," he says with a grin.

He pays for the miniature spear with a tiny metal brooch that he took from an enemy in battle and soon we are off to the fields near our fort for an afternoon of mock battle exercises. I love these days with Father. He shows me how to hold the spear and throw it with precision into a nearby tree. Of course I miss, but with much practice I am sure to master it soon.

After our exercises, Father lays out a lunch of meat and flat bread for us and tells me wonderful stories of Celtic life. One of my favorite stories is of a very fat Celtic woman who was stronger than any man in her village and all were afraid of her. Another is about our ancestors, who were great musicians. They used to sing to the enemy until they fell into a deep sleep, then they would steal their weapons.

We ride back into the fort in the early evening and find that the dinner feast is ready and everyone is preparing to eat. Afterward, many of us sing together and dance around the great fires that burn through most of the night. I sit close to Father and beg him to tell me stories as he whittles away at small pieces of wood and carves me beautiful treasures that I promise to keep forever.

Often before I go to my little straw bed to sleep, Father combs my messy hair for me. Mother wants to cut it, but Father says I should keep it long, as it is wild and strong and a sign of power. Sometimes he lets me comb his hair too, but I find it hard, as his hair is so thick.

Mother is watching us this night as Father combs my hair. She rarely sits with us, as Father is usually joined by other ladies who live in the fort. I often forget that she is my mother as I notice Father kissing and tickling two other ladies more than he does Mother. I also notice that Mother does not like to play much and Father certainly does.

He once told me that when he first found her abandoned in our land that she was the fairest woman he had ever seen and that he loved her immediately. But he soon found that their differences were far too great for them to stay happy for long. She came from a land across the northern sea where they did not have any horses, so she never learned to ride. She was taught that women were to be quiet and gentle unlike the boisterous and sexual women of our Celtic community.

He often tells me that he does not want me to grow up being quiet and shy but rather powerful and strong, like a Celtic goddess.

The years pass quickly in our community and soon I am ten. Inside the fort in the middle of a winter afternoon, Father's large room fills with the glowing warmth of the sun. Through the two small but long windows, the crisp winter air beckons me. I long to spend my days outside, riding and cavorting with Father and learning to fight like a soldier.

Many of the girls in the village laugh at me behind my back, but I do not care. They are childish and soft. They could never protect themselves in case of attack. One day I will show them and they will be glad that I have learned of battle so well.

Mother is ill again. I rarely see her, as she spends

most of her days lying in bed or sewing with her lady friends. It is not a wonder that she is ill, for she never goes outside in the crisp winter air. She wants me to come and sit with her and learn to sew, but I refuse. Sewing is for gentle ladies, not for a warrior.

My father is a warrior—and a great leader. Everyone in the village says so. I am proud to be his daughter. All of the men in the village want to be his friend.

As the day passes I join Father outside for our daily mock battle. Dressed in my tan-colored boy's tunic made of heavy wool and leather and my tall boots, I look like any youth in our village and am proud that I do.

Amid the leafless trees, Father stands behind me and shows me how to hold my dagger. I am very proud of my dagger. It is one foot long and a little heavy for me, but I am determined to manage it. Father moves in front of me and with a large, long piece of wood he swoops around in circles, showing me how to move the blade. I imitate him with great enthusiasm, spinning and thrusting my dagger at his piece of wood. Most of the time he knocks the dagger out of my hand, but I am determined to continue. After a while he falls on the ground in pretend tiredness and I jump on top of him, trying to beat at his chest with my tiny fists.

I squeal with delight as Father rolls onto all fours and lets me ride on his back. I grab at his hair and pull hard and he shakes his head quickly from side to side as I try in vain to hold on.

The afternoon passes quickly and dusk falls around us. Sad that the day must end, I mope a little, but Father reassures me that we will practice again tomorrow. For now we must return and eat.

Back at the fort, we enter the eating hall. Mother is there today with many of her friends, and the air becomes tense as Father sits down and I find my place between the two of them.

Meals are a communal event in our village, and I sit beside Father at our large table in the new eating hall. The hall is large and comfortable, with a long tall table that I barely can see over and benches all around. Father sometimes allows me to sit on his lap, but not tonight because Mother is here. I think she is angry that he spends so much time teaching me about battles and allowing me to wear boy's clothes.

As we sit at the table, Derwyn keeps speaking of the northern Picts and their vile ways. He tells of torture and rape. Strangely, I notice Mother becoming upset by these tales, probably because she is so frail and does not like talk of blood and battle. I love it. Father always tells me of his battles and how many men he has slain. Often when Mother is in one of her fragile moods at eating time, I pretend she is not there and devour my food or stab at it as though it were the enemy. This makes her even more upset, and she often leaves the table as she is doing now.

After she leaves with her friends, Father hoists me onto his lap and allows me to drink some local ale with him. I even have my own special bronze cup, which I keep hidden in the kitchen. Almost a hundred people live in our fort, and we have four servants who take care of our house. The cook, a young woman who Father likes to pinch and kiss; a washerwoman, who comes each day but lives outside the fort; a man, Olar, who cares for the wood and heat in the house; and Gwelynne, who spends most of her time taking care of Mother. I enjoy following Olar around the house, as he is always singing songs of our people and their struggle against invaders.

At the end of the day I go to sleep in my little room,

close to Father's, which is filled with objects I have collected from outside, rocks and metal and bones that old warriors have left behind. Father often brings me jewelry and brooches from the enemies' clothes. I keep them on a small table by my bed. They are my treasures.

Over the last five years I have spent much of my time studying battle strategy and some Latin with my Druid teacher. He says the Latin is important, as many of the southern Britons still speak a rough form of it.

It is too cold this day to spend out of doors, so I am sitting in Father's room at his table, diligently creating a plan for an attack on the Picts in the north.

My teacher is a middle-aged thin man of thirty who is gentle and wise. He is part of an ancient tribe of men called Druids who spend much time writing and teaching the ancient secrets of the earth from hundreds of years ago. He comes to be with me every few days in the winter to teach me. I give him my parchment paper and wait quietly as he inspects it. Proud of myself, I sit tall and patient but find it difficult to watch him inspect my work.

"Is it good, sir?"

Thinking carefully, unmoved by my impatience, he finally looks at me with a smile. "It is, my lady."

From the doorway of the room, Father looks in and surprises us.

"Of course it is good. She is a smart child."

Excited, I jump upon my chair and passionately shout, "I am not a child, I am a WARRIOR!"

I raise my hand in the air defiantly as Father comes up behind me and rubs my head with his gigantic hand. I try to grab at his hair but he pulls away too quickly and laughs, then tells me to be quiet so the Druid can continue.

"Peaceful warrior, Gwynnefwar. One should always use power to keep peace in the world," the Druid says patiently.

Not quite understanding his meaning, I question him. "But what of battle?"

Father watches by the door as the Druid continues to explain.

"The warrior may engage in battle only when necessary. To protect his people and lands. The true warrior does not fight for revenge or to prove his might."

Startling us all, an excited Derwyn rushes into the room and walks to Father. "The Picts come, we have seen them on the river. I have given word to the men, they wait for us now," he says anxiously.

Father turns and walks calmly toward me and looks at the Druid. "Take Gwynnefwar and the other women quickly, to the underground caves," he says and then looks at me with a serious face. "You will be safe there. I must leave you for a time and fight the northerners," he says and winks at me as he caresses my cheek.

He turns and quickly leaves the room with Derwyn close behind. I feel both nervous and excited. The Druid takes my arm and beckons me to follow.

"Come, Gwynnefwar, we must go!"

We rush quickly outside and the Druid grabs a large bone horn that hangs at the main door of Father's house. He blows it once, and within moments women and children come running toward us. The Druid quickly tells them that we must go to the underground dwelling. The women look frightened but act with speed, running back to their huts and gathering food and blankets. A few of the remaining men gather pots and oil for fuel and warmth. My mother and Gwelynne look nervous and upset.

A few minutes later we all walk quickly out of the fort and down a hill toward a large grove of trees. Through the trees toward a big hill we continue until we come to a cavelike opening. We move inside with precision and down into the depth of this hillside. It is dark and damp, but this is much more fun than doing battle strategy. As we move deeper through a tunnel it opens to a large earthen room. It is already filled with crates and straw to lie on. Soon the lights of our oil pots fill the room with warmth and smoke and the people begin to make themselves comfortable for the long wait ahead, settling in corners and talking quietly amongst themselves.

Iryanne moves about nervously and Gwelynne helps her settle, as she seems weak. Merewyn, now a plain-looking woman of twenty, stands quietly in a corner of the room, holding a small pyramid in her hand, her eyes closed. She is alone now, as her mother died a few years ago.

I watch excitedly from the center of the room, having great difficulty remaining still, my heart wanting to be with Father rather than trapped underground with a bunch of weak women. I decide to walk over to Mother and speak firmly.

"I want to go with Father, please let me go?"

Mother looks at me in horror, as if I had stabbed her. "My dear child, your father has gone to battle, to protect us. He will be back soon. You need not be afraid."

Disgusted at her calling me afraid, I stand back, putting my hands on my hips and raising my face a little to show my strength.

"I am *not* afraid!" I say defiantly.

I turn and walk away from her, hurt at her words.

She knows nothing of who I am. She calls to me as the women watch carefully. "Come sit with me, Gwynnefwar."

I turn and look at her, my nose in the air to show my contempt. "I am busy," I say, trying to remain firm in my lack of need for her.

Mother looks distressed and turns to see a lady bringing her some flat bread. Annoyed at her weakness, I walk to my Druid teacher and look up to him, speaking loudly so everyone hears me.

"I hate all northerners! One day I will kill them all!"

Suddenly, I am grabbed by an old woman and turned quickly around to see her face fill with shock and anger.

"Quiet, child," she says curtly.

She turns to Mother and notices her embarrassment as the whole room becomes quiet and watchful. I look at Mother too and bite my lip a little, realizing I have said something terribly wrong. She lifts her hand toward me, motioning for me to come closer.

"Come here, daughter," she says softly.

I obey and she takes my hand and pulls me close. I look down at her white, frail hands and she begins to speak softly to me as everyone listens.

"One day, Gwynnefwar, I hope there will be peace between your father's people and my people. Do not hate, Gwynnefwar. It only causes pain."

Suddenly someone says, "Quiet," and we all become still, awaiting further sounds.

Footsteps inch their way closer, as though someone were making their way through the tunnel, and we all hold our breaths in anticipation and fear. We are braced for the worst and everyone waits anxiously as the footsteps grow increasingly louder. I look around and notice Merewyn in the corner rubbing her pyramid calmly with an odd lack of concern. I wonder if she knows something that we do not.

I continue to look around at the terrified faces until I come to Mother's and notice her eyes wide with apprehension as she brings her hand to her throat, as though protecting it. I look up at the Druid for guidance, but he motions for me to be still.

Everyone is frozen as time seems to pass ever so slowly. A woman gasps as the door bursts open and we see Father, his face grinning with excitement. My breathing relaxes and I notice him holding something red and bloody in his hand. The whole room sighs in relief and the people turn to one another as Father yells loudly, "We are victorious! We have driven the Picts back to their own lands! Where is my Gwynnefwar!"

I push through the people and run joyfully into Father's arms as he bends down and pulls me close to him. Then letting me free, he holds out his hand to me and shows me a bloody heart. Iryanne gasps and turns away as do others while I look at it with growing curiosity.

"This is the heart of the enemy. I give this to you to honor you. This is a gift of power. Hold it now," he says.

He puts the heart in my hands. My eyes widen with excitement and my pulse pounds as I hold the warm heart.

"Can you feel it—the power?" Father says hopefully.

I look at it carefully, then back to him as a mounting feeling of pride races through my body. This is the enemy's heart in my hands. I find it difficult to speak.

"Yes . . . I feel it," I say very quietly as my whole being fills with a sense of awe.

"You are becoming a leader just like me," he says with pride.

With those words I feel like I will burst with joy and I peer into his eyes. "Can I be, Father! Can I be just like you?" I beg.

He laughs. "Yes, my little one, yes. I will teach you the way of the warrior so you need never fear."

I take a deep breath and try to show my strength to him. "I will make you proud of me, Father. I promise," I whisper, my pulse still pounding.

Father then lifts me up around the hips and carries me outside and back to the fort as the women and children follow us.

Dusk is falling, and once inside the courtyard the people become exuberant with victory. Father walks to the center of the crowd of people, still holding me in his arms, as excitement overwhelms me. He calls out loudly to everyone, "PEOPLE, YOUR SILENCE! . . . Men, we are victorious!"

The people cheer excitedly as I continue to hold the bloody heart.

"Men, kneel and raise your swords!" Father orders.

The men kneel, raise their swords, and the whole crowd becomes silent as Father speaks with gentleness.

"I proclaim this battle in honor of Gwynnefwar, my daughter and your future leader!"

I look around at all the people and lift the heart up high in the air, feeling excited and triumphant as the people cheer. I smile brilliantly as I experience my first taste of power, with everyone looking at me. This is where I belong. Father looks up at me with pride for a long moment then turns back to the crowd.

"Now is a time for feasting and dancing!" he yells. "To the hall then!"

Everyone cheers wildly and we begin to rush into the main meeting hall attached to our house. Father leads the way, still carrying me high in his arms. As we enter the hall, women and young boys begin quickly running about grabbing cups and jars to fill them with ale. We lead the way to the head of the table and Father puts me down in the seat beside his. I place the bloody heart on the table in front of me and a woman quickly brings me a bowl to wash my hands. As I clean myself, the hall begins to fill up with laughter and enthusiasm. Everyone begins to drink and musicians fill the air with lilting flute playing. I drink down my cup of ale and enjoy the sensations that it sends through my head and body as Father sits beside me and watches with pride.

Later that evening, I take the heart to my room and sit in front of it, replaying the day's events over and over in my mind. The most important one is when Father honored me with the battle, telling his people that I was their future leader. My heart beats a little faster as I remember the feeling that ran through me. I gather a bunch of my rocks from the corner of my room and bury the heart within them. This corner is slowly to become my altar of power. On it I will place those things that represent power and strength. As I look at it, I close my eyes and feel my body become tall and straight. The wind outside blows against the shutters and I pray to the spirits of power.

"Earth Goddess, be with me. Goddess of Wind be with me. Help me to be strong and wise. Help me to be powerful like Father."

I crawl onto my bed and lie awake staring for hours, pondering my role in the universe.

6

❁

Arthur's Power Begins

AT SALISBURY FORT, ARTHUR'S FATHER, HEAVY NOW AND
with lines burned deep into his forehead, sits writing
in a vast room filled with maps and tables. With an
elegant round bronze oil bowl lit beside him on a ped-
estal, he squints to read his words. A knock on the door
is followed by the entrance of Arthur, now sixteen. Tall
and strong, he stands with an air of might about him.
He pauses a moment, feeling unsure of his welcome,
then walks to his father.

"You sent for me, Father?" he asks firmly.

The duke looks up with concern on his face. "Yes,
yes ... Come sit with me."

He motions for Arthur to take a chair near him, and
Arthur sits down. The duke rises and walks around the
room as he talks while Arthur watches in silence, unsure of how to act in his father's presence.

"Arthur, I must return again to Rome on the next

ship," he says, then pauses a moment to think before he continues.

"My army grows small . . . I need more men to defend this land. I have hopes that the Romans will see the wisdom in giving me soldiers to keep the heathen invaders back."

Arthur listens intently, as though knowing what is about to come.

"Arthur, we as Britons may be few, but we are mighty. We have the only soldiers on horse in the land." He pauses and looks out of the window a moment as Arthur waits. He then turns and looks directly at his son.

"It is a dangerous journey that I begin, Arthur. I must travel through Scot territory in the southwest and I will be gone a long while. I am giving you command of my army and lands until my return."

Arthur's eyes widen with shock, and he stands, not anticipating this honor. His father walks over to him and places his hand on Arthur's shoulder.

"I trust in you, my son."

Elated and surprised, Arthur breathes deeply and kneels in front of his father.

"I will make you proud, Father."

"I know you will, my son. You are a leader as I. I tell you now that it will be a difficult time for you. The Saxons move quickly. We have had a long peace, but no longer," he says, looking around thoughtfully a moment, then tenderly to Arthur.

"I have not been a great father for you, my son, duty has interfered with that, but what I have given to you is my Christian blood. That is strong, I am sure. The many people of this land are not learned in our ways. We must teach them as we know best. The Saxons and Picts are heathens. They must not be allowed to rip the souls out of our people and land. Rely on our Lady—the Holy Mother. She is our savior."

He turns and walks toward a wooden trunk in the corner of the room. Opening it, he takes out an embroidered red tunic. He looks at it a moment, then takes it over to Arthur and hands it to him. Arthur takes it and stares at the embroidery as his father explains.

"They are the images of our Holy Mother and the mighty eagle. They will guide you in your journeys through life. Carry them with you in your heart and soul and you will be safe."

Arthur holds the tunic gently in his hands and looks at his father with love. For the first time they stare at each other a moment without words but with complete understanding. "I will carry on the teachings, Father. I will continue to bring this land together, as you have. The invaders will not take it," he says, then turns and leaves the room and walks to his own room down the long timber hallway.

He sits in his small room alone and stares at this red tunic emblazoned with the golden images of the Virgin Mary and eagle and his heart fills with a great pride in his father and his quest for a united island.

Taking off his old tunic quickly, he then puts the red one on and stands in front of a large polished metal mirror that stands against the wall. Gently, he fingers the embroidery as he stares at himself. He is suffused with a sense of duty as he lingers there for a long while, knowing his life is about to change. The boy is gone and the man is awakening.

7

Gwynnefwar, The Warrior

TREE LEAVES RUSTLE GENTLY IN THE WIND AND A RAVEN FLIES
about as spring fills the air in Northumbria and the
morning sun awakens all in the land.

Standing silently behind a tree and brandishing a
long dagger and a brightly painted round wooden
shield, I wait with anticipation. With a surge of energy,
I yell as I burst out from behind the tree.

"AHHHHHHH!!!"

I lunge forward as Father appears in front of me, also
holding a shield and a large stick of wood. He beckons
me to lunge at him, and I do. I am fourteen now and
more adept at using my dagger. We begin a mock battle
amongst the trees. Father knocks the blade out of my
hand a few times, but I am undaunted and try again.

After an hour of constant struggle, a new energy
surges in me and I spin quickly around and with one
fierce blow I knock the stick of wood out of Father's

hands. Surprised, he stops and looks at me with pride. I stand tall and slip my dagger into the bronze ring on my waist belt and smile confidently. I have finally proven my skill at battle, and Father comes toward me and slaps me on the back roughly.

"You are ready, my Gwynnefwar. I have taught you well. Let us ride now."

We make our way back to our horses and I pull myself onto my small brown horse's back with ease, aware that Father is watching me carefully. Taking hold of the leather ropes, I ride swiftly away with Father fast on my heels. We ride down to the nearby creek and across it toward a large plateau, enjoying the exhilaration and freshness of the wind in our faces.

Once upon the plateau, Father beckons me to race him, and I nod in agreement. He gives me a head start as my horse is much smaller than his, and I burst ahead with speed, hunching myself low over the front of the horse and holding my knees tight against its sides and back. My breath quickens and my body begins to sweat and my pulse race. I long to go faster and faster, to push myself to the limit as I become one with my horse. Together we are unbeatable as we race across the countryside, the wind whipping at my hair.

Never looking behind me, I continue onward when I hear Father's horse close behind to my left. I quickly turn right to throw him off and ride downward toward a clump of trees. Once there, I jump off my horse and sit against a tree as Father joins me, laughing at my cunning. He dismounts as well and we sit for a moment as the horses rest and we catch our breath.

After a while of blissful silence, he looks up at the sky as dusk begins to fall and points to the first few visible stars.

"There is much power in the stars. Someday you will

learn more of them and the lines of energy in the earth."

"What lines?" I ask with curiosity.

"Lines of energy, they join throughout the lands of earth and awaken our inner selves. It is an ancient power. Your Druid teacher will tell you more if you ask him. Now we must return as night falls."

We ride back to the fort with a new bond between us. For the first time, I feel that I am truly ready to be a leader, to be acknowledged by my peers in battle.

Back at the fort, I leave Father to go to the communal washing area to clean myself. It is a small building with large vats of steaming water hovering over fires that are kept going all day.

It is busy today, many of the younger girls are here washing and talking together. They spend so much time talking and playing with their clothes and hair. I find it difficult to understand them. Can't they see the excitement in riding horses and fighting? I feel sad for them, they miss so much. As I begin to wash at a tub I overhear some of the girls giggling and talking about me. One of them speaks loudly.

"Have you been playing Battle again, Gwynnefwar?" she says laughingly.

I stop washing and find myself becoming irritated at the tone in her voice. "Battle is not play, someday you will be glad that I am strong and skilled in warfare," I retort sharply.

"We have men enough for that," the girl answers back.

I notice all of the girls staring at me, becoming quiet as they watch. "So what is your great purpose in life?" I ask cleverly.

"To love and give birth," the girl smiles dreamily.

I laugh at the silliness of these girls, then notice some

bugs along the ground and answer her swiftly. "Insects do it better!" I say, then pause as I notice I have everyone's attention, some of them giggling now at my answer.

"I have a greater purpose like my father. You will see. I will rule this land someday with Lord Penryth. You may continue with your silliness while I speak with the men," I say with satisfaction.

I turn and walk out of the room, partially annoyed with myself for allowing them to arouse my anger. As I leave, the girls gather closely and talk about me.

"She was birthed into the wrong body," says one.

"I feel sad for her. She never feels anything. She only thinks and fights," says another.

I walk toward my room to change but stop when I hear Mother moaning in her room. I carefully peek in, not wanting to be noticed, and see her lying in bed as smoke permeates the stale air. Her wooden shutters never seem to be open. Her healer, Gwelynne, sits beside her, bathing her face with a cloth.

Why is she always ill, I wonder, has she no strength at all? If she arose and walked outside sometimes she might get stronger. I find I have no pity for her. It is almost as though she wants to be ill, she gets more attention that way. I feel embarrassed that I am her daughter. I wish I could forget her.

Suddenly, from another building, I hear screams from a woman giving birth. My body shivers and fury builds in me at the thought of the illness all around me. I run toward the eating hall and bump into Merewyn on the way. I look intently at her for an answer.

"Merewyn, are women always in pain?" I ask.

She laughs softly and touches my hand.

"No, my dear lady, no. It may seem so, sometimes,

but there is much joy as well," she says with a gentle smile.

Doubting her words, I continue on into the hall, my thoughts racing as I notice all around me there are women and babies. I gather a large plate of meat and bread from the kitchen and settle myself at a table to eat, all the while noticing drooling babies and children all about. Why are there so many suddenly? I have never noticed them before. As I watch a mother breast-feeding her child nearby, I find my appetite disappearing. I rise and return to my room and again ponder why I seem to be so different from other girls.

I spend the next morning planning a battle strategy in Father's room. Daylight filters through the windows and casts a haunting shadow across the table of papers. The Druid inspects my last piece of work as I continue to plan, my mind wandering to the memory of knocking the wood out of Father's hand. Bringing me back to the present, the Druid reaches across the table and takes my paper. He looks at the drawing then puts it down on the table again, pointing at it.

"You see, Gwynnefwar, the Saxons come from here and here. The Picts and Scots from here. The Britons, your father, and the other chieftains and high kings hold this wall here to the south, so we must find a way to push the Saxons back to the eastern sea and hold the Picts from here," he says.

He draws some lines and x's to show me the advancement of the various tribes and enemies and what land they hold as I watch with great interest. The maps are forever changing as even the Celt/Britons sometimes fight amongst themselves for land. No one seems to trust anyone.

He sits back in his chair as I go back to work and wonder why I must continue to sit in this room while other boys go with their fathers on scouting trips. Then, almost as though he read my mind, he speaks.

"Any man can fight in battle, Gwynnefwar. You have a greater skill, to plan that battle. To plan for peace. You have a wise mind, do not waste it on thoughts of blood and victory."

I remember Father's words of the stars and question my teacher.

"Father spoke to me of the stars. Will you teach me more?"

He nods and searches a moment on a side table for some maps. Bringing them over to me he lays them out. They are covered with unusual lines that cross the page. He also brings out another sheet of paper, but this one is covered with unusual charts and drawings. He points to the charts.

"Our Earth moves around the universe like this," he said, pointing to the chart. "It is pushed and pulled by magnetic forces that you cannot feel. There are many such planets as ours and stars that you see in the skies. They all affect our Earth."

He moves to the map with the curious lines. "These lines show magnetic energy under the land that is pulled by the stars and planets of our universe. When they cross each other as they do here"—he points to a spot very near our fort—"then a great power lies within the ground. It is wise to sit there, and the great power will awaken the same power inside of you."

Strangely overwhelmed by all of this new information, I find myself drifting through the rest of the day, questioning the purpose of life and trying to understand what this power is that my teacher and Father speak of. I know only of physical and mental power, not of this inner power. Does Father have it? Do I? Confused, I decide to go for a walk along the riverbed, my mind wanting only to understand how to regain the wealth and prosperity of this land and to rejoin the many tribes and build the stone cities that I have heard were here in the old times of the Romans. This is true power is it not? To lead and build.

I walk for a long while, glad for some peace, then stop as I notice Merewyn, barelegged and wading through the shallow part of the river. Fascinated, I sit behind a tree and watch her. Clothed in a simple green linen robe with her thick brown hair tied back with a leather string, I realize that she isn't like the others. She doesn't care for beauty or flirting as the other women do and she spends most of her time alone, yet she seems happy. Actually, she rarely talks to anyone except the spirits.

As I watch her gentle movements and the loving way she plays with the water, I begin to feel closer to her. Like me, she is different. Many of the ladies in the community fear her, for she has the gift of inner sight and she knows much about plants and spirits. I often hear people whispering about her, but I never question them for I am glad they aren't whispering about me.

Suddenly, she begins to sing, her voice high and lovely, then just as suddenly she stops and turns to look right at me through the trees and my breath becomes quick. How did she know I was here? My face begins to redden and I decide to walk out of the trees and say hello. She smiles at seeing me.

"Gwynnefwar, I am glad you have come. It is time."

"Time, for what?" I ask with reluctance.

"For us to become friends," she says as she walks toward me.

Gathering up her thin leather sandals, she beckons me to a blanket she has laid on the sand. Intrigued, I join her, and she begins to speak in her gentle and knowing tone.

"We are much alike. I know about you. I see you in my thoughts and my dreams," she says as her voice seems to float on the very air itself, as though not of this world.

Hearing this, I feel somehow comforted rather than invaded. I continue to listen to her lovely voice and find myself enchanted by her.

"You will be a powerful woman one day, Gwynnefwar. I would be honored to help you."

"How?" I ask.

"I understand your struggle with your body and with the women of the village. Your body is changing and so will your choices. I do not judge you. I only wish to help you have ease in your life."

Somehow her gentle wisdom makes me feel warm. I trust her even though I hardly know her. I know she was there at my birth and that she watches me often. I want to know more about her.

"How do you come to have these gifts, Merewyn?"

"The spirits have blessed me with them. I am one with the universe. My mother was a seer and healer as I am. She too was at your birth."

Realizing that she is reading my thoughts, I feel as though I don't need to speak. She smiles and I smile, then we turn and stare at the river, allowing ourselves to become lost in the flow of water. A fish jumps about, searching for its dinner and I smile at the simplicity of its life.

"I have dreams of you and a man," she says, piercing the silence and surprising me.

"A man, who?"

"I know him not. But he is gentle and kind. A large man with powerful hands and black curly hair. In the dreams he is longing to love you and help you."

"Love me!" I reply in disgust. "I have no time for such things."

"You will," she says, quite sure of herself. "Not for a while. It is in your future."

"Is he a warrior?" I ask hopefully.

"A great soldier," she replies. Then stretching, she rises and says it is time to return.

Disturbed by her words, I spend the walk back deep in thought about this man. How could he help me? Who is he? When will he come?

A few months pass and I awaken with a sickness in my belly. I decide to stay in bed for the day but then am horrified to see blood on the bedclothes. I jump from my bed and rip at my clothes, trying to find my wound, when I realize the blood comes from inside my body and down my legs.

"I bleed from inside!" I cry aloud.

Gaining my composure, I breathe deep as I realize the blood comes slowly and the pain is inside. I must have been wounded in my sleep. Someone must have come into my room. I quickly pull a long tan wool robe about me and run to Merewyn's hut, where I open her door without knocking and find her busy preparing a pot of food over her fire.

"Help me, Merewyn, my body bleeds! I have been wounded!" I plead.

Surprised at my words, she quickly comes to me. "Where, where are you wounded?" she says as she looks hurriedly over my body.

"Inside my belly, my body bleeds from inside here!" I point to my womanhood.

She stands back and smiles gently at me, then sighs with relief as I stand there confused and worried. I have never bled so much before. Surely, I must be dying from inside.

"You are not wounded, Gwynnefwar. Come, sit here," she shows me a stool.

She then moves to a trunk in the corner of her room and takes out some rolled-up linen cloths. Bringing them to me she instructs me to stand. I obey and she ties the rolled-up cloths under my legs and hooks them into a smooth leather strap that she ties around my waist. She then motions for me to sit again as she pours two cups of herb brew for us to drink. Calmed by her ministrations, I relax a little and listen to her words.

"Gwynnefwar, when a girl becomes a woman, she begins to bleed each cycle of the moon," she says and points to her own body and spends the next while teaching me about my menstrual cycle. Fascinated and repelled, I listen until I am unable to contain myself.

"I will have this for the rest of my life?" I ask in terror, and she nods her head.

"It is a gift of fertility from the Goddess of the Moon. The blood that comes from your body is filled with the goodness to nourish a child. The old women of our past used the blood of the body to nourish the crops." She pauses and realizes she must think of something to say that will appeal to me. "It is a power that is awakening in you."

"A power?" I ask with excitement but still feel bothered by it all. How can I go to battle if I must think of this blood?

"How long will it last? Will I have it every day?" I ask nervously.

"No. For six nights. Then it will stop until the moon moves full cycle again." She gives me more cloths and promises to help me if I have further questions.

I leave her hut and walk back toward my room. I notice a woman nearby holding a baby, and an odd tingling sensation arises in my breasts. What is happening to me? My life has most certainly changed.

8

※

Arthur,
Duke of the Britons

IN SALISBURY FORT, ARTHUR STANDS IN A GREAT TIMBER hall with a tall vaulted ceiling. It is large enough to hold hundreds of people, with beautiful hanging tapestries of the Holy Mother Mary and the Christian cross hanging on the wall behind three long carved wooden tables with benches and chairs all around. The room is decorated with swords and shields hanging on the walls, and tall pedestals with great bronze oil bowls sit throughout the room as well as oil bowls that hang from the ceiling beams. A giant stone fire pit sits in the center of the hall, and many soldiers, clad in their best brightly colored green and gold uniforms, stand about in silence.

News has come that Arthur's father was killed by the enemy upon reaching Gaul, and Arthur is about to be sworn in as the new duke.

Arthur stands rigid at the head of the room beneath the tapestries with a cold, empty look on his face and dressed in the red embroidered tunic his father gave to him. A tall man dressed in a fine green and gold tunic places over Arthur's head a large gold medallion, then reaches for a sword from another man.

"Lord Arthur, duke of Britain. Do you swear to uphold the duties of military leader of the army of Britain?"

"I do swear," Arthur replies with no emotion. He takes the sword in his two hands and holds it facing upward in front of his body as he turns and kneels in front of the tapestry of the Virgin Mary. The soldiers then kneel and raise their swords and yell in unison, "ARTHUR!!"

They all rise and the soldiers begin to jostle for the privilege of congratulating Arthur. Arthur, feeling numb, turns to see his best friend, Gulwain, beside him. A large, gruff man now of twenty-four, Gulwain pats Arthur lightly on the back.

"You have thoughts of your dead father?" he asks softly, so as not to be overheard.

"Yes . . . I did not wish to take his place so soon," Arthur replies with his voice near cracking with emotion.

Arthur and Gulwain look around and watch the crowd, both of them feeling detached as the people try to celebrate the coronation of their new duke. Gulwain tries to comfort Arthur.

"He was a great man. The people will miss him. It is a difficult time, Arthur. The heathens invade this country. There is no time any longer for games and fun."

"No, you are right, my friend. I must think now of Salisbury, now that I am leader of our army." He turns to Gulwain and speaks gently. "I count on you, my friend, to be by my side."

"That I am honored to be, *my lord*," he says with a little sarcasm.

They laugh together at the serious title and Gulwain continues. "It will take some time for me to call you that."

They laugh again and try to lighten their mood. Looking around they see women coming in to join the soldiers. Gulwain glances at Arthur and Arthur nods.

"Let us laugh with our women. We are not in battle yet," he says with a wink of his eye to Gulwain.

They move toward the center of the room and join some young women. Arthur, now twenty, finds many women attracted to him and eager to gain his attention. He and Gulwain fill their glasses with ale and enjoy the evening as best they can when another of their friends, Lancirus, joins them.

A quiet young man two years older than Arthur, Lancirus finds himself torn between fighting and writing. A gifted poet, he spends much of his time writing in solitude and speaking with Merlin of poetry.

Lancirus usually does not enjoy festivities, but tonight he is drawn to the women and drink. His curly, bright red hair and beard are irresistible to flirtatious fingers. As he laughs at Gulwain's Saxon jokes, though, he finds himself wanting more in life than this.

They all drink themselves into a stupor and each wakes up in the arms of a village woman. They gather together in the great hall in the late morning, their hangovers preventing them from enjoying their food, and share stories of the women they bedded. All except Lancirus, who keeps his words for his writing.

Gulwain, the most boisterous, brags of his lovemaking feats as Arthur and Lancirus laugh, knowing he was too drunk to be of much use to any woman.

51

9

❧

Time to Grow Up

IT IS TWO YEARS LATER IN NORTHUMBRIA AND A FIRE BURNS in the stone hearth in the corner of Iryanne's room. The room is dark and the air heavy with the aroma of burning herbs and oils. Iryanne lies on her bed, weak and very ill, her hair wet about her forehead. Gwelynne lifts her head and helps her drink some hot liquid.

"Come, my lady, try to drink a little," she pleads softly.

Iryanne moans as she struggles to drink. It is hard for her to swallow, so Gwelynne places her head back down.

Standing just outside of Mother's room, I am tense and cold. Mother has called for me. I know she is ill but I detest being in a room full of sickness and death. I am sixteen now and have an intensity in my presence that causes the other young women in the village and fort to avoid me. I open the door and stand just inside the doorway. Mother looks at me and smiles weakly. She hasn't seen me in a long while.

"Gwynnefwar!" she calls to me then turns to Gwelynne. "Leave us."

Gwelynne backs away and whispers to her, "Yes, I will be near."

I stand pensively by the door as Gwelynne comes to me and ushers me toward my mother. "Go to your mother, Gwynnefwar, she wishes to speak with you."

She then walks out of the room past me. Mother holds out her hand and I walk to her. She takes my hand and pulls at me to sit beside her. My mind is screaming at me to leave. I feel no closeness to this woman who struggles to speak to me.

"Sit with me . . . my beautiful daughter. I see you so little. You are so lovely. Why do you hide your body in that brown tunic? You are slim and beautiful and you should show your beauty," she says, fingering my clothes.

My body tightens with annoyance at her frivolity. All she cares about is beauty. She knows nothing of my skills.

"Your father has taught you well. You hide your feelings like a man."

Angry that she should speak of Father in an unpleasant tone, I long to pull away and avoid looking at her, but instead, I focus my attention on the wall.

"The end of my days is near. I wish you to remember always that part of you is northern," she says, trying to get my attention.

I wince at the very thought of any northern blood in my body and pull my hand away, as though to go, but she grabs it and pulls me back.

"Listen to me! I want you to remember me. To remember where I come from." She pauses a moment, then continues in a whispering voice, barely audible, "Your father has raised you to be a boy. You are very strong and very wise, but soon you will be a woman, and I will not be there to teach you of the joys and mysteries of womanhood," she says, wincing in pain and catching her breath.

Confusion begins to seep into me. I know she is dying before my eyes, yet I am trying very hard to hide this strange emotion that is rising in my body. I begin to tremble slightly as she continues to speak.

"Remember always, Gwynnefwar, you are a woman ... never forget. I know you wish to be like your father. I know I have not shown you how to be a woman, but there are many women here who wish to be your friend, do not push them away."

I pretend that I am bored and tap my foot on the floor, trying hard to detach myself from her.

"Let them help you. Let them teach you." She sighs in pain, her speech weakening. "Know that I love you."

She closes her eyes as I focus on tapping my foot. She draws her last breath and dies while I look at her in confusion and alarm. I touch her carefully, unsure of how to react or what to do.

"Mother ... Mother?"

I back away, and her hand drops on the bed. I look at her as anger creeps into me.

"I do not need you," I say aloud, wanting her to hear me.

I straighten my back and my body begins to ache with a feeling of sickness and pain. No, I say to myself. I am strong. I care not for her. She means nothing to me. She was weak. I walk quickly from the room and slam the door behind me. I lean against it for a moment as my body screams with emotion. I breathe deeply and push my emotions down inside. I am a warrior, I am strong. I walk away from Mother's room and outside to the courtyard. I look around, trying to decide what to do, then run over to the stables and tie the cloth and leather saddle around my horse. I pull myself easily up onto his back and ride quickly outside of the fort and into the fields nearby.

The wind in my face feels wonderful as I race faster and faster and my horse breathes hard as we jump small bushes and dodge trees. After a while, I begin to laugh at myself as I enjoy the speed of my horse. How silly I was to be so affected by my mother's death. I have seen death before, it happens often around here. I must become stronger, fierce. A true leader must be fierce. This is my goal.

I continue to ride for a few more hours until my horse and I are both exhausted, then I wander back to the fort and find that the people milling about are staying far away from me. By now everyone knows that my mother is dead, and they do not know what to say to me. I am quite happy to be left alone.

I dismount and brush my horse for a long while, enjoying his muscular body. Father received him as a gift from one of the western Celtic high kings as thanks for sending men to assist against the Picts. He is smaller than Father's but powerful and fast with a soft golden sheen to his coat. I like to think that we are somewhat alike, both strong and fast.

I notice Merewyn standing in front of her small hut, and drawn to her, I walk over and say hello. She invites me into her hut and offers me some steaming herbal brew. Without me asking anything, she begins to speak, again reading my mind.

"Death is a confusing thing, is it not?" She makes herself comfortable beside a tiny table and offers me a chair. I sit and drink the tasty brew she has given me.

"This drink is good. What is it made from?" I ask.

"Berries and leaves. It soothes the soul." She pulls her brass pyramid toward her and fondles it. Curious, I can't help but ask her about it.

"What is that?"

"It is an ancient pyramid from the place of Babylonia. It was given to me by my mother. She was given it by her mother. It carries with it the spirits of wisdom and truth. It helps me understand what is beyond our earth."

I find myself in awe of Merewyn and her pyramid and also a little afraid of her power. It is so different from mine and yet I feel that she is very capable of protecting herself from harm.

"Your mother is with spirit now, she is in joy with the Goddess of the Skies," she says, bringing my mind back to that unpleasant subject.

"You need not know much now. Her spirit will help you in your future. You are not wise to push her from your thoughts. Your life will be filled with unrest if you continue to fight your emotions and true self."

Annoyed with her last words, I rise and walk out, stopping to say a few words before I go. "My true self is well and strong! You need not fear for me!" I say curtly.

I walk with purpose toward my room. How does she know about my true self? I don't want my mother's spirit helping me. She could never even help herself, let alone me.

I spend the next few weeks in intense concentration with my maps and battle strategies. As I work endlessly, I am aware of Father and the Druid watching me with both pride and concern.

The months pass quickly and I find myself no longer having any thoughts of death or my mother. Summer is here and the air is warm and sweet with the smell of flowers. I go to the stable and ready my horse for a morning of riding.

Through the lush fields of flowers I race my steed, happy to be outdoors and in motion. I ride swiftly through the hills and up a small slope, enjoying the sense of power that racing gives me, then come to an abrupt halt near some trees at the top. Shock and surprise pierce me and my breath seems to stop a moment as I look in the distance and see a group of thirty men in metal helmets getting out of a large wooden rowing boat on the river. I dismount quickly and tie my horse to a tree a few feet back from where I stopped. Then turning and looking at the men again, I seethe with anger as I see them on foot now, carrying swords, weapons, and provisions off the boat.

Suddenly, I am seized from behind by two large arms and hands as one wraps around my throat and the other grabs at my chest. They belong to a large rough-looking man. A Pict! He wears the same metal helmet as the others. He laughs as he pulls me around to face him and holds my two arms with one of his hands. He places his other hand around my throat and pushes me roughly up against a nearby tree.

My mind screams with rage and disgust at this brutal boar of a man, and I fight and squirm for freedom but am pinned by the largeness of his body. I gasp for air as he pushes against my throat and my heart quickens its pace. The tree at my back digs into my skin and I try to bite and kick at him. How dare he, doesn't he know who I am? My father will kill him! I will kill him! He pushes his ugly face close to mine and breathes on me with foul breath as he grunts and pushes his body against me.

"What a treasure I have captured!" he grunts in a

strange accent, similar but somehow more coarse than our own language.

I try to make a sound but nothing will come out as he continues to stare into my face, smiling. He pins me harder against the tree with his whole body, his hand on my throat, making it difficult to breathe. I try to fight but am unable. He groans at me and I try to kick at him, but his body is too big to fight.

"A fighting girl, you are. We will see how hard you can fight me," he says with mocking pleasure in his voice.

He pushes harder still and my back feels the pain of the tree. I refuse to look at him and instead turn my eyes away, trying to look toward the sky as my body becomes icy and an odd numbness permeates me. I focus on the sky, staring at it as he rubs his head into my neck, grunting. I wince and clench my jaw as he rips at my clothes. Something strange is coming over me, a detachment and greater coldness.

The sky is so blue and I feel so cold as he forces his body into mine and pushes hard. I am aware of pain but it feels far away, as though I am apart from my body. I hold myself rigid and focus my mind. I am a warrior. I am a warrior. My body is trying to throb but I won't let it. I cannot let it. I think of Father. I must be strong for him. I will kill this man, I will kill this man. You will not hurt me. You will not weaken me. He grunts out a final moan and pulls out of me. Then he stands back and straightens his clothes. I stay pinned to the tree, unable to move as I continue to stare at the sky. He looks at me and grunts aloud. Then he sees my horse and laughs.

"I will have your horse as a gift of thanks."

He mounts my horse and takes one last look at me as I stay frozen against the tree, still staring at the sky.

He rides away as a rage mounts in me. My body begins to tremble and my hands form into fists and I falter for a moment, almost falling, but quickly steady myself against the tree and try to regain my senses.

Blinking finally, I begin to relax a little and bring my hands up to the front of my body. I touch my ripped clothes and close my eyes, aware of a strange smell about me. Sickness rises in me and I lean back for a moment against the tree and try to calm myself. Then, opening my eyes wide, I think of Father and those men, the Picts, that are coming our way. I must hurry back to the fort. I must get help. We must stop them.

I push myself from the tree and walk to the point where I can see the enemy coming, then I quickly turn and run down the other side of the hill toward home.

Unaware of the tiredness of my body, I seem to be partially floating beside myself. My energy is building and I run faster and faster, thinking only of getting home and telling Father.

I arrive home soon thereafter and run toward Father's house. I burst through the door, breathless, and find Father and Derwyn sitting at the table, eating and drinking. Father turns as he sees me and I run to him as my body finally begins to give way. Out of breath, I falter, and Father grabs me as I fall and stands me upright. I balance myself and try to catch my breath. Father's eyes fill with fear as he looks at my clothes and face.

"What is it? What has happened?" he asks urgently.

"The Picts ... they are back.... They come by foot ... one has my horse!" I say breathlessly.

"Your horse?"

"Yes ... quickly, we must ride!" I begin to breathe a little easier and Father turns to an anxious Derwyn, motioning with his hands for him to go.

"Ready the men for battle!" he says, then looks at me with concern. "Which way do they come?"

"I will show you!" I say firmly. "I am going with you!"

Father looks at me as though to say no, but I stop him. "I AM GOING WITH YOU! Do not stop me, Father! I must go!" I say with severity.

He touches my face gently and I stand firm, trying desperately to hold myself strong. My body cries out to fall and be held, but I know now that I must show my strength. I force myself to think. I am a leader, I am a warrior. Father nods in agreement.

"You will come, but you will stand behind us. Show us the way, quickly."

In the courtyard, Derwyn is quickly rousing the men for battle. They gather spears and shields and battle knives in a hurry and Derwyn motions for a scout to go on ahead and I point the way. I shake a little as I look down at my body and continue to smell the Pict's semen and odor on my clothes. My stomach wrenches and I force myself to focus on killing the Picts.

Our horses readied, we mount them and race out of the fort toward the hills and river. As we move closer to the Picts anger fills me and my body begins to warm again. The scout comes back toward us and tells Father where the Picts are. Father then orders us into a nearby wooded area and we wait silently, our horses anxious to move, our spears at the ready.

In the stillness, a small ground animal looks around, nervous with our presence. My breathing is so heavy and fast that I am sure it must be heard by the others. Slowly, the Picts enter the woods carrying their bundles and weapons on their backs. The large man who raped me comes up behind, walking my horse.

Through the trees, we can see them. Their noise

makes it impossible for them to hear us. Before long they are amidst us and Father yells, "Forward!"

Instantly, from all around, Father and our men, all on horseback, explode out from the woods and attack the Picts, piercing them with our spears. Shouts and cries of pain abound as our men fight the enemy, slaying them one after the other. I watch from the trees. I jerk my horse forward and join the others, my dagger ready in my hand.

A man grabs at my leg and tries to pull me from my horse, but one of our men thrusts a spear into the side of his neck and the blood spurts everywhere. Screaming, the Pict falls and I watch in amazement.

Dismounting from my horse, I look up to see a fierce man holding a large spiked weapon aimed directly at me. He swings and I duck and thrust my whole body toward his. With my dagger in hand I push it swiftly into his stomach. He grabs my body as he falls and pulls me down with him. I struggle and regain myself and stare at his dead body, then looking around me I see the fight coming to an end.

It was a short and swift battle, and our men begin to tend to our few wounded men.

I start to walk through the dead bodies as though in a trance. Coming upon one man who is facedown in the earth, I bend down and roll him over, hoping for him to be the one who raped me. Disappointed, I continue to look through the bodies. My heart beats faster as I see a man lying by a tree. Walking to him, I recognize the dead rapist lying faceup. I stand over him and step on his abdomen, my body beginning to tremble in anger.

"I told you I would kill you," I hiss at him.

I take my dagger and point it toward his nose, then slowly move it down to his heart, remembering the heart that Father gave to me as a child and that he must have cut it from the enemy. I realize that I could easily do that now, my hatred is so deep. With my dagger over his heart, I change my mind, take a slow, deep breath and tighten my jaw. I continue to move the point of the blade downward, taking my foot off of his stomach, then past his abdomen and stopping above his penis. Rage engulfs me and my whole body shakes. I bend down and grab his penis tightly through his clothes and swiftly chop it off. My breath intensifies and my mind screams with satisfaction as I hold the clothed penis in my hand.

Hearing someone, I look around to see Father coming toward me. He stops in shock when he sees what I have done and slowly his face becomes sad and his eyes fill with tears. He stares at me a moment tenderly but, unable to speak, he turns and quietly walks away, feeling powerless in the face of my pain.

The men begin to gather themselves together and throw the bodies in a pile to be burned later. Reclaiming my horse, I put the penis into a small bag attached to my waist and mount him. I follow the others home, allowing myself to lag behind. My mind is so confused. Why is my body feeling so numb and empty? What is wrong with me?

As we arrive back at the fort, I leave my horse at the stable and wander about for a moment, lost. Soon I find myself at Merewyn's hut, standing in front of her door, unsure of whether to go in or not. I linger for a long moment, then open the door and see her sitting on a stool by a table filled with pots of dried berries and plants. She turns to see me entering.

I stop and close the door behind me, my body trembling. Looking closely at me, she comes to me and stops. Peering deeply into my eyes and touching her fingers to my forehead, her eyes widen in shock. She brings her hand up to her mouth as though in pain and almost cries.

"Ohh . . . , my lady! Such pain! Are you all right?"

I look at her and open my mouth to speak, but for some reason, I cannot. She touches my arm and looks sadly at me, then she becomes angry.

"Such a beast deserves to die! I will gather some men, they will find him and kill—"

I stop her with my hand and hold out the bag with the penis in it. Confused, she opens the bag and takes out the clothed item. Opening it, she freezes and stares, then looking up at me, she nods as I stand silently.

"Yes . . . I will prepare a ceremony. All will be well." She touches my face tenderly, and I try hard to hold myself together.

"I understand," she whispers with tenderness in her voice.

We look at each other a moment, she fighting tears and me fighting to control my trembling. She then leads me to her stool to sit, takes the penis and walks over to her pots above the fire and places it in one of them. She then comes back to me and helps me out of my ripped and dirty clothes. Without looking at them, she throws them into the fire and brings me a tan-colored robe of soft cloth. She places it gently around me and I shiver. My body feels foreign to me and fragile. I don't understand why I feel so weak.

I sit silently on the stool as she moves quickly about the room, busily gathering plants from clay containers and brewing two pots over the fire. The room grows hot and is filled with the aroma of incense. Standing in front of her worktable, she picks up a bowl of burning plants and walks around me. The smoke swirls throughout the room, filling it with a wonderful smell. I inhale deeply and find myself relaxing and drifting, my mind softening its hold. She places the bowl back on her table and picks up another smaller one, then walks over to her fire. There she stops and looks back at me, and sighing to herself, she holds back some tears and turns back to her pot.

She dips her bowl into the pot where she placed the penis and walks back and stands in front of me. We look at each other a moment and I know that I trust her completely. I can tell her anything now. She raises the bowl in the air with one hand and raises her other hand high in the air and speaks.

"Spirits of the heavens, come now. Spirits of healing, come. Release from Our Lady Gwynnefwar's body, the evil of this man."

Lowering her hands, she removes the robe from my shoulders and it falls around me. She then dips three of her fingers into the bowl and anoints my right and left shoulders, breastbone, and the tops of my legs with the warm liquid as she continues.

"With this water, the spirits of the sky, the spirits of the earth, give back what was taken from you." She anoints my forehead. "We give you your power, your strength."

Merewyn puts the bowl down on the table and picks up her pyramid. Then walking behind me, she places one hand over my forehead and the pyramid over my heart area.

"Close your eyes?" she asks softly.

I close my eyes and she hums a single high-pierced note. My body jolts uncontrollably for a moment, then becomes still. Lightness and peace seem to seep into me at long last and I allow myself to relax. Merewyn walks over to her table and replaces the pyramid with a cup filled with liquid, which she gives to me.

"Drink. With this brew you will not carry a child."

I look at her a moment, then drink the brew quickly.
I give her back the bowl and we stare at each other as
her eyes fill with concern for me.

"Rise, lady, you are whole again."

I take a deep breath and stand as my mind clears,
then turn to look at her.

"I lost control, Merewyn. I could not think out there.
A leader should always be in control. My father taught
me so. I have disappointed him."

Merewyn shakes her head and touches me tenderly.
"No you have not. You are also a woman. You acted
as you needed," she says with a loving smile.

"I must be stronger, Merewyn. I must not allow my
feelings to rule my actions. A true leader must act from
wisdom and strength, not emotion."

I begin to make my way toward her door, aware of
a renewed strength awakening in me.

Merewyn gives me a worried look as I leave her hut.
Once outside I make a vow to myself. Never again will
I be weak, I will guard myself carefully. I must become
stronger and detach from my emotions. I watch the
people moving about the courtyard and find myself
strangely separate from them.

I notice one of our men flirting with a young girl
nearby. She giggles as he tries to tickle her and I feel
angered at his actions. I decide to go to the stable and
gather my shield, which I left there. I enter and find a
rugged-looking stable hand brushing my horse. He
turns to me as I gather my shield and my senses are
instantly invaded by the smell of sweat that comes from
him. My stomach churns slightly and I back away hurriedly and make my way back to my room.

Once there, I stare for a long while at my altar in the
corner. For so many years I have collected treasures
from battle that either I have found in the field or that

Father has given me. I wish I were a child again, running through the grass with Father. Life was so pure and happy.

I look down at my body and find myself angered at it. If I were a man, I would never have been invaded. This female body is a weakness to me, I must disguise it better.

With a burst of genius, I decide to race out of my room and the fort and make my way to the metal workers' buildings nearby, I enter one of the buildings and find three young men working hard at making weapons. They stop as they recognize me and I speak with a command in my voice.

"Make me a full tunic of mail," I say as I describe the chain mail tunic that I want to cover my torso and head.

I will disguise my body and hair inside my battle dress so that no invader will think that I am female. Only some of our men wear chain mail, as they find it heavy and awkward, but it is the only way to hide my womanhood.

10

❖

A Call for Help

WALKING SLOWLY AMIDST THE STILL TREES IN THE VALLEY
beside the fort, Father stops and stares at the setting
sun. Sadly, he rubs his beard and ponders the cloudless
sky. All around him there is stillness as the day comes
to an end.

"Oh, great spirits of the sky, I have received much
in my life but I ask one gift of you," he says as he
starts to walk slowly, his mind searching for the right
words to ask the spirits. He turns and looks at the sky.

"My daughter, Gwynnefwar. I fear I have failed her."

He questions the universe. "Was I wrong to raise her
as a son? I fear that I cannot help her now."

He wanders around and seeing a deer nearby,
watches it for a moment as it stops at a stream to drink.
Ever alert, the deer raises its head as it sees Father and
twitches its ears. Recognizing something of me in the
deer, he continues to watch it, fascinated by its strength

and gentleness, yet knowing it is fragile. Suddenly, it leaps across the stream and bounds out of sight. Father turns again to the sky.

"Help her . . . help her find peace in her soul. Help rid her of the pain that torments her."

He closes his eyes for a moment, as though in prayer. Behind him, Derwyn approaches quietly, careful not to surprise him. He coughs slightly to announce his arrival. Father turns and sees him. Not really in the mood for words, he hopes to make the conversation quick so he may continue speaking with the spirits.

Derwyn smiles broadly as he speaks. "My lord, I bring you good news."

"Good news?"

"Yes, lord. Your young friend from the south, Arthur, duke of the Britons, rides this way."

Thrilled with the news, father places an arm around Derwyn's shoulder and pulls him around to look at the sky.

"This is good news, indeed. It has been many moons since I have seen my friend." He looks at Derwyn, releasing his arm. "When does he arrive?"

"Tomorrow, my lord. He rides swiftly with six others."

Happy again, Father looks at the last bit of setting sun.

"We will prepare a feast of welcome for our friends," he says, slapping Derwyn on the back. "Tell the cooks and the others."

Derwyn turns and leaves as father looks across the valley of hills and smiles. He closes his eyes, and in his mind he thanks the spirits for bringing some hopeful change into the community.

He makes his way slowly back to the fort and his room. Glad that the day has ended, he sleeps deeply.

11

❖

The Meeting

Morning comes with much excitement in the community. People busy themselves for the arrival of Arthur
and his men. The day is bright and sunny and the feast
will take place outside as the men place the long narrow tables together. In the center of the courtyard a
great pile of wood is being laid for the fire. Dogs run
around excitedly, and the ladies take out their most
brightly colored linen dresses and robes for the
occasion.

I spend the majority of the day wandering down by
the river. There is a small wooden boat that I often use
and I want to be alone and adrift this day. The courtyard is far too busy for me and everyone is so happy.
I, on the other hand, still feel lost inside. It seems as
though my body is filled with a black substance. I feel
heavier today.

I push the boat out a way and jump into it. Sitting

low inside it toward the rear, I lie back and let the sun burn into my face. Somehow it helps me forget. It feels warm and comforting, and I feel some of the blackness disappear inside me. I hear people nearby, probably young men gathering more wood. I hope they don't see me. I don't want to speak with anyone today, I want to isolate myself and think of battle plans. When I plan a battle I feel strong again, in control of the earth and my people. This is what I must focus on.

Sleep comes over me and I drift for some hours in the boat until again I hear voices. A group of people from the nearby farms are walking to the fort for the feast. It must be late.

I paddle my boat back to shore and take a hidden pathway to the fort. Through the back entrance I sneak in and quickly go to my room to tidy myself. I wish I didn't have to go to this celebration, although I have heard that Arthur is a fine leader. His father was a powerful man who brought much peace to this land for a long while, and they say that Arthur is like his father. Maybe we can speak of strategy together. I decide that I will try to enjoy myself as I leave my room and go to the courtyard.

Fire pits are ablaze and people dance and sing about the courtyard, which is filled with tables of food and drink. Off to one side, four men play wooden wind instruments and a drum and another sings softly. At a large main table, many men sit as father engages them in laughter and jokes. Some women stand about them, and Father pulls one of them onto his lap. She laughs and he pulls her lips to his in a passionate kiss. His men cheer and he lets her up. She laughs again and runs over to some other ladies who are flirting with the men.

I enter the courtyard from the side wearing my

brown leather tunic with my hair tied back. I stop and look around, undecided as to where I want to go. I feel reserved and distant as I watch the people. I often notice how free the women seem to be with their bodies. They flirt openly with men, even if they are married. It is quite common in our Celtic culture for a woman to bed more than one man, especially if she is married to a high king or chieftain or a daughter of one, for often their mates are away at wars and they long for companionship. One of the ladies in the group walks up to me.

"Gwynnefwar, you look so beautiful this night with the moonlight on your hair. Why do you not dress like a woman? The duke of the Britons arrives soon. I hear he is a handsome man, and unwed," she says, looking at me devilishly.

"I want no man!" I return coldly.

I walk away from her, and she looks after me with a raised eyebrow. Another lady joins her and starts to pull her back to flirt with the men.

"Leave her, she wants to be a man, remember."

The two laugh together and walk back to the others. I wander over to a table and choose some food, annoyed that those women are only concerned with sex and flirting. I detest them. They know nothing of what is important. I walk over to a side table and sit and play with my food, trying hard not to be noticed.

At the entrance to the courtyard there is a big commotion and people begin to gather. Father rises from his table and walks toward the entrance as seven riders enter. The lead rider is on a magnificent gray horse. He has an air of power about him, he is Lord Arthur. Resplendent in a red and gold embroidered tunic over a longer tan one and with an odd-looking short metal skirt, he sits tall on his horse with a large dagger hanging from his side and tall brown boots on his feet. He carries two spears on his horse and a great round shield covered in leather. He leads his men, who are clad in green and gold tunics with the same metal skirts and breastplates, to the center as excited people gather around them.

Arthur stops and Father walks over to him. I watch curiously as Arthur dismounts and Father goes up to him and hugs him. They laugh and exchange greetings. I decide to walk over to them as the rest of Arthur's men dismount. As lady of the community, it is important that I greet honored guests. Father, his arm around Arthur, leads him forward just as I come up in front of them. Father stops and dropping his arm from Arthur, extends his hand to me, pulling me to him.

"Lord Arthur, this is my daughter, Gwynnefwar, the joy of my life. Gwynnefwar, I give you Lord Arthur. The leader of our Briton Army."

I smile slightly and look deep into Arthur's eyes. Somehow I find it difficult to look away from him as he penetrates my eyes with his. Much time seems to pass as we stare transfixed, then Arthur, still staring into my eyes, takes my hand gently and brings it to his lips, tenderly kissing my fingers. My eyes widen and I pull back my hand in nervousness, but he continues to hold it a moment as his mouth forms an endearingly crooked smile. I can't help but be aware of the mischievous boy peeking out from inside of him. I don't understand why I feel so strange. I feel torn, part of me wants to run far away and the other part wants to stay here looking into his eyes. He begins to speak softly to me.

"My lady, your beauty is a joy to the eye after a long journey."

Confused, I squirm a little. Father thankfully interrupts and slaps Arthur on the back. "Arthur, come join us. We have prepared a great feast in honor of you and your men."

He pulls Arthur toward the head table, and Arthur reluctantly goes with him, looking back a moment at me and smiling. Still confused but determined to regain myself, I turn quickly and walk the other way, my breath short and fast as I find Merewyn standing by a table, watching the whole scene very carefully. She smiles as I approach her and looks to where Arthur and Father have settled themselves at the main table.

"He is the one, lady," she whispers.

My mouth drops open and my heart seems to jump and I grab at my chest. I turn to Merewyn, feeling almost afraid of what she is going to say and she continues.

"Remember, I told you long ago, the one I have seen in my dreams."

I turn back and look at Arthur. Something begins to change in me, I feel both dread and a sense of energy rushing through me. My body straightens as I remember what Merewyn means. That I will be with this man.

"Merewyn, what do you think of this man?"

"He is a handsome man. He looks at you with love in his eyes."

I realize she is right. "Yes . . . he does."

"He will not hurt you, my lady."

My body tightens at her words and I feel an anger rise in me as I snap back at her.

"No one will *ever* hurt me again, Merewyn. No man will ever touch my soul. I have one purpose in life. To lead our people."

Surprised at my words, she backs away slightly. Smiling and straightening myself, I decide to join the men. My mind begins to feel focused. This man will help me. We will join our people and build a better land. He is a leader and I am a leader, that is all. That is why we are alike. I walk up to Father's table and he turns and smiles, glad to see me.

"My daughter, come, join us." He makes a place for me to sit between him and Arthur.

Arthur's right-hand man, Gulwain, speaks in a low voice. "The northern Picts, have you forced them back to the mountains?" he asks gruffly.

Father replies, "We have, they will not return this way."

Arthur takes a long drink of ale and Father speaks to him as I listen carefully.

"What of the Saxons, Arthur, have you driven them back eastward?"

Arthur cocks his head sideways as a boy fills his cup with ale. "For a time, but I fear they will return soon. I hear they gather forces with the Picts and Scots," he says seriously to Father. "I need assistance from yourself and the other high kings of the land if we are to regain this Island."

Father turns to me. "My daughter, what do you think of this?"

I sit erectly, thrilled to be asked my opinion in front of our guests. I notice Arthur and his men looking surprised as they glance at each other, then back to Father. Gulwain grunts under his breath and tries to control a laugh, and I shoot a wicked look at him as Father interrupts.

"I have skilled my daughter as a leader. She has learned well of battle and strategy. Speak, Gwynnefwar?" he prods.

I look at all the men, Father, and then to Arthur as he watches me intently.

"Yes, Father. The Picts will not come this way for a time." I take a small drink of ale and continue, holding all of their attention as Gulwain rolls his eyes.

"They will try to move south, along the shore, then join the Saxons near the sea in the mid-South. The Picts will bring horses from the north where the Saxons cannot, then together they will continue the quest westward."

I notice Arthur as he sits back in his chair, smiles, and looks around at his men, then at Father. "You have taught her well," he says looking at me. "What do you recommend, dear lady, as a plan for victory?"

Pleased and growing in confidence, I look right at him. "We should join our men together and fight the enemy where they meet, in the mid-South. Then we will defeat them all and once again the land will be ruled by the Britons." I turn to Father. "Father, will you meet with the chieftains and high kings in the West? If they join with us we will be sure to be victorious."

Father smiles proudly at me. "I will, my daughter," he says and looks at Arthur. "She speaks wisdom, Arthur, this daughter of mine."

Smiling, Arthur continues to stare at me as Father raises his cup and stands.

"Men, raise your cups in honor of our union."

The men stand, raising their cups and I join them.

Father speaks loudly. "Together we will be free of the heathen raiders and return this land to the wealth and splendor she was before the Romans left."

We all raise our cups high and I take a slow, deep breath and smile to myself. Father, sitting down, turns to Gulwain and begins a private conversation as the other men begin to talk amongst themselves. Arthur turns to me and looks tenderly into my eyes. I feel a bit uncomfortable and try to remain composed as he whispers.

"You have great strength, lady. I wonder, where do you hide the woman in you?" he asks softly.

Startled at his words, I shoot him a cold look but cannot seem to hold it as I am met by his gentle gaze. I think for a moment then speak. "She is deep inside."

He looks lovingly at me in silence as my pulse begins to race a little. My mind keeps repeating—I am a leader, I am a warrior.

Father rises, motioning to the people dancing in the center of the courtyard. "Let us dance, celebrate!!!"

Leaving the table, the men begin to dance with the women as Arthur takes my hand and pulls me to join the others. I resist firmly, as I have never danced, but he is persistent and we dance together as he swings me around. I tell myself that I am just being a good hostess.

Gulwain, spotting Merewyn nearby, walks up to her. They look at each other a moment, then smile as though they have been friends for a long while. They move to a table and talk quietly together. The whole crowd enjoys the music and Arthur pulls me close to him and whispers in my ear, "I will find the woman in you."

I pull back from him a little and look at him wide-eyed and confused. He raises an eyebrow in a mischievous way and smiles that crooked smile, and I turn my face away, unsure of what to do. We continue to dance and drink the night away. I try to engage him in talk of strategy, but he only wants to dance. I resign myself to it, knowing we can speak more tomorrow.

The women flirting with Father find they are quite welcome in his arms. He dances and kisses them and soon they are quite drunk. The warm evening air has brought with it an intoxicating effect, a gentle mix of moonlight, music, and drink. I am caught between enjoying myself for the first time in a while and fighting for control of my emotions.

I cannot show my weakness to Arthur. He must see me not as a woman but as a leader, a skilled strategist.

As the men drink more and more I find myself becoming very tired and confused.

I find a moment where everyone is engaged in laughter and I sneak away to my room. Curling up on my bed, I notice the moonlight streaming across my altar. I ask the spirits of the night and moon to help me be strong and true to my people and the land. I also ask for help in convincing Arthur to trust me. As I lie there, I find my head begins to spin a little from the drink, although I don't want to sleep. I want to think, to plan, but sleep comes and I drift off.

I awaken the next morning and dress in my green tunic, putting my dagger through my new silver ring on my new silver belt, which Father has given me. It was stolen from the Pict leader. I feel excited and nervous at the same time. What will happen this day, what will Arthur be like to me? Will he listen to my plans or treat me like any other weak woman?

I walk into the eating hall and find people milling about the tables where food is set. A dog barks noisily and a young man chases it through the hall. At the main table, Father is gathered with Arthur and his men, eating their breakfast of meat in relative silence. Father rubs his eyes and then his chest and stretches, then rises in time to greet me walking into the room. I walk toward him and greet him with a kiss.

"Father. How do you fare this day?" I ask.

I sit down and choose some fruit and bread and a young man pours me a steaming berry drink. Father sits back down beside me and shrugs.

"I fear I am a bit weary," he says hoarsely.

I turn and look at Arthur, proud that I am remaining detached.

"Lord Arthur, what of you? Are you well?" I ask and he looks up from his food and smiles at me.

"Indeed so, lady. I had wondrous dreams," he says with a longing sexual tone in his voice.

I turn away from him, hiding my rising nervousness, when Father suddenly pounds his fist on the table and startles us all. "I have decided!" he shouts.

He pauses to take a drink, then turns to me and takes my hand, pulling me up to stand beside him. "You will join us," he says to me, then shouts to the room, "we will take a large gathering of our men and ride south to Salisbury! We will ride in one day's time!"

The people all look to one another excitedly. I look at Arthur and he rises to stand beside me. He smiles a loving smile of conquest and I look away from him, trying to hide my confused emotions. He acts as though he has just won a prize. I sit back down to finish my food and Arthur leaves to talk to his men. I watch him out of the corner of my eye and occasionally he looks over at me. The more I think about the journey to Salisbury, the more excited I become. This will be my chance to prove to everyone that I am ready to lead and to fight. There is much more fighting now with the Saxons and Scots in the South than here against the Picts.

I hurry and finish my food then rush back to my room and look around. I realize that I haven't that much to bring with me. I gather a bag made of animal hide and fill it with my tunics and battle gear when Olwy, a young woman helper in the house, enters the room and sees what I am packing.

"Please, my lady, that is not all that you take."

"It is, nothing else is needed."

"My lady, Salisbury Fort is much larger than our own, the people dress in finery. We must gather some of your more suitable clothes," she pleads.

Confused, I continue, "I have no finer clothes, this is all I wear." I point to my tunics.

"Oh, you do, my lady. Long ago your mother in-structed her ladies to make lovely dresses for you on each birth day, to be kept in a trunk should you need them. They are in your mother's old room. I will ask one of the men to place them on a cart." She turns and leaves before I am able to stop her.

Oh well, I don't care what she brings along. I will never wear them. I can't ride a horse in a dress. What silliness!

I spend the rest of the day making sure everything is ready with the other people. I help to groom my horse and check with Father to see that we bring enough weapons and maps along.

12

❖

The Journey
to Salisbury Fort

THE NEXT DAY, DAWN COMES QUICKLY. WITH THE SUN BLAZ-
ing on a summer morning, I jump out of bed at the
sounds of people readying themselves for the journey.
I dress in my best green tunic and carry my bag, filled
with clothing and chain mail for battle, and my new
shield, dagger, and spear, which I will tie to my horse.

Out in the courtyard the crowd is gathering. About
thirty people, mostly men—there are but a few women
joining us—ready themselves for the trip.

Father has instructed some ladies of our house to join
us—Olwy and Rhianne, a frivolous young girl of sixteen who seems interested only in giggling. Merewyn
is also coming along as my companion and as healer
for our people. I am glad she is joining us; she is my
one true friend.

As we leave the courtyard to the sound of cheers and
some tears from the families whose men are leaving, I

am exhilarated and anxious to get to Salisbury. It is at least a four-day journey, maybe longer with the carts and supplies we bring with us. Father and Arthur ride up front whereas Arthur's right hand, Gulwain, has gone ahead to scout the way.

The day moves by easily enough. I find myself meandering off a little from the others, wanting to experience the countryside without the constant chatter of people. Later in the afternoon as we come to the edge of a plateau, I ride up beside Father and Arthur and lean forward so that Arthur can hear me speak.

"How far is Salisbury from here?"

Arthur looks at me and points ahead. "Three days from here, across those hills to the southwest."

I look around, excited by the magnificence of the hills and valleys of thick forests and rivers that meander out of our sight. "The land here is beautiful."

Arthur and Father both nod in agreement, and Arthur replies, "It is God's country, that is truth."

What an unusual thing to say. I have heard from the local people that Arthur's spirituality is different from our own. That he lives by the rules of the Roman Christians. Surely, it cannot be so different, everyone knows that we are one with the Goddess of the Earth and Spirit. I am not sure what he means by "God's country."

I find myself drifting in my thoughts again as I look at the countryside, noticing old stone buildings now in decay and wondering if they were part of the old Roman cities. Dusk is falling, and we find a place to rest for the night. Although tired, I am far too excited to sleep.

As we finish our food and sit by a fire, Father and I enjoy a moment of quiet together. He points at the stars above and relates to me the story of our civilization's past.

"The ancient ones come from the stars. They came and created our land and seeded it with plants and animals. They made us a part of our earth. We must always honor it and remember we are spirit first."

"Does Arthur not understand our ways, Father?" I ask, needing to know.

"His ways are different, yes. He has been taught the Roman Christian ways of one God, superior to people and ruler of all."

"Superior to people, not one with people, how can this be?" I ask, surprised at the difference.

"They follow the ways of a teacher from ancient times."

"But what of the earth spirit or the moon spirit?" I say, feeling compelled to question more. "Does he not feel one with them? How do their crops grow if they do not honor the earth spirit?"

"No, it is true, he does not. Maybe you will teach him of our ways," he says smiling.

Tired, I decide to ponder this more in my mind as I move to my makeshift bed inside our small cloth tent. I will speak about it more to Merewyn; she will help me.

The next morning arrives and we pack our belongings, continuing the journey southward. The following two days are filled with new scenery and lush green lands and forests. We continue to pass many small villages and old stone ruins and Roman roads along the way, and I find myself fascinated with this part of the world.

Along the way, Gulwain chases a wild boar and easily slays it with his spear. It makes for a wonderful meal, and Arthur gives me the tusks for a gift. He tells me that their many craftspeople will be happy to make something lovely out of them.

As we come closer to Salisbury the excitement in me grows. Over the past few days I have watched Arthur most carefully and am aware of him watching me. I wish I could get inside his mind. Of course—Merewyn. I will ask her. I ride close to the cart that Merewyn rides in and I ask her to come close to the edge as I whisper, "What does Arthur think about when he looks at me?"

"I cannot invade his thoughts, my lady," she says, then pauses to think for a moment. "I can say that he thinks much of you, his body yearns for you and you fill his mind with fantasy and lovemaking."

Disturbed by this, I question her further. "Does he not think of me as a partner in battle? To join our peoples, to rid the land of invaders?"

"No, my lady, he does not. He thinks only of ways to bring the love out of you." She smiles to herself, knowing this is just what I need.

I drift back from the cart and become more disturbed at Merewyn's words. Soon, we come upon much farmland and small timber houses. People begin to wave at us as we move nearer to Salisbury Fort. Large hairy cattle roam the many farms as do sheep and pigs.

As we ride on we come upon more people and more timber houses in what seems to be a large village. In the middle of a large group of people there are loud voices shouting. We slow to a stop as Arthur and Gulwain ride into the group. Father and I ride closer and try to see what the commotion is about.

I notice a large man in a green and gold soldier's uniform beating an older, poorly dressed man and pulling at a sheep that the old man is tied to, neck to neck. The soldier continues to shout at the man until Arthur dismounts and interrupts the scene. Arthur commands the soldier to stop and instructs Gulwain to untie the man from the sheep. I watch with building curiosity, wondering what Arthur will do, when the soldier speaks.

"He owes this sheep for rent on his land, my lord, it is our due."

Arthur turns to the old man, now bleeding from his neck and arms, and bends down, then asks a nearby woman to bring some water. Everyone seems to be frozen around them, waiting for the old man to speak. Finally he does, with a weakened voice.

"I have but one sheep left, my lord, . . . please, may I keep it?" he begs. His head falls to one side as a woman gives him some water.

Arthur holds the man upright and turning, glares at the soldier as loathing fills him. Without saying a word, the message is clear. The soldier backs away in fear of Arthur's wrath, then Arthur turns back to the old man.

"You shall keep your sheep . . . and more. You will be repaid for your troubles, old one," he says, then calls for some men to help the man onto one of the carts. Gulwain ties the sheep to the cart and the crowd begins to disperse.

As we continue on our way, the people wave at Arthur, obviously thrilled to see him. I am glad to have seen Arthur's fairness with that old man. He has a tenderness for those in need, like Father. That pleases me.

There are small wooden huts with women outside weaving wool, and many huts filled with metal or leather and other goods of various kinds.

Fascinated, I look carefully at the wares the people offer as we ride on what seems to be an old road of stone. In the near distance there is a huge flat-topped hill with trees all around it from the ground up. On the top I see a vast wooden fortification. Excited, I push through the riders and catch up to Father and Arthur in front.

"Is that Salisbury Fort, Lord Arthur?" I ask excitedly.

"It is," he says with pride. "It was built by my father. It has many comforts that you will not find anywhere else in the land."

I drift back to Merewyn's cart, eager to share my excitement with her. She smiles happily when she sees me.

"Is it not wonderful, my lady? So many people. So much wealth!"

I nod in agreement, taking in everything, most of all how the people seem so fond of Arthur. We begin to climb the steep and difficult road to the hill fort. There are deep ridges in the land around the hill that men can hide in in case of attack and that make it impossible for any man to ascend easily to the fort. What a brilliant idea! To see such a well-thought-out fortification thrills me. Here are a people that understand how to protect themselves and prepare for battle. I am going to enjoy staying here and learning from them.

As we reach the top, we come to a large stone wall four feet high with long timbers built still another six feet higher on top of it and with a large covered entrance gate with two guards standing watch on top. Passing through it, I notice the wall is very wide, wide enough for men to walk along the top and watch for the enemy. Inside the main wall there is a space broad enough for three horses to ride easily before the main structure of the fort begins.

I stop for a moment, awed at the sight of a two-story timber building that follows the outer wall. Wooden shutters on the second floor open to see over the outer stone and timber wall.

We enter the center of a huge courtyard, and I look around, captivated by it all as people come rushing up to us. Many attached two-story buildings have been built around what seems to be the whole plateau of the hill. The top story has a balcony or covered hallway that stretches all along it. It seems to house the majority of people, as the bottom floor has various craftspeople and at the entrance of the fort, stables. As I look in front of me, I am stunned by a beautiful timber building, a giant meeting hall. As tall as the others, it has two great carved doors in the center.

The entourage enters the vast courtyard and people begin to cheer and gather around us. I look ahead to see Arthur and Father.

Arthur enters the center and the excited people cheer him. He moves toward Father and the people as they help him and his men with their horses. I dismount and walk to the cart to help Merewyn and two other ladies out. Arthur and Father look around through the people, trying to see me. Arthur spots me by the cart and motions for his men to help me. The people take our supplies and horses, and Merewyn, noticing me staring at the huge fort, comes to my side.

"This is your home now," she says with joy in her heart.

"My home? We stay only until the enemy is defeated, then back to Northumbria," I reply in confusion.

"No, lady. You will stay here for many years," she says, shaking her head.

Suddenly I am aware that my life is changing very rapidly. Looking around carefully, I am glad that I will stay here. This is the center of planning for our country and it is right for me to live here. I smile to myself.

Some women come up to me and usher us to follow them as men behind us carry our belongings. We follow them up some stairs above the stables and along the long covered hallway toward our rooms. We enter a large, well-furnished room with a huge carved bed on one side covered in a red and gold embroidered blanket similar to Arthur's tunic. There is a large table in the center of the room and comfortable wooden chairs with red and gold cushions on them. By the far wall is a long narrow table with a large square of polished metal hanging above it. I touch the strange metal and laugh as Merewyn comes over to see what I have found.

"Look, Merewyn, I see myself in this metal."

Amazed, she touches it too. "It is quite enchanting."

Looking down on the table, I find lovely hair combs made of silver and bone. In the corner of the room is a large stone hearth. The room is also filled with exquisite round bronze oil bowls with delicate markings on them, much nicer than the ones we have at home. I walk to the window and look out across the valley. The view from here must be the best in the whole fort.

A large, gruff man enters, carrying a wooden trunk and places it down, then leaves as another man follows with more supplies.

"It is a great room, lady," Merewyn says. "It has been Arthur's room."

Surprised, I look around carefully and wonder aloud, "Why does he give it to me?"

Olwy and Rhianne enter and begin busily to unpack the bags and trunks.

"I have never seen such a large place," says Olwy.

"The people, so many," adds Rhianne, giggling.

"The women have such beautiful clothes, did you see the one in gold?" Olwy motions with her hands how it flows to the ground.

"Yes ... yes ... Lord Arthur must be very rich—"

Annoyed at their frivolousness, I interrupt. "Must

you speak of such things?" I walk over to a trunk. "What is in here? This cannot be mine."

"These are the clothes I spoke to you about," Olwy explains. "There are also many fine things that your mother had made for you. Will you look at them now?"

Bored by the very idea of clothes, I decline. "No, I wish to see more of this magnificent fort. Merewyn, will you come?"

Merewyn's eyes light up at the prospect of exploring the fort. "Yes, yes!"

We rush out of the room, glad to be away from the giggling Rhianne and her obsession with appearances and begin to wander about the fort. With the doors to the rooms mostly closed, it is difficult to look inside, so we walk farther down the hallway. Hearing women's voices we walk down the nearby stairs to the bottom floor. Near the back wall of the fort we enter a large room and find ourselves shocked at what is before us.

We both freeze as we see two giant circular tubs made of pink marble filled with steaming hot water. On the floor, exquisite azure blue tiles cover the ground. All around are large marble pedestals with giant oil bowls that create a warm glow throughout.

The room is full of naked ladies wandering about from one tub to the other. Along one wall, there are three tables with women lying on them and other women rubbing oils onto their near-naked bodies. The air is heavy with heat and the smell of perfumes. The women talk amongst themselves and seeing us, two of them come forward.

"My ladies, you are not from here. Are you guests of our Lord Arthur?" she asks and waits for our reply.

I am unable to speak amidst all these naked women,

and Merewyn replies for us. "Yes, we are from the North. We have just arrived with Lord Arthur."

"Welcome then. Will you bathe now?" She looks at us and waits for our reply.

"Bathe?" Merewyn asks.

"Yes," the confused woman replies. "I will take your clothes."

Disgusted at the thought of taking my clothes off and swimming with these strange women, I turn and walk immediately out of the room as Merewyn says, "Not now, I thank you."

We both stop outside the room, look at each other and laugh together, then continue on to the next room. Before we enter, I question Merewyn.

"Maybe we should not look at any more rooms. Their ways here are very strange. How do you think they make all of that water so hot? They must have large fires."

Suddenly, we turn quickly to find a woman behind us. She speaks, obviously having just heard our words.

"The water is from the ground, my ladies. The Romans built many baths near here and the water moves through the ground in pipes from nearby. There are few left, we are very lucky to have them. It heals the ills in the body."

Embarrassed, we thank the lady for her understanding and move quickly across the main courtyard to the other side of the fort. Realizing that we must find a room for Merewyn, we go back to my room and ask a lady nearby where Merewyn will stay. She shows us a room quite near to mine.

It is much smaller than mine but equally comfortable. Merewyn is extremely pleased and she begins to unpack her many herbs and pots. Bringing out her pyramid, she places it on a large eating table. I decide to bring up the subject of Christianity with her.

"Merewyn, do you know of Christian beliefs?"

"Little, my lady. They are different than ours. Arthur is Christian and worships a god and his mother, Mary. She is embroidered on his tunic. She is simply another form of our Goddess of the Earth, Arianrod. The Christians worship something that is outside of themselves rather than that which is a part of themselves."

I listen carefully as she continues to unpack her many things.

"We believe we are one with the earth, that the earth and spirit are our mothers. They believe they are conquerors of the earth, that one God rules over them. They believe they must please their God or they will be punished. We believe our earth and spirit mothers and fathers love us and wish for us to prosper and love one another. It is sad, for they do not understand the love of being one with the universe."

Suddenly a worried look comes over Merewyn and she turns to me. "Remember this, my lady, a woman in their beliefs is a mother. The man is the leader."

Horrified and doubting of her words, I stand up abruptly. "This cannot be so!"

"It is, my lady, I tell you this so you are careful in your choices. To win the respect of these people you must do so with care."

I decide to return to my room and rest for a while. Lying on my new bed, I feel an uneasiness about my new life. Can Merewyn be right? If she is, then I must make these people understand me. I must show them that a woman is powerful. I sleep for a while and am awakened by Rhianne and Olwy knocking on my door. I ask them to enter and they do, full of excitement as always.

"A feast is being readied, my lady, it is time to join the others," Olwy exclaims.

Stretching and walking over to the wall table, I notice a large bowl of water and cloths. I wash my face and clean myself quickly. Olwy and Rhianne are both dressed in their best blue and cream-colored dresses. Feeling tired, I cannot help but wonder what lies in store for me this night. I turn to the women.

"Where is my green tunic?"

"Lady, please, why not wear the blue dress?" cries Rhianne.

"It is a celebration. Do you wish Arthur's people to think you poor?" pleads Olwy.

I walk to the table with the dresses draped across it and touch them, questioning their logic. I realize that they are probably right, the people expect it of me. How I wish I were a man!

Olwy stands and holds the dark blue linen dress with silver embroidery along the sleeves and neckline. She lifts it up in front of me and I notice it falls almost to the floor. How can anyone walk in such a thing?

"It is beautiful, lady, and you have never dressed in it."

"Very well, help me with it?" I say, resigned to this frivolity.

I reluctantly allow her to help me dress. She combs my hair as I continue to question in my mind the religious differences between my people and Arthur's. Feeling uncomfortable and awkward in the dress, I try to think of a way out of it. I rub my arms.

"It is too cold for this dress. Give me back my tunic."

Becoming upset, Rhianne cries out, "No, my lady, it is warm this night, you need not fear the cold."

Angered by her words, I snap at her, "Fear? I fear nothing!"

Merewyn enters the room and comments on the dress.

"You are beautiful. A woman of your beauty should always wear a dress."

"I care not for beauty, as you do," I say angrily.

I grab my short brown cloak and wrap it tightly around my body, tying it at the waist, and leave the room, slamming the door in disgust. Merewyn shakes her head in concern, wanting only for me to be accepted by Arthur's people.

I walk toward the main hall and enter from the side door, through the kitchen. It is a massive room, filled with bustling people. I am enchanted by the smells of cooking. Four giant hearths span one whole wall and are filled with many pots. Through the center of the room are long and wide tables with many cooks around them busily chopping and arranging food. I savor the moment before moving onward out into the main hall. There I stop and look around in wonder. There are giant tapestries like nothing I have ever seen hanging from the walls and flags with eagles on them draped from posts at the doors. Giant oil bowls hang from long chains secured in the ceiling beams and a large fire in the center of the room surrounded by stones two feet high sends sparks upward and out through an opening in the roof.

The tables are crowded with people eating and drinking. I notice Arthur and Father at the head table. A beautiful tapestry with mother and child on it hangs behind Arthur. This must be the Christian mother Merewyn and Father spoke of.

The people all wear their finest clothes this night, many of a shiny thin material that is foreign to me, as well as much heavy jewelry around their arms and necks. The women all have long multicolored dresses with long sleeves and braided gleaming rope that winds around their breasts and waists. The people seem happy as they fill their mouths with food and drink. A young boy carrying a large jug walks to the main table and places it down in front of Arthur and Father.

"My friend, will you have some wine?" Arthur asks. "It comes by boat from Gaul. It is the finest anywhere."

Father nods eagerly, holding out a cup. "I will. Fill my cup. Tonight I celebrate," he replies joyfully.

Arthur fills Father's cup, and they drink as Father looks around the room.

"You have many lands and riches, Arthur."

"Much I have received from my father. He was honored in the Roman Court, and I am proud to continue his quest for wealth and peace in this land," he says as they drink.

Father looks around the great hall and his eyes light up as he sees me enter by the side door. I walk toward him as he stands, his hand outreached to me.

"My daughter, come, sit with us," he beckons.

I take his hand and he pulls me closer. Arthur, standing as well, looks at me closely up and down and noticing my cloak, he questions me.

"Are you not warm?" he says with a note of sarcasm.

"No!" I snap in return.

I sit in a place Father makes for me and pull my cloak tightly about me as Arthur smirks and sits beside me. Father sits on my other side.

"Will you drink some wine with us?" Father asks me.

"Yes, Father," I reply.

He pours me some wine and a young man brings me a large plate of food. Hungrily, I eat as father and Arthur talk about the fort and the people who live in the surrounding areas. I listen closely, fascinated by the vastness of Arthur's land. I learn that the Romans had once created massive cities with roads and sewage, but that over the past one hundred years most of it has decayed from lack of upkeep. There was no longer enough money or supplies from Rome to rebuild the cities. Even those in the East were nearly gone from warring with the Saxons.

Arthur continues to speak of how their center of command used to be in the eastern cities, but since the Saxon invasion, they have withdrawn westward. He speaks of his desire to push back the Saxons and retake the cities and rebuild them to their past splendor.

As we continue to feast and speak of daily life in Salisbury, musicians begin to play lovely music with drums and flutes. Some of the instruments are strange to me, and I find myself drifting from the conversation, enchanted by the sounds wafting through the room. I notice the women here are quite different from those at home. None of them are dancing or being sexual or flirtatious with the men. In fact, even the men seem quite well behaved. I wonder if they are always this way or if they are just being docile because we are newcomers.

Entering through the main door, Gulwain comes to Arthur's side and whispers to him as Father and I continue to watch the people. Nodding to Gulwain, Arthur leans across toward Father.

"I have heard from my men that the enemy approaches. I have sent men ahead, we must prepare ourselves quickly. Will you join us?" he says to Father.

Father puts his cup down and nods and my heart quickens at the thought of battle. Arthur stands and quiets the room with a motion of his hand.

"My men, ready yourselves for battle! We ride at first light!" he commands.

The people quickly begin to move about, leaving the

hall. Arthur turns and walks out with Gulwain while Father and I both stand to leave when I look at him anxiously.

"I will ready myself to ride with you, Father," I say and start to leave but he grabs my arm.

"No. You will stay here," he says, looking down a moment, then taking both my hands in his, he looks tenderly at me as I fill with confusion.

"This is Arthur's battle. It is not your place to go," he says tenderly.

I cannot understand his words, it cannot be.

"You taught me to lead. Now you leave me here?" I question, sure that I have heard him wrong.

He pulls my hands to his heart.

"Gwynnefwar, I was wrong. Forgive me. You must be a woman now," he says with a disheartened voice, realizing I will not be accepted here as a warrior.

I wrench my hands away from him. Enraged, I turn and run from the hall. Racing back to my room, my heart pounds and my head throbs with anger. How can this be! My father, how can he say this to me! I have been waiting for this, I am ready, more ready than ever!

I burst into my room and walk to the large table in the center, stop and pound my fist on it in frustration.

Merewyn stands in the hallway, looking worried. "What is wrong, lady?"

I scream, "Leave me!!!"

Startled, she pulls back and leaves the doorway. I pace around the room in frustration, trying to think. I must think! I look down at my dress and in an angry rage, start ripping at it, pulling it off. I move to my trunk and root through the clothes, pulling out my riding tunic and chain mail. I will go, they cannot stop me. I have earned the right to fight for my land. I will show them all.

I dress in my battle clothes, hiding my figure beneath the chain mail covering my head and torso, and lie on my bed in wait for morning. My body is rigid with anger and I am unable to sleep.

Night passes quickly and before dawn I rise and finish dressing by lacing up my boots. I grab my round shield and spear and stand in front of the metal mirror. No one will think that I am a female in this battle dress. I take my dagger, slipping it into the ring on my waist belt and wait in my room until I hear the men preparing in the courtyard. Silently, I creep out and down the hallway toward the steps to the bottom floor. I wait in the shadows of predawn until I hear the men leave.

As soon as they are all gone, I run across the courtyard to the stables and quickly tie a new cloth and leather saddle on my horse. Moments later I am out of the stables before anyone notices. Seeing only a young stable boy walking about, I ride with an air of confidence that suggests to the boy I am one of Father's men.

I ride down the road from the fort, careful not to catch up to the men. As I move swiftly, my breathing quickens with the thought of a battle against the Saxons. Finally, I will be able to prove myself and no one will know until afterward that it is me. I follow a good distance behind until I come to the top of a hillside where I stop suddenly, seeing Father, Arthur, and the men about to engage in a battle in the valley below. I am too late, it has already begun. I dismount and let my horse graze as I watch closely.

About eighty of Arthur's and father's men rush forward on horseback, spears and small swords pointing forward, toward about thirty Saxons on foot. The Saxon leader yells at his men to raise their weapons.

My excitement mounts as our men, their skills superior, slay the Saxons, easily killing them. The Saxons try in vain to defend themselves by pulling our men down to engage in hand-to-hand combat, but Arthur's soldiers are far superior to them. Maneuvering their horses expertly, they turn quickly to face one then the other as Arthur's voice cries out, his face ablaze with triumph as he thrusts his spear through the Saxon leader's neck.

Seeing this from the hill, I jump up with excitement, cheering aloud. Then I see Father struggling on the ground with a large Saxon.

"Oh no, get up, Father, get up!" I scream.

Fear fills me as the Saxon seems to have the advantage. He pushes a large knife toward Father's throat.

"STOP!" I cry, but no one hears me.

Suddenly the Saxon's eyes widen, his mouth spewing blood, and he falls to the side just as Arthur pulls a spear out of his back. Father stands and smiles at Arthur and the battle comes to an end.

Suddenly I hear footsteps behind me. I pull my dagger and turn to face the enemy but instead I find an old man walking toward me. He stands beside me and looks at the battlefield. Surprised to see this old man, I question him.

"Who are you?"

"I am Arthur's friend and counselor. My name is Merlin."

I ignore him and turn to watch the men as Merlin comes close beside me.

"It is a small battle. They have easily won."

"Yes." I smile to myself. Of course they have won. He looks me up and down slowly.

"You long to be with them?"

"Yes," I reply, annoyed with his intrusion.

He smiles and walks around to the other side of me, then he quickly pulls the chain mail off of my head, freeing my long, curly hair. Angered, I turn and glare at him, then look back at Arthur. Merlin grins, then runs his hand down my arm.

"Gwynnefwar, you are not meant to be with them."

I turn and back away from him, angered at his rudeness and speak sharply. "You—know—me—not!"

He looks at my body again as I say defiantly, "I am strong enough! I can fight as well as any man!"

"Indeed, yes," Merlin says seriously.

That's better. I ignore him and turn back to see Arthur and his men tending to their minor wounds.

"But you have more inner power than any man," he adds suddenly.

I laugh at that statement, still annoyed with his intrusiveness. He touches the side of my face and I pull back, though I do not want to insult Arthur's friend.

"Why do you touch me?"

"Do you not see, Gwynnefwar?" He takes my hair and drapes it around my shoulders. "Here . . . here lies your strength. Look at your body, look at your spirit."

I don't understand what he means. My strength is in my hair, my body? He turns then and pointing to Arthur and his men, speaks gruffly.

"Your destiny lies not with them. Look, here," he says and touches my arm, then points to my heart as I try to understand what he means. He raises an eyebrow and smiles at me, then speaks softly.

"Look closely and you will see."

I turn away, convinced that this man Merlin is mad. I see Arthur's men preparing to leave the battleground. I turn to my horse and quickly mount. I look around for Merlin, but cannot find him. Where could he have gone so quickly? What kind of man comes and touches a strange woman so freely? What power does he speak of?

"Merlin?" I call, but there is no answer.

I shrug and ride back the way I came. "You have more power than any man." What am I not seeing? Back at the fort I quickly dismount and run to my room. No one has recognized me, except of course, Merlin. Will he tell Arthur that I followed them? I hope not.

Rushing into my room, I close the door and find Merewyn sitting by my table, waiting for me.

"Lady . . . where have you been?"

"Nowhere, I am well," I reply absently.

She looks at me with disappointment. She well knows where I have been! I walk to the polished mirror on the wall and stare at myself, trying to understand Merlin's words.

"There was a man, Merlin, Arthur's friend," I say. "He spoke to me with strange words. He told me I was stronger than men. What does he mean?"

She smiles, as though she knew all along.

"He means your inner strength, your body, your womanhood."

My mind begins to race as I realize what must be done. I will not be ignored and forced to wait here with the other women as he goes to battle for our lands! I turn to Merewyn.

"You say that Arthur loves me?"

"Yes, he will do most anything for you, especially if you are his wife."

Wife! Of course, that's it! A wife has more power. The people must listen to me if I am Arthur's wife. I must make him see me.

"Merewyn, how do I become Arthur's wife?"

Stunned, she jumps up. "Oh, my lady, are you sure?"

I grin in response and she runs to the trunk of clothes. Immediately, I understand her meaning.

"Quickly, help me dress. My most beautiful dress," I say as I begin to feel a new and different power race through my body.

Merewyn excitedly pulls out a gorgeous red sleeveless dress that drapes to the floor. Even I am surprised at the vibrant color. I have never seen other ladies wear such a brilliant red. I quickly change and Merewyn finds some jewelry in the trunk while I tie a golden rope around my waist.

Around my forehead and under my hair she places a thick golden band and on my bare arms two gold armbands. Over my right shoulder she pins a thin white sheath of cloth, which drapes to the floor. Standing there in this finery, I begin to feel different. Not weak as I would have thought. I think I am beginning to understand Merlin's wisdom. Arthur is enchanted by my looks, so I will seduce him first, then convince him of my importance as his partner in driving out the Saxons.

13

A New Strategy

I HEAR THE MEN RETURNING FROM THE BATTLE AND ENTER-
ing the courtyard, and I slowly walk out of my room
and down the hallway. I must think carefully now. I
must not show weakness, he must come to me.

Arthur and Father and the men are exhilarated after
their battle and the people come running to meet them.
They laugh and talk excitedly of how easy it was to
defeat the Saxons. Arthur and Father dismount, giving
their horses to stable boys, then turn and stop, their
mouths and eyes opening in astonishment as they see
me at the top of the stairs.

I stand very still and regal in my flowing crimson
dress. My red curly hair rests around my shoulders.
The whole courtyard becomes quiet as everyone stares
at me. Nervous, but in control, I breathe slowly and
deeply, a feeling of triumph coming over me. It's working, I have everyone's attention.

Arthur, regaining his composure, walks quickly to me and I walk a few steps down and wait for him. As he comes to the stairs he holds out a hand to me, his face filled with awe. I look around as everyone watches and smile slightly, not wanting to show softness but enjoying the moment fully. I feel like a goddess. I continue to descend, taking Arthur's hand. We stare at each other a moment and I realize my victory over him is complete. Taking my hand, he leads me through the crowd to the center of the courtyard and onto a small platform. Standing on the platform, I look around and see Father staring at me, his face full of pride. Is this what he truly wants of me? Arthur looks at me lovingly for a moment, then turns to the crowd.

"We have pushed the enemy back, we are victorious!" he cries.

The crowd roars as Arthur looks at me with a deep longing, as though asking me something. I smile, feeling my hold over him tighten with each passing moment and he turns back to the crowd and raises his hand.

"People, hear me!"

He turns to me and the people become quiet. I remain stoic, trying to ignore the twinges in my stomach as Arthur says softly, "Gwynnefwar, I ask you to be one with me, to join our spirits and people in unity, to join us with the land as far as the eye can see."

He takes both my hands and pulls them close to his heart. My own heart starts to beat faster and a tingling sensation floods my chest.

"Gwynnefwar, I ask you to be my wife."

I look at the tender love in his eyes, then around at all the people and I smile triumphantly. I did it.

"Yes, Arthur," I reply.

Thrilled, he pulls me close and kisses me passionately. Shock runs through me. What is he doing? He wraps his arms around my waist and lifts me into the air exuberantly. The people cheer wildly and even Father nods with approval. I push against Arthur's shoulders, wanting him to put me down. I am trying to behave with dignity and he is acting like a child! What will the people think? He finally sets me on my feet and calls out loudly, "Let us feast, let us celebrate this great day!"

His eyes fill with the excitement of a boy with a new spear and he picks me up around the hips again and starts to carry me to the great hall. Disgusted at his behavior, I begin to wonder what I have done. Am I really going to be married to this child? Unable to convince him to put me down, I look around with embarrassment as the people watch. What are they to think of me if I allow Arthur to carry me around like this?

Everyone is laughing and talking as we enter the hall. Arthur carries me toward the head table and yells, "Food! Drink! . . . Music!"

Finally placing me down, he pulls me close to him again and kisses me with abandon. Frustrated and yet disarmed, I look around for help. Father then comes up to us both and slaps Arthur on the back.

"This is indeed a great day!"

He sees my embarrassment and takes my hand and kisses it tenderly. "My dear daughter, you fill your father with joy this day."

"Do I, Father? Is this what you want?" I ask with confusion. Does he really want marriage for me?

"It is."

I smile at him and again feel joy run through me. Father's happiness means more to me than my own. We look at each other for a long moment then are interrupted by Merlin, who walks up to Arthur. Arthur grabs Merlin's arm and excitedly pulls him close.

"Merlin, come, join us. I wish you to meet my future wife, Gwynnefwar."

I smile as Merlin looks at my clothing and hair. His eyes twinkling, he smiles back, taking my hand and kissing it.

"My lady, you are enchanting," he says.

He stands back and walks to the other side of Arthur. Many people begin to settle at the tables and musicians begin playing in the center. Arthur's men gather around him. A young handsome man of twenty-four with long red hair and a beard moves through the small crowd to congratulate us.

Arthur, seeing him, says, "Lancirus, my friend, come congratulate me."

Lancirus comes closer and stops, looking at me with puppy dog eyes, his mouth slightly agape. I laugh at him with kindness in my heart. He seems so much like a cuddly puppy. He continues to stare at me and I cannot resist teasing him.

"You stare, Lancirus."

Embarrassed, he pulls back a step, his eyes downcast. Arthur, seeing his friend captivated by me, pulls me close and laughs.

"She is enchanting, is she not?"

Lancirus looks up at me again. "She is that, my lord."

Arthur pats Lancirus on the back as he did the others and turning, motions for him to sit. As I watch him, I realize that I have ensnared Lancirus as well as Arthur. What a strange power I am acquiring! Arthur continues to speak.

"Drink! We celebrate this day."

Lancirus steps to the side and finds a place beside Merlin, who pours him some ale. Father moves to sit with Merlin and Lancirus continues to stare at me. I look at him out of the corner of my eye and am smiling when Arthur suddenly picks me up around the hips again.

I hide my embarrassment well as Arthur playfully embraces me, praying that he will not always be this way. My own parents certainly did not behave so demonstratively.

Nearby, Gulwain stands up abruptly from his seat. He already looks slightly drunk as he raises his cup and shouts loudly, "To victory!!!"

Roars of joy sound all around as Arthur puts me down and raises his cup to cheer boisterously with them. I remain quiet and again notice Lancirus staring at me. I give him a seductive look, practicing my new power and realizing that this man will be a valuable ally. I will be sure to continue to entice him. He turns from me in embarrassment at having been caught staring again. I laugh, and a young lady comes up beside me and whispers that she has an apple and that I should bite it, as the Christian beliefs teach of Eve biting the apple. I laugh with the young lady and take an apple from her. Then I taunt Arthur with it as everyone oohhs and aahhs. Arthur, enjoying the game, grabs it and bites it furiously, then throwing it away, he pulls me close to him again, ravaging my neck with his kisses. I throw my head back, finally realizing what the crowd wants, and they cheer. We then sit in our chairs and enjoy the entertainment.

I look around and notice a woman hiding behind a wooden pillar. Morgana, a small woman with straight light brown hair pulled back severely, pulls a cloth in front of her face when she notices me looking at her. She stares at me a moment then looks away quickly. I turn back to the entertainment as Arthur takes my hand

and kisses it, then fills my cup with more wine. Lingering around the tables nearer to me, Morgana suddenly appears, taking some food.

Arthur, spotting her, calls out, "Sister, Morgana!"

She turns and he waves her over. Looking scared, Morgana slowly makes her way to us as I turn to Arthur.

"Sister?"

"She is my half-sister."

Arthur stands behind me and places his hands on my shoulders as Morgana comes up to us. A strange tension fills the air between her and I. She looks at me with squinted eyes and jealousy in her face. I recognize her hatred immediately, for I have seen it at home, so I stand. A good bit taller than her, I am now able to look down at her with an air of strength. She stares at the floor, retreating from my gaze.

Arthur, unaware of the tension, is filled with joy as he squeezes me slightly from behind.

"Morgana, welcome my beautiful Gwynnefwar. She will be the lady of the land now."

Morgana offers me a false smile and says, "Welcome, lady. I wish your stay to be happy."

Surprised by her words, I reply sarcastically, "Stay? My stay will be for always, dear sister."

Arthur turns to answer a question from one of his men as we stare each other down for a moment. I give her a fierce glare and she finally looks away and leaves. I smile and sit back down. Again, I have won. What a glorious day this is.

As the evening wears on, Arthur and Father engage in talk of battle as they try to outdrink each other. I yawn and stretch a little, tired from the day's events.

I notice Morgana staring at me and return her look with fury. Shocked at my expression, she quickly turns away and scurries from the room. Shaking my head, I turn to tell Father I am going to bed just as Merlin stands to leave as well. Arthur seeing this, stops him.

"Merlin, have you any words of counsel for us?"

Merlin takes our hands and joins them together. "Look into each other's eyes."

Arthur's eyes are filled with love while I try to avoid this moment by staring at his nose.

"See not the outer shell, for it is enchanting to you both. See behind the eyes and you will see truth. Beware the shadows that cover the truth."

I quickly look away from Arthur and turn to Merlin, nervously wondering if he can read my thoughts, as Merewyn does. Merlin raises his eyebrows and turns to leave. I look back at Arthur.

"I must sleep, Arthur. I am weary," I say, pulling my hands from his and walking out of the hall as Arthur, quite drunk, sits back down.

Back in my room, I savor the day's events. So much has changed! It is a new beginning for me and for our country. We will surely push the heathens out now and renew the cities. Soon we will be able to rebuild more permanent structures of stone as the Romans did.

The oil bowls light the room with a warm glow and I find myself humming softly. Looking into the polished mirror I check my face. Am I beautiful? I do not know. What is beauty? My hair is unruly and long, but everyone seems to like it. I noticed both Arthur and Lancirus admiring it. I had always thought I understood men. I understand Father, but these men seem to be different. They think often of women rather than battle. I cannot help but begin to question their strengths. Surely Arthur has been taught that the land comes before all? As I watched him in battle today he showed great strength and fury fighting the Saxons. Can he also be gentle and kind? Why not? Father is. If he is like Father, we will certainly have a wonderful life together.

Gulwain, on the other hand, is quite different again. He is truly a warrior. Women do not seem to be important to him, although he and Merewyn have spent much time exchanging words and looks. He seems to be a ruthless warrior and therefore a powerful ally.

Now Lancirus, what a sweet boy he is! I do not remember seeing him fight today. I will certainly befriend him.

I lie down to sleep and awaken to find the day rainy and cool. Olwy and Rhianne knock on my door quite late in the morning and bring me food and a steaming herbal brew. Excited by the news of a wedding, they congratulate me and ask what I will wear.

"Wear?" I reply. "It matters not what I wear, you may decide for me."

Thrilled at the prospect of choosing my attire, the ladies start to chatter endlessly about wedding plans. Merewyn enters a while later and congratulates me as well on the news, although her thoughts seem to be somewhere else. I decide to let the three of them bother about the preparations while I go for a ride in the valley below. I pull on my tunic for the day, grab my dagger and hurry down to the stables.

As I ride out of the fort, I hear Arthur call after me, but I ignore him. I need to be alone with my horse and the countryside. The rain has lightened a bit and I enjoy the gentle spray against my face as I make my way through a heavily forested area. The cool air feels pleasant to breathe and my horse and I are invigorated by our run. The forest is magical this wet day as small birds and animals scurry about, seeking cover. A group of young deer gather amidst some bushes ahead of me.

I stop and watch them a moment, fascinated. They quietly move along as they hear me come closer.

I slow my horse to a gentle walk as I ponder my wedding, which will take place in two day's time. Father seemed so proud of me yesterday. I only wish he was as proud of my mind as he is in my ability to entice Arthur. Surely he must understand the purpose for this marriage and admire my cunning!

I come upon an old road and begin to follow it for a long way. It leads me to some overgrown bushes and trees. I make my way around the dense bush to find a large circle of giant stones, almost four feet high. Thrilled at my discovery, I dismount and tie my horse to a nearby tree. The rain begins to fall harder now and I pull my hood over my head. Walking amidst the stones I run my fingers across them and think of Merewyn. I must show her these. She has spoken to me of stone circles before and their power of drawing energy from the moon and sun and distributing it to the people and crops.

I sit by one of the stones and lean against it, allowing myself to absorb its strange energy. Oddly, I feel very ancient, as though time itself were nonexistent. I sit there for most of the day until dusk calls me back to the present. Reluctant to leave this sacred place, I decide that this will be my secret hideaway. I will tell no one but Merewyn of it.

I untie my horse and make my way back toward the fort, forgetting just how far I had gone. The journey home is a long one and when I return, I find that people are looking for me. Irritated by their overprotectiveness, I assure them that I am very capable of caring for myself. Gulwain approaches me with a stern look.

"Lady, it is not wise to ride alone."

"I am very able, sir," I retort and turn away from him.

Obviously annoyed by my self-assurance, he grunts and spits behind me, then walks toward the great hall. I leave my horse in the care of a young stable boy and return to my rooms to see that food has been placed on my table for me.

The next day I return again to my secret circle. I am enjoying my last moments of solitude as the people at the fort prepare for the wedding.

On the night before the wedding, I am again alone. Merewyn and the others are busying themselves with details and understand my need for privacy. I do not see why there is such ceremony over the joining of a man and woman. I long for it to be complete.

14

❖

Gwynnefwar,
Lady of the Britons

A SUMMER MORNING LIGHT FILTERS THROUGH MY ROOM AS
Rhianne picks up a silver comb and some fine gold
chains from the table. She walks toward the bed, where
I sit dressed in a sleeveless cream and gold colored
sheer dress with gold braided bands across the breasts
and around the waist. The dress hangs to the floor and
gently sweeps the ground behind me as I walk. Rhianne
and Olwy begin to comb my hair and tie the fine gold
chains into the top strands. It doesn't feel as good as
when father did it when I was a child. Rhianne and
Olwy giggle as I sit, bored, on the bed while everyone
rushes about me. All of this fuss for an afternoon ceremony! I wish it were finished. Olwy moves to my feet
and begins to lace delicate white leather thongs around
my legs. How uncomfortable they are!

Merewyn looks almost pretty in a light blue dress
with flowers in her hair as she sits at the far table, her

astrology charts in front of her. She looks up toward me with joy in her face.

"My lady, the stars are kind to you. Your union with Arthur is a union of spirit. You are birthed under the same moon. Your souls will be joined through eternity this day."

I open my eyes wide and smile at her, then speak as Rhianne pulls at my hair. Impatiently, I push her and Olwy away.

"Leave this," I say angrily.

I grab the comb and chains from Rhianne and throw them on the bed when there is a knock at the door. Olwy opens it and we all become silent as we see Lancirus standing there, dressed very formally in a tan embroidered tunic, with a rolled-up parchment in his hand. Glad to see him, I invite him in.

Standing in front of me, he unrolls the parchment paper. Merewyn, a worried look coming over her, watches closely as Lancirus begins to speak, a slight quiver in his voice.

"It is my Lord Arthur's wish that after the ceremony of marriage this day you be honored and welcomed as lady of the land," he says as he looks at the parchment and pauses a moment.

"I bring to you words from all of the people of this land. . . . We will honor you as Arthur's wife and as our lady. As the sun rises, your beauty has come to bless this land and nourish it."

I inhale deeply with pleasure and smile as Merewyn walks a little closer, looking more worried still. She looks closely into Lancirus's eyes, then suddenly opens hers wide, having seen the future.

"Come closer, Lancirus," I say.

His face full of love, he kneels in front of me, takes

my hand and kisses it. A little embarrassed but feeling empowered, I look around at the others.

"Leave us . . ."

Merewyn comes closer, insistent. "Lady, we have not time . . ."

I flash a look of irritation at her. "Leave us!"

Upset, she lowers her eyes and walks out the door, taking Rhianne and Olwy with her. Lancirus looks up at me and I tenderly touch his sweet face.

"Lady, I am enchanted by your mystery. When I see your eyes, I am filled with love for you."

A sad look comes over him and I cannot help but cup his face in my hands as he continues. "I will not dishonor you, nor Arthur. Know simply, I am your devoted servant."

I smile gently and pull him up. "Stand, Lancirus. You are a gentle spirit. I am in need of a gentle spirit. Always be my friend."

He kisses my hands, lowering his eyes, then turns and walks out of the room. Merewyn returns anxiously, staring at me and trying to read my eyes. I walk to the window and she calls after me, "Careful, my lady."

I look out at the summer day and assure her. "I am not a fool," I say as she walks closer to me.

"You are playing with that man."

How dare she question me! "He is gentle and kind. He pleases me."

Merewyn shakes her head. "He is weak and you feel superior. Therefore he is safe."

I turn angrily to her, irate at her presumptuousness. "I fear no man!"

Merewyn raises her eyebrows and looks directly at me, as though to challenge me. "You fear Arthur. For only he can stir the passion in you. With Arthur you *must* be a woman."

I laugh at her silly words. "You know nothing of such things. No one knows what I feel."

I turn back to the window, my mind suddenly recalling the day I was raped. I begin to tremble when there is a knock at the door and see Father, handsome in his green tunic, his hair combed. He enters and stops before me, breathless at my appearance. I am overcome with dismay when he kneels before me. Why kneel, you are my father?

"My daughter, today I give you to Arthur with my love. Today you step into power, use it well. You are no longer mine, you are Arthur's."

I pull back a moment at the idea of being any man's, then put my hand on his shoulder. My heart wants to hold him and be his little girl again but another part of me feels suddenly mighty and wise.

"Rise, Father."

As I look at him standing in front of me, his face both sad and happy, I feel bereft and find it hard to hold back tears.

He clears his throat as his emotions begin to overwhelm him, and he turns to leave as Olwy and Rhianne rush in to tell me it is time to go.

We leave my room and enter the courtyard to find a tiny, beautiful cart strewn with ribbons and flowers and pulled by two men in soldier's uniforms, breastplates covering their chests and odd-looking metal helmets on their heads. Father and the women run off ahead and I sit carefully inside the cart, part of me feeling that I am being led to my execution rather than my wedding.

We make our way down the road and into the valley below. The day is warm and the sun filters softly through the trees, lighting up flower petals strewn along the road by the village people. It seems as though I am dreaming, everything is moving so slowly. The trees are decorated with bright colored cloth and as we come closer to the ceremonial place, I pass the faces of hundreds of people. They all stare, fascinated with this new lady of the community.

I see Morgana hiding by a tree, and I look ahead and find Arthur and an older Christian bishop waiting for me. Apprehension comes over me as I move closer to them. Arthur is resplendent in his red and gold tunic with cream-colored breeches and tall brown boots. An exquisite gold medallion hangs about his neck. He comes toward me as the cart stops, and takes my hand.

He stops to look into my eyes for a moment as he helps me out of the cart. I smile nervously, and he leads me to the bishop.

The bishop is a serious-looking man with brightly embroidered golden robes. He seems rather a funny figure to me, so stiff in his many robes and gold medals. So much finery on a man would never be seen in Father's fort. I look quickly around and see Father and Merewyn watching from close to my left, and on the other side behind the crowd is Lancirus, his face straight and cold. Arthur and I turn to face the bishop as he begins to speak in Latin.

We stand in front of him and he takes an embroidered piece of cloth and, placing my hand on top of Arthur's, he binds our two hands together. I resist a little as he continues reading the ceremony and notice that Arthur keeps looking at my sheer dress. He is so easy to read. My mind wanders a little. I cannot understand the bishop very well because he speaks a formal Latin, and having my hand bound to Arthur's makes me feel uncomfortable, although I force myself to keep still. I wonder whether this marriage is real in the eyes of my people, as it speaks only of Arthur's Christian god and not the spirits of the universe nor the goddesses of spirit and earth.

A young, timid-looking priest enters my field of vision from the right. He is dressed in cream-colored robes and carries a bowl filled with water. He stands by the older bishop and holds the bowl out to him as the elder dips his fingers into the water and then blesses the air with his hand. He then touches my forehead and Arthur's, blessing us both. Realizing this ceremony is similar to the one Merewyn performed on me, I begin to relax. The bishop continues the ceremony in our mixed Briton/Celtic language, and the young priest moves aside and watches.

"As a disciple of God, I herewith bind you, one to each other and each other to God for eternity as he unites all people under his eyes. He joins your souls to each other."

Father watches with pride and Morgana's face becomes increasingly distraught. She turns to run from the ceremony and bumps into Merlin. As she looks up at him, her eyes are filled with tears, and she runs away back toward the fort. Merlin raises his eyebrows and smiles to himself, and the bishop continues by placing his hand over mine and Arthur's.

"Arthur, you are herewith to honor Gwynnefwar as part of yourself."

He blesses the air with his hands and motions for us to turn and face the people. Very slowly, the crowd of onlookers kneel before us. Gulwain comes forward carrying a medallion of gold on a chain of gold, the same as Arthur's. My eyes widen with anticipation as Gulwain approaches Arthur and he reaches for the medallion. Lifting it, Arthur nods to Gulwain and Gulwain retreats backward a few steps. Arthur places the necklace over my head and looks deep into my eyes, causing my heart to race.

"Gwynnefwar, as duke of the Britons, I honor you as lady of the Britons. Together we join our souls. I give to you my power, my wisdom ... my love."

Arthur's men kneel and raise their swords in unison, and I turn to look at them and raise my right arm, inviting them to rise.

Suddenly, I begin to feel dizzy and I sway slightly, trying to control myself. Arthur swiftly places his hand under my elbow to steady me. I don't know what is wrong. I feel so weak! I look to Arthur for support and become even weaker and falter. Without missing a beat, Arthur catches me in his embrace, and the whole crowd cheers as he carries me down the path and back to the cart. Quickly, he orders the men to pull us up to the fort as he holds me in his arms. My vision fades and my body feels hot as I hear Arthur command his people.

"Let us feast!"

Feast! Not now, I cannot stay awake. He must be trying to maintain calm.

Inside the great hall the tables are filled with huge platters of beef and ham surrounded by many types of vegetables and flat breads and tall jugs of wine. Arthur carries me to my chair at the main table beside his and places me gently down. He kneels beside me but I can barely keep my head up.

"What is wrong?" he says, but I barely hear him.

"The day has been too much for me," I whisper.

Arthur looks behind me and suddenly looks concerned.

"What ... what is it?" I ask in desperation.

Arthur starts forward calling, "Morgana!"

Morgana runs from the hall and Arthur turns to me. "What have you eaten today?"

"Some ladies brought me food and drink," I say in confusion as I try to remember.

"Did you note a strangeness in the food?" he asks anxiously, holding both my arms with his hands.

"No ... no ... it was just a drink, why?"

"Where do you feel weak?"

"My head, it spins ... to breathe ... is difficult."

Father walks up behind Arthur, concern creasing his face and says, "What is wrong?"

"She feels weak. I must take her to our room."

Arthur lifts me and the whole crowd of people cheer all over again. Father shouts to them as Arthur carries me out of the hall.

"Drink, the lovers wish to be alone!"

The people laugh and continue to feast as Arthur carries me up the stairs to my room.

Inside I try to speak but my head keeps falling against Arthur's shoulder. I am overwhelmed with dizziness. Merewyn follows quickly behind us.

"Lord, what has happened?"

Arthur gently places me on the bed and Merewyn comes around the other side. Frustrated with his inability to help or protect me and fighting the idea that Morgana could have caused my suffering, Arthur looks angrily at Merewyn. Perhaps *she* is to blame! He comes quickly around to where she stands and grabs her roughly, pushing her up against the wall. I try to gather my strength.

"No, stop, it is not her. She did nothing," I sputter.

He holds Merewyn roughly by the shoulders, questioning her. "What have you done? This is your fault!"

Merewyn looks fearfully at Arthur, unable to move.

"I have done nothing," she falters.

I drag myself across the bed toward Arthur and grab at his clothes. "Let her go, it is not her," I plead.

Arthur, knowing he is wrong and feeling helpless, lets her go and rubs his face with his hands. He turns to me on the bed as Merewyn composes herself and begins to check my eyes and tongue, murmuring softly. Arthur stands back a little and allows Merewyn to continue her examination.

"How do you feel, lady?"

Arthur raises his head to the ceiling and unable to ignore the growing realization of Morgana's guilt, he whispers aloud, "Morgana . . . yes."

Merewyn turns to me. "What have you drunk today?"

Drifting, I say feebly, "Just the drink some ladies brought to me."

Merewyn looks toward Arthur and nods. Arthur quickly leaves the room as I call after him.

"Where are you going?"

"To find Morgana!" he replies sharply as fury begins to build in him.

As he storms out of the room, I look to Merewyn for help and she caresses my face tenderly.

"All will be well. I have something that will make you stronger."

In a small room filled with herbs and plants hanging from the beams, Morgana is crushing herbs with a pestle. She is humming happily to herself and dancing around her table with demonic glee. Suddenly, Arthur bursts through her door, his eyes wild with rage and his chest heaving.

Morgana turns quickly to him and her eyes widen in surprise as Arthur grabs her by the throat and pushes her backward over her table. Filled with terror, she tries to speak but is unable to and Arthur towers over her, pushing her still farther back onto the table.

"What have you done? Tell me, what have you done to Gwynnefwar?" he questions angrily.

Terrified, she stares at Arthur, unable to utter a word. He shakes her, determined to get answers.

"Speak!"

He loosens his hands a little as Morgana begins to smile mischievously, like a child. Arthur's eyes become small and he looks closely into her face.

"If you have harmed my wife in any way, you will *never* see light again," he threatens.

He pushes her to the floor in disgust and she crawls to the corner of the room.

"She will not be ill for long," she stutters. "I gave her something to make her weak, that is all."

She pulls her legs up to her chest and Arthur looks at her with disgust. "You have evil in your soul, Morgana. I will not forget this," he warns.

He gives her one more disgusted look and walks away. She slowly rises and walks to the door to be sure Arthur is gone. Closing it, she turns around and begins to dance in glee around her table, thrilled with herself and completely unaware that she has just made a mortal enemy.

Back in the room, I am sitting up in bed as Merewyn gives me something to drink. Arthur walks in and sits beside me. He looks at me for a long moment, noticing the sweat on my face, then turns to Merewyn. Merewyn smiles at him, forgiving him for his outburst.

"She will be well soon. There is no need for worry. She must rest a while, that is all."

Merewyn walks over to the table and begins to gather her medicines."

"Was it Morgana?" I ask weakly.

"Forget Morgana, I will make sure she does not harm you."

He gets up and readies himself to leave. "Rest a while. I will return later so we can be together."

He smiles and kisses me on the mouth, then leaves the room and Merewyn follows him. I sigh to myself and lie back down to rest, vowing revenge on Morgana. You will learn, Morgana! Petty poisons will not kill me. I will be forever at your back from now on. You will never rest from worry.

As sleep comes over me, I dream of revenge on Morgana. Too soon, it seems, Merewyn enters and awakens me. I sit up and stretch as she talks to me.

"Lady, are you feeling well now?"

"Yes, Merewyn. A memorable wedding day it was. Will you bring me some water? My throat is dry."

"It is the poison that makes you so thirsty."

We both look at each other in silence, thankful that I am well, She goes to the table and begins to pour some water from a pitcher. The door squeaks open and a young girl of twelve enters. Her face is covered in boils and her hair is unruly and long. I invite her in.

"Hello," I say. "What is your name?"

She looks at me with awe and speaks shyly. "Arius, my lady. I wish to bring you food and drink."

"Come," I say softly, my heart going out to her.

She seems so innocent and gentle, yet afraid of showing her face. Her hair hangs over much of it, covering her eyes. She walks in and places some food on the table.

"Do you live here with your parents?" I ask.

"My mother, lady. My father is dead. He was a soldier like Arthur."

I motion for her to come closer. She moves beside me and I touch her chin. "Do you miss your father?" I ask kindly.

Her eyes look softly at me. "Yes, my lady."

My heart swells with sympathy for her as I sense her

loneliness. Something inside me longs to take her under my wing. I notice she dresses in boy's clothes.

"Why do you where a tunic and not girl's clothing?" I ask.

"I wish to be strong, like the men," she replies quietly. "The girls do not like me."

I find myself angered at this, understanding her completely. "Well, my dear Arius, you may be my friend if you wish. I will teach you how to plan a battle as the men do."

Arius's eyes light up with excitement. "Oh, thank you lady, thank you. I will go and tell the others."

She runs excitedly from the room and I smile to myself as Merewyn brings my water over.

"You were very kind to her," she says.

"She reminds me of myself," I say, drifting back to memories of my childhood.

15

※

The Wedding Night

THE DARK OF EVENING CASTS LONG SHADOWS ACROSS MY
room as Merewyn finishes lighting the oil bowls. I drink
my water in silence while I watch her gentle movements,
so graceful and serene. She must think me clumsy.

She moves to the far side of the room and pulls a
sheer robe from a trunk and smiles a little wickedly as
she brings it toward me.

"We must ready you, my lady."

My body tightens. It is time. My wedding night.
There is nothing I can do to change it. I again remember
the rape and feel a cold chill run through me. I force
the memory out of my head, trying to remember that
Arthur is gentle and kind. All will be well. I will simply
detach myself from my body.

I rise and walk to the table with the wash basin on
it. Taking a cloth, I bathe my face as Merewyn comes
up behind me with a small leather bag. She reaches in

and takes out a bottle. Opening it, she smells it and smiles, then pours some liquid onto her fingertips and dabs it onto my forehead.

"Scented water! Mmmm," I say.

She dabs the perfume above my breasts. Then motioning for me to undo my robe, she dabs some between my thighs. Surprised at this, I look down at her and we laugh together.

"Remember, my lady, you have great power now."

I look at her sceptically and she continues.

"Over Arthur. Be careful with it. He loves you dearly," she says. She is concerned that I may have entered this marriage for the wrong reasons.

Feeling a little overwhelmed by the day, I listen to her without argument.

"The body can offer you much pleasure, my lady, allow yourself to enjoy it . . . to enjoy your womanhood."

Enjoy it. How could I enjoy it? Ice seems to creep through my whole body. "I care not for bodily pleasure. It is weak," I say coldly.

Merewyn looks at me with worry and pleads, "Do not be so cold, my lady. Arthur only wishes to love you. You were not born a man . . . you were born to *receive* a man. Your body is your treasure."

"Treasure? You mean curse!" I say, turning around to finish dressing.

"Why did you marry Arthur?" she says, confronting me.

I straighten my back at the insolent question, wanting greatly to avoid it, but knowing that Merewyn will see the truth anyway. "Together, we can rule this land," I say truthfully.

She shakes her head sadly, knowing I am heading for trouble. "I fear for your heart, my lady. You throw away a precious gift."

She turns and leaves and I am glad to be alone. I am combing my hair absently when I hear footsteps coming toward the room. I lean back against the table, my nervousness rising.

Arthur opens the door and seeing me, stops, breathless for a moment as he feels an immense love overtake him. He recognizes my nervousness and vows to himself to be gentle and tender. He balances two cups and a jug in one hand as he closes the door behind him and walks toward me, his eyes never leaving mine. He hands me a cup and pours some steaming brew into it. I smell it and smile.

"Spiced wine, my lord?" I ask, knowing the answer.

He smiles lovingly in return, his body beginning to warm with the thought of making love to me.

"Indeed so, *my lady*."

He looks deeply at me, as though right into my soul. "Gwynnefwar ... with you by my side my life is full. Soon we will have peace in Britain and I will spend all of my days and nights in bliss with you," he says with sincerity.

I raise the cup to my mouth while holding Arthur's gaze and sip the hot wine. A small trickle escapes the cup and wets my lip. Delighted at the chance to touch me, Arthur lifts his finger very gently, still looking into my eyes, and wipes the droplet from my lip and chin very slowly. I seem to sway slightly, losing my balance for a moment as a strange warmth runs through me. What is this odd feeling, I wonder?

He puts his cup and the jug on the table behind me and then takes mine from my slightly trembling hands and rests it on the table as well. He then softly traces my lips again with his hand and starts to move his hand down my throat and toward my breasts. I try to compose myself but find I am having great difficulty as my head and body feel like they will explode.

Arthur, realizing he must awaken what has been dormant in me, seems to know just what to do as he opens the front of my sheer robe. Slowly kneeling in front of me, he gently presses his lips to my belly and pulls me close to his mouth. I look down at him and gasp quietly, placing my hands on his hair and thinking, what is he doing?

Fear comes over me as I realize I am losing control. I try hard to fight the heat that is rising in my body but find it a losing battle. As I look down at him I am almost terrified at what might happen next. As if purposely trying to break me, he rises and lifts me into his arms in one rapid movement. He places me on the bed and quickly removes his clothes as I try to think of what to do.

I must allow him to love me, yet I need to detach myself from it. Why isn't it working? He bends over me on the bed and begins to kiss my neck and breasts as he whispers gently, "Gwynnefwar, I have waited forever for this moment. You leave me weak, like a boy."

Lying there, I smile to myself at the thought that I leave him weak, but I am weak as well. As he presses his kisses along the length of my body, a strange tingling arises in my womanhood. My body is on fire and a part of me wants to pull him to me, but I mustn't. This must end soon, I must hold on. As he positions himself on top of me and slowly enters my body, I go rigid with dread but somehow this doesn't feel the same as the rape.

Arthur pushes farther into me and we begin to move in rhythm together. Passion builds in me and my breathing becomes erratic. I try desperately to think of something else, but I feel overcome. I am lost, I cannot control this. Immediately, my body is washed by a wave of intense energy and I realize that I must be dying. I grab the bed and dig my fingers into it. This is the end, I cannot breathe, why does he not stop? I gasp and cry out as my body explodes and then it is over. I release my hand from the bed and try to catch my breath as Arthur continues to thrust himself inside me. Then he too seems overcome by energy and moans loudly and I am shocked to feel his body spasm as mine did. Spent, he comes to rest beside me on the bed.

I turn and roll away from him, bringing my hand up to my mouth to stifle a cry. I begin to shake with emotion and try to keep it inside but my eyes well with tears anyway. I don't understand, I thought I was dying. I lost myself with him. He overcame me.

He turns to me and reaches for my face, pulling it around so that he can see me. Seeing the tears, he becomes concerned.

"My love, why do you weep?" he says with tenderness.

I compose myself quickly and become cold. "I do not weep. It is the potion Morgana gave me."

I turn my head away and close my eyes, trying to forget what just happened, but he presses close behind me and surrounds my body with his. He felt my fear and my pleasure.

Very satisfied with himself for finding the woman in me, he holds me tightly until he falls asleep. I try to pull away from him, but each time I do he awakens and pulls me back into his arms. I am frustrated and cannot sleep as morning seems to take forever to arrive. I lie there and wonder if I should have married this man. Something must change, this cannot continue. I must have control back. I am the strong one.

We awaken in the morning and I quickly jump from bed as Arthur smiles to himself and shakes his head, realizing it will be some time before he can break down my walls. He whispers to himself, "I will find you, I will make a woman of you."

Hearing something as I comb my hair, I turn to him. "Did you speak?"

"Only thinking aloud, my love," he says, deciding to break down some barriers. "Was I tender enough last night?" he says with that devilish grin on his face.

Frozen, I want only to avoid this conversation. "Yes, my lord. You must be hungry. Shall I ask Arius to bring you some food?" I say, walking to the door as he calls me.

"No. You need not bother Arius. I will find my own food," he replies in frustration. Realizing how difficult getting close to me will be, he is resigned to a long but playful struggle and laughs aloud as he dresses and I wait at the door.

"You change words very quickly, my love. We have many years to find each other," he says, coming very close to me and taking my chin in his large hand. "I am not going to hurt you. You need not fight me," he says tenderly and leaves the room.

I relax and drop on the bed for a moment, relieved that the night is over and we can now get on with the purpose of our lives. An elderly woman bursts into the room and stops abruptly.

"My lady, I am here to help you with your bath," she says, then waits formally.

"My bath?" I shriek. "I need no bath!"

"Oh yes, my lady. All women here bathe. I will assist you, as Lord Arthur tells me that you have not enjoyed our custom of bathing before."

Lord Arthur spoke, did he? Well, I am sure he feels quite powerful this day, ordering me about. I will show him! If that is the custom of this land, then I will try it. I am not afraid of being naked with the other women. I pull my robe about me and follow the elderly woman to the baths.

Once inside the steamy room, I am pleased and relieved to see that no one else is in there. I turn to the lady.

"Where are the other women?" I ask in surprise.

"Oh, no, my lady. The bath is for you alone whenever you wish it. I am here only to assist you." She then begins to help me off with my robes and leads me to the hot, steamy water of the bath.

The creamy pink of the bath stone is soft and slippery as I run my fingers over it. I am filled with a sense of luxury. As I look closer at the tiles on the floor, I notice they are painted in many beautiful shades of blue. I walk up two steps then down one into the bath. With a cry of pain, I jerk my foot back out.

"It is too hot! I cannot sit in this!"

The elderly lady smiles knowingly and pushes me gently with her hand. "It is right that way, my lady. You will see once you enter. It is hot for only a moment. It heals the body and pulls the ills from the skin," she says, motioning with her hand for me to try.

Stepping in it again, I cannot help but think that the Romans were mad! Surely this cannot be truth. I will burn in this water. Still, I must not show weakness in front of this woman, for she will tell all of the community. I hold my breath and enter the tub, then sit down and the water rises to my neck.

"You see, my lady, all is well," she chatters. "I will now add some perfume to the bath."

She takes a blue painted jar from one of the tables

nearby and opening it, pours some lavender liquid into the water.

The smell is exquisite, like exotic flowers, and I inhale deeply, allowing the fragrance to intoxicate me. I rest my head back and the lady quickly grabs a tiny pillow for my neck, then blows out some of the oil bowls that rest on three-foot pedestals nearby. Moments later she places some cloths and jars of liquid beside me on the ridge of the marble tub.

"Here are some soaps, my lady. I will leave you to yourself and return soon," she says quietly and sneaks out of the room.

As I look around this place, I realize just how lovely it is. No wonder the people enjoy coming here. The many oil bowls create an otherworldly atmosphere. I linger in the bath for a long time, enjoying the strange sensation of heat that the water brings to my body. I feel almost sleepy again and I allow myself to close my eyes and rest. Finally, after what seems like hours, the elderly lady returns with a large bowl of fruits and breads. She rests them on the marble tub and leaves the room only to return quickly with a jug of fruit drink as well.

"You must eat now, my lady. Your body will weaken with the heat," she insists.

Realizing the truth in this, I sit up straight and enjoy the food she has brought to me. I finish my food and she returns to stand behind me with some large softened wool cloths to dry me.

I rise from the tub and allow her to help me dry off. This is what the old Roman queens must have felt like. Renewed, I am ready to charge the Saxons with vigor. I realize that she has also brought me a dress from my trunk. I laugh a little at the thought of having to wear a dress every day and shake my head.

"No, I will wear my green tunic this day," I state with assurance.

I gather my robe around me and make my way back to my room, where I dress myself. Then I go down to the great hall, where people are busy eating. I walk apprehensively into the center of the room, take a pitcher and pour some steaming brew into my cup. The people stare at me and smile politely and I am very aware of everyone's eyes upon me. I straighten my back as I walk toward the main table with what I hope is the air of a queen. Seeing Morgana amongst some ladies, I decide that this is a good time to confront her.

Walking directly up to her, I stare into her face while she tries not to show fear, standing frozen as I smile wickedly.

"I know what you have done. But you will not win, Morgana. Arthur is mine, remember it well. If you do, I *may* let you stay here."

I give her one last intense glare and turn and walk away. Drawing a relieved breath, she turns and leaves the hall.

Back in her room, Morgana fondles her plants and potions, frustrated at not having frightened me. Her mind races with ways to get me to leave. "Arthur was meant for me, not her," she says aloud.

Desperate, she tries to think of a way to convince Arthur that I am wrong for him. She thinks back to her childhood and smiles at the memory of caring for Arthur as a baby.

"You are mine, Arthur. I am the only one who can care for you. I promised Mother I would protect you always. She does not love you. She only wants power. I must learn the potions that Merewyn knows, then I will show you, my lord. I will prove that I am worthy of you."

She wanders over to a mirror that stands in the corner. It is a beautiful old polished metal mirror that she can see her full body in. She caresses herself and tries to forget that it has become heavier and older.

"I am still beautiful. Her beauty is cold, mine is soft," she says as though trying to convince herself, pulling her hair back fiercely from her face.

Although she is still young, Morgana's face is weathered from spending much time outside, and her hair has become thin and lifeless. Realizing this, she turns quickly from her mirror and runs out of her room and into one of the rooms on the lower floor.

It is a well-furnished room with many chairs and tapestries of the Christian Mother Mary. In the front of the room there is a large altar with books and various articles on it. Morgana walks up to the altar and kneels.

"Help me, God. I have no one. I must have Arthur. I must have him," she pleads. Humming again, she starts to rummage through one of the books, searching for some answer that will help her.

16

Finding My Power

BACK IN THE GREAT HALL I WALK TO THE MAIN TABLE AND join Arthur as he talks with Father. Anxious to spend some time with Father myself, I move between them and they rise to welcome me. Arthur takes my hand and guides me to my chair as Father says gently, "My daughter, . . . you are beautiful this day."

I smile at him, wishing we could go outside and create a mock battle like we used to, but I bite into a piece of fruit instead. Merlin enters from the side and motions for Arthur to come and join him at the food table in the center. Arthur rises and Father takes my hands and looks sadly into my eyes, his heart welling up with emotion.

"My dear one, I must leave you," he whispers tenderly.

My heart skips a beat with alarm before I gather my composure, knowing I must show my strength to him now.

"Will you not stay awhile? What of helping Arthur?" I plead softly.

"No, I must return north. My men are needed there. I have heard that the Picts are close to our lands again. Arthur understands."

He shakes his head, knowing we are both hurting inside at the thought of separation.

"You are a true woman now, you do not need a father any longer. You have a new man in your life," he says, almost wishing it weren't true.

Sadness overwhelms me but I force myself to smile as my throat chokes a little.

"Will I see you again?"

He tries to avoid my eyes and sighs heavily. "Someday. Remember your strength, Gwynnefwar. Look around you. These people are not your enemy. Make them your friends. They are not so different from our people. If you do this, you will always be safe. You must trust in Arthur now, he will not betray you."

I look around at Arthur then to Father, then back to Arthur. I take a deep breath and remember my mission. I am a leader and I must lead. I can no longer rely on Father. I must stand alone. I turn to him with purpose.

"I will miss you, Father, and I will make you proud."

"Go now, be with your husband. I leave in the morning," he says, trying to avoid an emotional scene.

He kisses my hands and we look at each other for a long moment. Holding my head high and suppressing the tightness in my throat, I turn and make my way to Arthur as Father watches me.

Some of Arthur's men have gathered around him. They are speaking of the coming of the Saxons, and I am aware that they do not want my intrusion. I must assert myself this moment or I will never have the respect of these men. I have to gain back what I lost last night. Arthur must hear me, and the only way to get him to listen is to use my body. Very well, if that is the only way, but this time, I will control you. I lift my head proudly and moving into the center of the circle that has enclosed Arthur, I place my hand on his arm. Lancirus stands beside Arthur and the expression on his face is sad as he tries to avoid my eyes. I look at Arthur seductively and speak firmly.

"Arthur, be with me now?"

Arthur looks very surprised and not a little suspicious of my motives. Merlin, who stands beside him, smiles to himself, knowing full well that I need to be the center of attention.

The men seem embarrassed as they move away and talk amongst themselves. Lancirus turns abruptly and walks to the other side of the room. Arthur looks at me and smiles, then takes my hand and leads me out of the hall and toward our room. Before entering, he hesitates.

"I want to show you something," he says and leads me farther down the hallway to another room.

We enter a large chamber with maps and charts strewn over tables and walls. In the center of the room is a large square table covered with maps. He motions for me to come closer as he points toward them.

"I must go with my men soon. The Saxons are coming from the East and the Scots from the Northwest. We must prepare for battle," he says with concern in his voice.

Excited, I grab his arm. "I can help you. My father taught me strategy. Let me see the maps."

I move closer to the maps and look carefully. Scanning them, I trace my fingers over certain areas, a plan coming to life in my head.

"The Saxons, they are here now?"

He bends over the table and looks at where I'm pointing, to the middle and eastern part of Britain.

"They are," he replies, nodding.

I frown for a moment in deep thought as I notice some problems in his battle plans. Then I point to the map again.

"You have too many men in one place. Look, you need to spread them out into smaller groups."

Arthur looks at where I am pointing, his curiosity piqued as I continue to show him.

"You see, this large group will come across the river Glein where it is most narrow, but the smaller groups may cross at other parts. When they do cross they will be tired. They have no horses, so they will need to rest. We need to surprise them before they can regain their strength."

I look to him for agreement and he rubs his hand through his beard, thinking. I look back at the maps.

"If you put all of your men in one spot as you have, they stand a greater chance of being attacked. If you put them in smaller groups, here," I say, pointing, "along these places by the river, then scouts here on the hills can signal each other by fire and alert the other groups, who can join together in the spot where the Saxons are," I say. "Do you see, Arthur?"

I wait excitedly for his reply, looking at him as he ponders what I have just said. He starts to smile.

"Yes, I see."

I take his arm with my hand. "It is much safer this way. What if the Saxons come across the river here instead," I say, pointing again. "Then you will miss them and they will make their way here." I pause for a moment to let him think, then continue.

"The signal fires will alert the men who can ride quickly by horse. The hills also rise above the mist of the swampy ground, so there is no fear that the scouts will not see the signal fires."

He stands and places his hands on his hips as he looks at me with a big smile. "I agree, my love, it is a good plan. You are a wonder to me."

He laughs a little, amazed and proud of me. I realize I must now make a move and so stand up and look right into his eyes.

"Arthur, . . . take me with you."

"Take you with me?" he says, astounded that I would even think of such a thing, a woman, in battle. He laughs slightly, mocking me.

"Your place is here, as my wife, not in battle."

He walks over toward the window. Anger begins to grow in me and my face reddens. "Arthur, listen to me. I am your partner, not only your wife."

He stares out of the window in disbelief.

"I can help you, Arthur. I have been in battle before . . . with my father. I need to be by your side . . . *Please.*"

He turns slowly to me, a look of concern on his face.

"No, I want you here. Someone must be in charge here while I am away."

I draw in a deep breath and close my eyes for a moment. I must try something else. I open my eyes again, and it is as though a seductress has suddenly inhabited my body. I look at Arthur and walk slowly to him by the window. I stand right in front of him and gently caress his neck and chest with my hand. He remains still, not quite sure of how to handle this change in me. I press my body closer to his and whisper, "Arthur, please let me go with you."

Arthur looks upward to the ceiling, understanding my game and becoming annoyed as I continue to try this new tactic.

"I know what I am doing, my love. I can be a great help to you in battle," I beg.

He grabs my arms and looks fiercely at me. "Stop this ... You are not going. These are my words," he says and pushes me gently away and walks back to the table.

I'm frustrated, but I haven't given up. Still playing the seductress, I decide on a new strategy. I come up behind Arthur and touch his back lightly.

"Arthur, I want you to make me your second in command. Your partner."

He turns quickly, amazed at my request. I continue before he can stop me.

"If I am to stay here without you, I must be second in command. If not, the people will not give me their loyalty."

He rubs his fingers through his beard, scratching it, and shakes his head, recognizing some truth in what I am saying but not convinced.

"Gulwain is my second in command," he retorts.

"Yes, but he is always with you. He will never need that command. I need it here. I must have the people's loyalty. They are your people now. If you make me second, they will become my people too," I say, looking at him firmly, knowing I am right. The people must respect me if I am to lead them. If he doesn't respect me, they certainly never will.

"Make me your partner, Arthur, you know I am worthy of it. I can plan a battle better than any of your men."

He turns to the table and fingers the maps, trying to make a decision. He turns back to me with an air of resignation. "All right, my partner, it will be so."

Triumphant, I move up close to him, and taking his hand, I rub his palm down the front of my body, glad to share myself now. I smile at him and kiss him on the lips. He sighs deeply and pulls me over to a cot by the wall.

"You have wicked ways, my wife," he moans as he pulls up my tunic and his as well.

This time I am in complete control as he thrusts his body inside mine. Glowing with pleasure at the prospect of being his second in command, I am barely aware of what he is doing. Quickly, it is over, and he rests on his side looking up at the ceiling and wonders why I want so much to be like a man. Recognizing that he will never understand it, he rises and leaves the room, calling for someone, then returns and sits at the table of maps. Fixing my clothes, I rise and move to the window and look outside, a smile of conquest on my face. There is a knock at the door and Arthur calls out, "Come."

Gulwain enters, followed by Lancirus. Arthur motions them toward the maps as I listen carefully in the shadows by the window.

"The plan has been changed, my men, look for yourself. Give me your ideas."

Gulwain and Lancirus bend down and go over the maps as Arthur watches me. Gulwain looks at Arthur with a pleasant surprise on his face.

"This is masterful, my Lord. I should have thought of it."

Lancirus stands straight and nods his head.

"Yes . . . yes. I agree. Putting men on the hills and forming smaller groups will enable us to cover more ground along the river."

I walk to the table with great dignity.

"Thank you," I say with confidence.

Gulwain and Lancirus look wide-eyed in amazement as they both stare at me and then at Arthur. Speechless, they wait for Arthur to speak. Arthur wanders around the subject and starts scratching at his beard as he becomes increasingly uncomfortable with the situation.

"Yes, yes . . . it was Lady Gwynnefwar's plan."

Turning around and rubbing the back of his neck, Gulwain is visibly disturbed. Lancirus, quiet and thoughtful, looks at the maps as Arthur continues, a little embarrassed.

"Her father skilled her well in battle, did he not?"

Lancirus speaks quietly, almost to himself. "Yes . . ."

Gulwain mutters something inaudible toward the wall as I walk behind Arthur and place my hands on his shoulders, looking directly at Gulwain's back. I realize I need to push Arthur into telling them his decision.

"Arthur, will you not tell them what we spoke of?" I push.

Arthur squirms in his seat and I wait a moment, then speak out, impatiently. "Our Lord Arthur has made me his second in command. I am his partner in every way now."

Lancirus chokes for a moment and turns wide-eyed and looks at me. Gulwain, silent, turns as well, his right hand clenched into a fist as he fights his anger.

"I ask you both now for your allegiance and loyalty to me as your leader as well as Arthur's right hand," I continue.

Gulwain looks at me with disgust as he stands back. "I will not."

Lancirus, confused, looks at Arthur. Gulwain also turns to look at Arthur, waiting for his words, and Arthur stands and rubs his beard even harder as he turns to look at me for a moment. I shoot him a stern look in return and he turns to Gulwain and Lancirus.

"I have made Gwynnefwar my second in command. I ask that you both swear your loyalty to her now. The people need to know that I trust her with command here at Salisbury."

Lancirus stands straight and looks directly at me. "Lady, I give you my allegiance and loyalty as My Lord Arthur's wife and second in command."

Gulwain moves restlessly about in frustration. He is filled with loathing for me. Not only does he not trust me but he firmly believes that I will bring Arthur down. He promises himself that he will watch my every move and make sure I do not control Arthur. Sensing his mistrust, I walk over to him and look him coldly in the eyes, one warrior to another.

"Gulwain, I am more skilled in strategy than you. I ask for your loyalty now. Will you give it?"

He looks hard at me and I remain firm. We stare at each other for a long moment. Gulwain's face is red with rage as he speaks icily to me with a clenched jaw.

"Yes, lady. I do here swear."

Standing back from him now, I feel triumphant even though I know Gulwain is not on my side. It doesn't matter. Arthur is, that is what's important. Soon they will see that I do this not to destroy them but to help them. I am a better strategist and I will prove myself. Soon they will all recognize my true skill as a leader.

Arthur sighs in relief. "It is done. We begin preparations this day for battle. We leave in four days."

Lancirus and Gulwain nod and turning, walk out of the room without uttering a word. Exhilarated, I move in front of Arthur and speak. "Thank you, my lord, I will not disappoint you. Together we will lead our people to victory," I say sincerely.

Arthur looks lovingly at me, knowing I am right but concerned about what these changes will do to his community and friendship with Gulwain. "You could never disappoint me," he says and we look at each other, both thinking different things.

Merewyn is busy inside her room tidying her things when Gulwain bursts into the room and she turns in surprise. He storms about the room angrily.

"That woman rules Arthur. He is no longer a man of power. She is wicked!" he shouts, hoping everyone will hear him.

Upset by his words, she counters him. "Do not speak of my lady in that way. She is not wicked. She is strong."

"Strong, HA! That woman has just stripped me of my command. She knows not her place."

Upset by his attitude, she says, "Her place is beside Arthur . . . in every way."

He stands with his back to her, angered. "We shall see how long Arthur puts up with her." Then turning and looking at Merewyn he begins to soften. "Your loyalty is commended, but I trust her not. Why can she not be like you? Kind and gentle. You are a true woman."

She smiles at him, realizing it will take some time for him to understand me. Gulwain reaches suddenly for her and pulls her down to the little bed as passion rises in both of them. He moans loudly, and outside the door, passersby stop and giggle softly as they hear the sounds of lovemaking.

17

❖

The Battle Begins

IN THE COURTYARD THE NEXT MORNING ARTHUR'S ARMY OF
men is busy preparing for the journey, and many people
rush about helping. The soldiers look glorious in metal
breastplates and skirts that cover their tunics. They load
their horses with spears and swords as well as large
round shields painted with images of eagles, the Briton
Army's power animal. I walk over to Arthur and his
horse, and notice some of the women looking at me. Few
of them actually speak to me. I wonder what they are
thinking. I often notice them watching me. Judging me
no doubt. Arthur turns to me and pulls me close.

"You are always in my soul and one with me in
spirit," he says, then kisses me. "We ride today in
your honor."

"I give you my blessing. Come back to me whole.
Bring me victory," I reply, excited, but disappointed at
having to stay behind.

As Arthur gets on his horse, I back away, then cry, "Arthur . . . bring me the heart of their leader?"

As they ride out of the courtyard led by Arthur, the army of about a hundred Britons looks magnificent and powerful and I am proud to be one of them. Gulwain passes behind me and I hear him grunt and spit on the ground. I turn quickly but he is already gone. He still does not trust me.

I follow them out of the courtyard and watch them descend into the valley, where they are joined by many more of Arthur's soldiers who live in the nearby villages. It is wondrous to see such a vast, organized group of soldiers riding to defend our lands and I linger to watch until they are out of my sight.

I make my way back toward the stairs when I notice Arius standing with some of the other young girls. I walk over to them, careful not to be seen and I overhear the girls taunting her.

"You will never marry, Arius, you're too ugly," one girl says.

"You will only be good for washing clothes, where no one can see you," another girl taunts.

Enraged by their words, I move closer so they can see me. I walk right up to them and notice Arius fighting back tears of pain.

"You wicked children!" I roar. "You think beauty is all that is important? You will certainly have an empty life if you do. Arius has much more power than you ever will. She is gifted and wise where you are weak and silly. I choose Arius to be my aide, as I know she is worthy and blessed," I say and turn to Arius. "Come, Arius, let us go to my room and speak of the world together. These girls are unworthy of you."

Arius, radiant now and smiling, walks with me toward my room. She turns back once to notice the other girls, who are embarrassed and unsure of what to do next. As we enter my room, I motion for her to sit at a table while I gather a few maps to show her. We spend the day talking about my adventures with Father and how the Saxons, Scots, and Picts must be pushed out of our land. I find an unusual joy in showing her what I have learned.

18

###

The Waiting

THE DAYS PASS SLOWLY AS MEREWYN BUSILY WORKS AT HER table preparing her herbal mixtures. My seventeenth birthday has passed without much notice. Merewyn reminded me by creating a picnic in the cool fall air, but I had little thought of celebrating. My mind has been on battle and little else.

I look longingly out her window at the rolling hills around us. Turning and running my hands through my hair in frustration, I pace the room.

"Why have we not heard anything? What has become of them? It has been many days. Can you not see how they fare?" I ask.

"Patience, lady, they fare well," she replies softly, continuing her work.

I mumble to myself as I play with herbs on the table. Then walking toward a wall, I place both hands against it and lean.

"I shall go mad here, Merewyn! I must go. I must see where they are."

Merewyn turns abruptly and gets off her stool. "No, lady. Arthur spoke his words . . . You must stay," she pleads.

"Arthur's words," I say sarcastically. "Arthur's words. What about what I wish? I want to be out there. I am tired of waiting in this dark place and not knowing if my plan is working."

"Patience must be acquired, lady," Merewyn cautions. "The people need you here."

I laugh mockingly at her and start to pace again.

"Need me, for what? So they have someone to look at. So all the ladies can come and comb my lovely hair," I say with a mocking tone, lifting my fingers through my hair in a dramatic manner. "So they can make me fine clothes. Oh, Merewyn, I am so tired of this."

A knock at the door interrupts us. "Come."

A young lady enters, looking excited. "There is a rider, my lady. He comes into the courtyard."

"Have him come to me, here," I reply excitedly.

Nodding, the young lady rushes off on her errand. I rub my hands together as Merewyn walks to the door and opens it just in time to see Lancirus about to knock. I motion for him to enter and he closes the door behind him.

"You bring me word?" I ask impatiently.

He stands stiffly in front of me, speaking formally. "Yes, lady, all is well. The men wait, as there is no sign of the enemy yet. Arthur asked that I bring you word."

Relieved, I sigh, then walk to the window and look out. I pause for a moment, then turn to Merewyn.

"Merewyn, leave us. I must speak to Lancirus alone."

"But, lady . . . ," she stutters.

I glare at her. Casting her eyes downward, she turns

and walks out. I motion for Lancirus to come closer, wanting some gentle attention from a man.

"Come, speak with me."

He walks tentatively toward me, his eyes filling with tenderness and love as he tries to keep his composure.

"Tell me more, Lancirus. Are the men in place as I planned?"

"They are, lady. They wait in the mist. They are patient and filled with anticipation."

I tenderly bring my hand up to his face and touch him as he tries not to give in to his love. "Why did you come? Why not a message boy?" I say, unable to resist teasing him.

"Arthur asked me, lady. I am not needed now." He turns from me.

"Do not turn from me, Lancirus. Speak your truth. You came to see me . . . did you not?" I bait him, feeling powerful again.

He turns and looks back at me with longing in his eyes.

"I offered to come, lady. I longed to see you . . . I think of you in the night. When I do not see you, there is emptiness in my soul. As I see you today, I am filled again."

He kneels in front of me, takes my hand, and presses his lips against it. Looking down at his head I pull him close to my stomach, stroking his hair. He is so much like a child!

"Dear Lancirus, you touch me in such a gentle way. Your face is like a boy's. Pure and free of wickedness. You fill me with joy," I say tenderly.

He pulls back from me, filled with guilt.

"Lady, I must not. I have lost myself in you."

I pull him close again, wanting attention, but only

if I can control it. "Lancirus, lose yourself, I will not harm you."

We look at each other for a full moment, then he pulls away and stands facing me, his face full of pain.

"I cannot, lady. I must go," he says with a shaky voice.

Angered by his refusal, my eyes flare as I wave my hand at him and turn abruptly, walking to the window. He is weak.

"Go then . . . Leave me!"

His voice pulls at me as I look out the window, frustrated.

"Do you have any words for your husband, Lord Arthur?" he asks tentatively.

Stiffening at the word *husband*, I turn and glare at him.

"Yes . . . Tell him I *love* him!" I say sarcastically.

He winces and casts his eyes downward, refusing to face me. His body seems somehow weaker as he turns and walks out of the room, leaving the door open. I sigh and tilt my head backward, closing my eyes and tensing my face. Suddenly, I whirl around and grab some herbs and throw them across the room. I need to regain my power somehow. I decide to go for a ride on my horse.

I burst with speed out of the courtyard and into the valley below, leaving the people of the fort staring in surprise. The rush of wind in my face and the speed of my horse fills me with happiness and vigor. I ride for a long while until I come to an open valley of soft grasses where I dismount and throw myself down to rest.

Hours later I am still lying in the grass, looking up at the sky, my horse lingering nearby. Even though the day is beautiful, I can't help but feel frustrated, knowing the men are out there, invigorated by the soon-to-be battle, while I wait, bored, here at the fort.

Soon, I hear a horse, and rising quickly, I see one of our guards. He rides up and dismounts, nodding to me.

"My lady, we have been concerned. You left with no guard."

"I need no guard. Leave me," I retort sharply.

He stammers and tries to speak as I wait impatiently for him to go.

"Well? Leave me," I repeat coldly.

"I cannot, lady," he says with embarrassment. "Lord Arthur ordered us always to follow you, in case of danger."

Fury courses through me and I stand and glare at him.

"Did he? . . . What else did he order?" I demand.

"To care for your every need, lady."

I raise my eyebrows and smile to myself, feeling the desire to overpower this man. I walk provocatively toward him.

"My every need?"

He looks ahead, becoming nervous and avoiding my eyes.

"Yes, my lady," he says quietly.

I move close to his body, enjoying myself immensely. He must obey me.

"My need is that you love me now," I command.

His eyes widen in fear as he loses his speech.

"Did you not hear me?" I taunt him.

"Yes . . . , lady," he stammers, nervously.

I remain icy and cold, suddenly furious at all men for abandoning me at the fort with nothing to do.

"Then obey Lord Arthur's wish. Love me."

Breathing hard now, he kneels down in front of me, then looks up at me with fear and I smile. I push him backward and position myself on top of him, taking him inside my body. The sense of power I feel is overwhelming.

I straddle him for only a short while, then, tiring of him, I rise and tidy my clothes, leaving him frustrated and relieved at the same time. I gather my horse and ride back to the fort. Upon entering my room, I throw myself down on the bed.

Why did I do that? Why did it feel so good to control him? I don't understand it, but I feel better. Stronger inside somehow, as Merlin said. I can control my body whereas a man cannot. Yes, that is what it is. I have a power that is different from a man's.

I find myself wondering about Merlin again. Determined to seek him out, I walk down the hallway and finding his door open, enter the room. He is writing at an old desk, but turns to greet me when he hears my steps.

"Gwynnefwar, come, join me."

I look around the room, noticing the large number of books strewn everywhere.

"So many books. Have you read all of these?" I ask.

"Yes," he replies, smiling at my interest.

The room is a small one but somehow it seems older than the others. I wonder how old Merlin is? My eyes try to take in all of the books and pictures and I notice a small cot in one corner. He obviously doesn't care much for comfort. I also notice a large open book with new writings in it and can't help but look closer.

"What is this, Merlin?" I ask inquisitively.

"These are my writings. Someday, when the world is ready, they will read my words and come to a greater understanding of themselves."

"From where did you come, Merlin?" I ask with continuing curiosity, hoping to unearth some fascinating secret.

"The same place as you," he replies with a wicked smile, as though knowing that I seek information. "The womb," he continues with a laugh.

"You seem to have many secrets," I hint, sure that I will uncover something soon.

"I have no secrets, Gwynnefwar. I am a simple man who leads a simple life. I am a man of words. My purpose is to bring my words and the words of the great teachers to the people."

He closes his book and turns to me.

"I see you have found your power."

Uncomfortably, I realize that he is trying to turn the conversation to me. Somehow Merlin has a way of seeing through me. I decide to play the game of discovery for amusement and smile as he continues.

"Careful. If you do not use it wisely, it can bring you harm."

"What do you mean?" I ask, curious now as to his meaning.

"You can go too far, Gwynnefwar, with this gift you have. Do not shut Arthur out of your heart," he says as he watches me carefully.

I turn away, pondering the books, feeling a little naked in front of this old man's wisdom. I don't understand how I can possibly go too far with my gifts and I decide to avoid the subject.

"Merlin, your words enchant me. You give me great pleasure," I say with a broad smile.

"You still hide, lady," he presses on.

I lower my eyelids, hoping that somehow he will not be able to see through me anymore as an uneasiness creeps over me. Why does everyone think they know me so well? They do not understand my quest or my feelings. Merlin continues to speak as I browse through his books, hoping he will change the subject.

"You take on the outer shell of a woman. You use that power to dominate men. It makes you feel strong, does it not?" He pauses but I do not answer.

"You still fear the true woman inside yourself. Gwynnefwar, do not try so hard to gain the respect of men. They will honor you when you show them your truth. You are a magnificent woman. You need not prove it so much."

He comes over to me and takes my chin in his hand. I feel as though I trust him, yet I do not fully understand what he is saying. I must gain Arthur's respect. He doesn't understand that my purpose here is to lead the Britons. Why do people always want to talk about my being a woman? I know that I am a woman. I don't fear it. I simply prefer to be like a man. It is much more interesting than sewing and raising children.

Merlin kisses me on the forehead and I pull away, frustrated at being treated like a girl. Kissing and softness! All these men want to treat me like a toy, all except Father, he understands me.

I smile at Merlin and thank him for his advice as I quickly leave his room, glad to be away from his perceptiveness.

I wander down to the kitchen and relax on a bench as I watch the cooks preparing food for the masses of people that live here. It is somehow comforting to watch the daily ritual of food preparation. Few words are needed. Structure and rules are followed with ease and delicious food is the result. How simple! Like a battle in a way. I linger in silence and pick at various dishes as the kitchen help bustles around me.

19

❖

The Strategy

ON THE TOP OF A TALL HILL ON A DARK NIGHT, TWO OF Arthur's men stand holding a blanket. They move it about in front of an enormous blazing fire. On a far-away hill another fire flickers back. One of the men turns to the other and motions urgently with his hand.

"Quickly! Go to Lord Arthur. Tell him the Saxons have settled by the old stone ruins near the river Glein."

The younger man races down the hill toward his waiting horse. Mounting it, he rides furiously through the winding pathways, lit only by the dim moon.

He arrives at Arthur's camp and searches through the masses of soldiers for his leader. He finally finds him sitting by a fire in front of a tent with a red flag beside it and dismounts in front of him.

"My lord. The Saxons have settled near the old stone ruins by the river Glein. We have just received a signal from Bowys," he says excitedly.

"Good, raise the men, we leave at once," Arthur says as he stands and looks up at the sky with a smile.

"You were right, Gwynnefwar," he says aloud to the sky.

He and his men mount their horses and make their way through the night toward the Saxons' camp. Silently, they surround it and wait for the right moment. As the last of the Saxons drifts into sleep, Arthur listens to the breeze rustling the nearby trees. He raises his spear and points it forward, and in a burst of movement his army of men charges into the camp of unsuspecting Saxons. Caught by surprise, the Saxons try to engage in battle, but Arthur and his men slaughter them with ease.

The battle won, Arthur and his men return to their camp and dismount, talking excitedly about their success at the Saxon camp. Although it was dark, Arthur figures they killed about sixty-five Saxons. A great triumph!

As the men settle around the fires and pour themselves some ale, Arthur hushes them.

"Men, raise your cups to our Lady Gwynnefwar!"

Gulwain and Lancirus look at each other, wondering what Arthur is thinking. Gulwain turns his head slightly and spits on the ground. Repulsed at the thought of honoring me but realizing he must, he raises his cup with the others. Arthur notices his hesitation and worries for a moment about me and his best friend before he continues his speech.

"Her plan has served us well. Soon we will regain this land and enjoy the riches of our fathers. Let us drink."

The men drink together and Arthur motions for Gulwain to come sit with him by the fire.

"Gulwain," he says sadly. "I fear you have anger toward my wife."

Gulwain's face tightens, knowing he must speak the truth to his friend, but not wanting to cause trouble. He hesitates and Arthur presses. "Speak. Are we not friends?"

Gulwain takes a swig of ale and sighs. "I trust her not. She is a woman of trickery."

Arthur fills with anguish as Gulwain continues.

"A woman's place is with home and child." Gulwain stand abruptly, and Arthur follows suit.

"I am your servant," Gulwain says, "but I will not be used by your wife. That is my truth."

He walks back to his men a few yards away as Arthur looks worriedly after him. Arthur turns to see Lancirus before him. He little guesses that Lancirus's mind is full of guilty thoughts of me. He turns away from Arthur without speaking, who wonders what Lancirus has on his mind. Arthur sits down again in front of the fire and thinks aloud to himself.

"Oh, Gwynnefwar, my love. Why do others not see in you what I see?"

Gulwain hears Arthur and shakes his head, wishing only that their lives were as they were before I came.

20

❖

Discovering Self

TWO WEEKS PASS AND I FIND MYSELF ASLEEP WITH MY HEAD
on the table of maps when Arthur bursts through the
door. Awakening, I am disoriented at first, but then I
see Arthur and my eyes widen as he comes quickly to
me and picks me up in his arms. He hugs me and
kisses me passionately on the mouth as I try to protest.

"Arthur, what has happened?" I ask, shocked by this
rude awakening from sleep.

He pulls me closer still and tries to kiss me again,
but I am insistent on news.

"Arthur, tell me, what has happened? Are we
victorious?"

He lets me down but holds me close to him and
kisses me on the neck. Annoyed, I wait impatiently for
his answer.

"We are, my love. For a time. You were right. The
signal fires worked well for us," he says passionately.

I am thrilled that Arthur appreciates my contribution to the victory. I can't wait to hear more, but Arthur is feverishly running his hands over my body, obviously thinking of something other than battle.

"How I have longed for you! For those fiery eyes and your warm breasts," he says softly, kissing my neck again. I close my eyes and surrender, realizing that he needs to make love to me first, before he will tell me anything.

Afterward, I press him for details of the battle as we lie in bed. He tells me everything and I find myself longing to have been there. Maybe now that I have proven myself he will let me ride with him.

After we have rested for a short while, I hear much commotion coming from the great hall. Arthur rises and dresses and urges me to do the same, as he has given word to prepare a wondrous feast in celebration of the victory. We make our way to the great hall, my heart full of pride at being a part of it all.

When we enter, the feast and celebration are already under way. Lancirus stands by a far table, watching me as Arthur and I take our seats at the main table. The hall is filled with excitement and I enjoy a tender moment as Arthur feeds me a piece of fruit. I am truly enjoying myself and revel in the celebration as I drink wine and laugh and sing with the others.

Arthur spins me around as everyone begins to dance to the sounds of drums and singers. After a while we sit and eat more and I realize this is a good time to talk.

"How long will you stay, Arthur?"

"Not too long," he says. "The enemy will soon return. I hear the Angles push westward with the Saxons from the Midlands. We must be ready for them."

He then takes my hand and we both look at our

hands joined together. Confusion wells up inside me as I feel this tenderness and heat rising in me.

At a side table, Gulwain sits with Merewyn, a look of hatred on his face. "Look at how she teases him. She loves him not. All she wants is power. She will destroy him," he says angrily to Merewyn.

Merewyn stands and stares down at him with disgust. "I will not listen to such words. Gwynnefwar does love him. Your jealousy is repulsive."

She storms out of the hall, and Gulwain turns back to his ale, gulping it down. I notice their argument and turn to Arthur.

"Gulwain has angered Merewyn. He probably speaks of me again. She told me of his distrust. You must watch him carefully, Arthur. He will try to turn you against me."

Arthur tilts his head back and laughs a little.

"I wish for you both to stop these words. I love you, my wife, and I do not wish to lose Gulwain from my side. He is a mighty warrior. I need him. Can you not make peace?" he asks.

I look at Gulwain a moment, realizing that I cannot trust him but knowing that I had better not anger Arthur. Besides, I am second in command now, and Arthur believes in me, which is all that is important. I turn to Arthur.

"Forget Gulwain. I have some new plans I wish for you to see. I believe the Scots are coming near from the West."

Arthur raises his eyebrows. "The Scots?"

I lean over to him and nod, eager to fill him in on my news.

"Yes. I have heard from the farmers along the western coast that more small bands of Scots are moving over from across the sea. I want to post some men along the cliffs as guards. Will you look at my plans before you leave?"

Arthur smiles and shakes his head.

"Is strategy all you think of?" he says, then pauses and looks lovingly at me. "Are your thoughts ever filled with me?"

I sigh and look at him awkwardly, unsure of how to answer his question. Why must people always speak of sex and love? There are more important things to worry about.

"Of course, my lord. But there are many days to fill. I cannot be idle as the others," I say, trying to be truthful.

He smiles and touches my face with his hand. "I will look at your plans," he replies with a gentle laugh, enjoying discovering me.

The next winter months are filled with many idle hours and much frustration. As Arthur and his men prepare for battle, I notice I am not welcome. Although Arthur has looked at my plans for the Scots, he does not seem to share them with Gulwain or Lancirus.

Arthur and I spend little time alone, as Gulwain and the other men always seem to have something they need to do or talk over with him. Our evenings are filled with drinking and socializing in the great hall, which suits me fine.

We make love only occasionally, as I often feign tiredness or else Arthur has drunk too much and falls into a deep sleep as soon as he enters the bed.

I decide to ride down to the small nearby river and spend the day wading and resting in a little wooden boat that is always there.

The day passes into afternoon and the sun blazes down on my fair skin. It is difficult to see, and I allow my boat to drift in the calm water of the river. Such a

peaceful day, far away from the business of the fort
and the men practicing their skills with their blades
and spears. They spend much of their time sharpening
formations of attack and playing at mock hand-to-
hand battles.

As I rest, I hear faint voices coming from nearby.
Curious and cautious at the same time, I row my boat
to the shore and listen, trying to figure out their source.
I get out of the boat to follow the sounds into the
woods. As I walk carefully through some trees, I notice
in the distance the back of a small woman, in a heavy
cloak, who looks to be Morgana and a large bearded
man with poor tattered clothes. I creep closer, careful
not to be seen or heard and hunch down and watch.

Morgana bends down and pulls something from a
hole in the ground, and the man stands beside her with
a shovel. I inch my way sideways a little to see better
and notice that Morgana has pulled a box from the
ground. She opens it and pulls out some rolled-up papers tied with gold string. Placing the papers on the
ground, she continues to take things out of the box
until finally she lifts out a bag. She opens it and shows
the man, who then reaches in and lifts out some coins.
Nervously, Morgana quickly places the papers back in
the box and hides it back in the ground. The man then
covers the box with the earth and the two leave quickly.

I try to follow and listen but am unable to hear more
than mumbles. What is she up to? I can't help but feel
that something is wrong. Why would Morgana give this
strange man coins and why does she hide them and
the box way out here? We don't use coins in our land
for exchange. The man must be from some faroff place.

Determined to find out what is going on, I wait patiently until I am sure they have both gone, then I
search for a piece of flattened wood and begin to dig

up the spot where they placed the box. I am glad to find the hole quite shallow and the box easy to lift out. I take it back to my boat and horse where I set it down and open it.

Anxiously, I look inside to find many papers and coins. The coins seem strange, unlike any I have seen, and the papers very important. I unravel some of the papers and find them filled with Latin writing that I find difficult to read. As I look farther into the box I also find beautiful brooches and gold wristbands with delicate markings on them. The jewelry is very heavy and more like a man's than Morgana's. Confused and curious, I decide to take the box back to the fort and show Arthur my find.

I lift the box onto my horse and secure it, then mount the horse myself and ride swiftly back home. Upon entering the fort, I notice the men are still engaged in preparations for their next journey. They seem almost unaware of me. I wonder if they actually ignore me on purpose or if they are afraid of me. No, how could they be afraid of me, they are all warriors. Then why do they ignore me? I dismount and take the box with me to my room to show Arthur.

As I walk down the hallway, I notice a haggard-looking Morgana running into the fort. I hide quickly so she doesn't see me or the box and I watch her scurry to her room. I can't help but wonder why she is so strange. It is almost as though she is in a different world than the rest of us. I must ask Arthur if she is unwell.

My room is empty and I place the box down and go to find Arthur in the map room.

"Where have you been?" he says when he sees me. "I have been worried. Gulwain and I have been over the plan you have for the Scots. It is good. But then all of your plans are," he says and kisses me on the cheek as I try unsuccessfully to interrupt.

"It is almost as though you were born in the wrong body, my love. You have the brain of a man," he says then releases me and begins to walk out of the door.

"Arthur, wait. I must show you something. Please come to our room." I beckon him and lead the way forward.

"Hurry, the men wait for me."

We go to our room and I point to the box. "I found it in the woods near the river. Morgana had buried it."

Anxiously, I open it and show him what is inside as I proceed to tell him of Morgana and the strange man. Concerned, Arthur opens the papers and reads them as I wait.

"These are my father's papers. You see, here is our family name, Aurelianus," he says with a look of concern as I prod him further.

"What do they mean? Why was Morgana hiding them and giving coins to the man?" I question him.

"I do not know. These papers are my father's letters from Rome. They are many years old, from when he first came to Britain. They speak of the mounted horsemen and of gold coins to be used for the army. These must be old Roman coins. They are quite beautiful." He purses his eyebrows and continues. "Why would Morgana have these? She must have found them after my father died."

"In the ground? Do you think that she hid them?" I inquire.

"Why would Morgana hide them? She has her own room. No one enters it. No, I think my father must have hid it long ago and forgotten it." He closes the box and stands.

"We will not worry about it now, she must have been

paying the man for some potion or something silly," he says laughing and walks out as I follow, unconvinced of Morgana's innocence.

"If it were a simple potion Morgana was buying why would she look so nervous? Why would she use coins? No one has any use for them here. I think that I should watch her carefully. I am not sure I can trust her. She hides too much," I say with concern.

Arthur smiles and stops as we enter the courtyard full of soldiers practicing.

"Gwynnefwar, do not worry about Morgana, she is harmless. She has always been very different and nervous. She does not have many friends. Why don't you become friends with her, then you will understand her ways better."

He turns from me and moves toward his men, but I can't help thinking that he is wrong. Morgana is up to something, I feel it in my bones. That man did not dress like any around here. He must be from far away. I wonder if he is a Saxon or a Scot. I must find out more.

Another few months pass and we find spring upon us. Arthur and his men are leaving for a long journey eastward. He turns to me and speaks softly.

"You will be always in my thoughts, dear lady."

"As you will be in mine. Fare well on your journey. I will wait for word of your victory," I answer.

Arthur mounts his horse and leads his soldiers out of the courtyard, turning back once to see me and wave.

After they leave, I wander the fort restlessly, looking for something to occupy my time. When I peek into Merewyn's room, I notice that she is busy working with her astrological charts. I knock and she beckons me to enter.

"Hello," I say.

"Hello," she replies, eyeing me carefully. "You are bored, my lady."

"How do you always seem to know what I am feeling?" I ask, wondering if I have any privacy at all in this fort.

"I am sorry, my lady, I do not spy on you. I have concern for you. You seem unhappy."

I wander around her room, curious about all the myriad things that fill every corner.

"I feel useless here. Back in Northumbria I was always busy with Father. He was always teaching me something new. We shared everything. Here I am alone. Arthur is always gone. I spend most days planning battles that may never happen and waiting for Arthur to come home and tell me how good my strategies are."

I walk over to her pot over the fire and taste with my finger an aromatic potion. Merewyn watches me patiently, like a mother. Suddenly I have a great idea.

"Let me take you to the stone circle that I found. You will love it, it seems very ancient. Will you come with me? It is not too far by horse." I look excitedly to her for an answer and she nods her head.

"Yes. I would love to see an ancient circle of power. Let us gather some food and drink first so we may spend some time there."

When we get to the stables I suddenly remember that Merewyn does not ride very well and I offer to have her on my horse behind me. She agrees and we set off for the day.

As we leave the fort and follow the old paths through the trees, I feel exhilarated at the idea of sharing my sacred spot with Merewyn. Of all the people in my life, I feel I can trust her as much as Father. I wish she were my mother. She is so nurturing and never angry and she always seems to understand my worries. We ride for quite a while before we reach the stone circle. Finally, we dismount and walk into the center of it.

Merewyn looks around and goes to each stone in turn, placing the palms of her hands against it and closing her eyes. A strange change comes over her as I watch, almost as though she is transformed somehow into an angelic presence. I decide to let her have some peace and settle myself against one of the larger stones and unpack our food and drink.

With the sun shining upon us, hours seem to pass like minutes and I suddenly wake from a light sleep. Surprised that I had fallen asleep, I look around for Merewyn and notice that she is lying at the center of the circle on her back with her arms stretched out above her head and her eyes staring into the afternoon sky.

At first her stillness worries me, but finally I notice her blink and I carefully cross the grass and sit beside her. She brings her arms to touch mine and smiles at me.

"This place is sacred. Much wisdom has passed through these stones. There are many ancient spirits that dwell here," she says as her face seems to glow.

I decide that I want to know more about this invisible world that Merewyn understands.

"What do the spirits say? Do they speak to you?" I inquire hopefully.

"Not in words, but in feelings. I feel their wisdom and their love move into my body and heart. Here, touch me."

She brings my hand to her heart, and I am startled to feel how hot her body is. "Why are you so hot? Are you ill?"

"No. I have never been so well. It is power. This

circle is a source of power and energy. If you open to it you will feel it too, here, in your heart."

"How do I open to it? What will it give me?"

Merewyn smiles gently and sits up. "You must simply trust. Trust that spirit is here and longs to share love with you."

Love again! What do I want with that? That can't help me rid the land of Saxons. I show my frustration.

"I mean power, how do I receive power?" I insist.

Merewyn looks at the sky, then back to me. "The power I speak of is not to win over another. It is not to conquer but to heal. To understand the universe and self," she says.

I find myself wondering about Merewyn and Merlin. They both seem to seek the same thing but by different paths. Merlin through words, Merewyn through spirit.

We make our way back to the fort in the early evening. I return to my room but am full of energy and unable to sit. I decide to go down to the baths and spend the evening there.

As I enter the luxurious hot bath, all thoughts drift away. Suddenly the enemies seem very far from me. More and more I find myself enjoying this ritual of bathing. The scented water and flame-lit room intoxicate my senses and allow me to move into a different, more exotic world. I stare into the colored water and feel somehow transported to a place of freedom. Water seems so natural to me. I can't help wondering why my northern people never bathe. It is so soothing. I think Father would enjoy it.

After what seems to be hours in the hot bath, I linger over some food in my room, finally uninterested in maps and strategy. Looking down at my near naked body, I wonder what Arthur finds so very stimulating. It is soft, yes, but is that enough to drive a man to frenzy? When I look at Arthur's body I am not driven to madness. I even remember Father when he used to look at some of the women in our village in the summertime. He somehow seemed different, more animallike. I have even heard of women who enjoy this act of sex. I cover myself and drift into the deep caverns of my mind, trying to understand what the mystery of sex is, but finding only sleep.

I am rudely awakened from my rest by loud noises in what seems to be the early morning. I sit up in bed as my door bursts open and Rhianne rushes in with a terrified look in her eyes. She screams at me, "The Saxons, they are here!!! Hurry, lady, we must hide!"

I jump from my bed and run to the window, then I turn to Rhianne as she hysterically screams again, "They are all around us!"

Maintaining my calm, I grab Rhianne.

"Quickly, arouse everyone, then hide yourself!"

Rhianne stiffens in fear and I yell at her, "GO! GO!"

I push her out the door, grab a cloak and throw it around me, covering my head. Then running to my chest, I open it and pull out my long dagger. Just then I hear footsteps coming closer. They stop a moment and I carefully tiptoe to the door and position myself behind it. I wait, holding myself still, but they move past.

I walk cautiously out the door and into the hallway, slipping my dagger into the sleeve of my cloak. Suddenly, I am seized around the shoulders by a large Saxon. I twist myself out of his grasp, but he quickly grabs my left arm and holds me tight.

"A fiery one you are," he grunts, laughing.

I glare at him with steely eyes and stay very still. He looks me up and down and removes my hood.

"A beauty too. I am lucky this day."

He grabs my waist with his other hand and pulls me

close. I explode with revulsion as he buries his head in my neck and kisses me roughly. Suddenly, I flash back to the time I was raped, and with one swift movement, I drop the dagger into my hand and stab him fiercely in the neck. Pulling back in shock, his hand moving to his neck, he falls against me and down to the floor. I pull the dagger out and run behind the door, trying hard to calm my hurried breathing.

Another Saxon then comes running, looks around and seeing no one, bends down to check his friend as I wait behind the door. I watch carefully without moving, waiting for the right moment. I know I need to kill him or he will kill me. He rolls his friend over and I jump out from the doorway and onto his back, stabbing my blade into the back of his heart. He throws me from him and I fall roughly against the wall, the wind knocked out of me. Falling, the Saxon takes his knife in hand and lashes out at my leg, wounding me slightly. Gasping for breath, I pull myself out of his reach as he falls dead on the floor. My dagger is still in his back and I pull it out. I stand and look around as Merewyn comes running down the hall, terrified.

"Gwynnefwar, are you hurt?" she asks with fear in her voice.

"No. Where are they, are there more?"

"I do not know . . . I think . . . outside."

I run into my room to the window and Merewyn follows.

"Stay here. I will return," I implore.

"No . . . no . . . you must not," she pleads.

I grab her arms and look fiercely at her. "Stay here!" I order.

I let her go and run out of the room, cautious as I enter the hallway and holding my dagger at the ready.

My mind races in anticipation of battle, yet another part of me dreads it. No time to think now, I must act.

Hearing the voices of our soldiers, I enter the courtyard. People run about in confusion and I look around and spot one of our guards standing over a dead Saxon. Running to him, I pull him around to face me.

"Where are they, are they gone? Where did they come from?"

"I do not know, lady. It has surprised us all," he answers in confusion.

I look around quickly and motion toward the stable.

"Quickly, get a horse. Search the hills around. We must find out if there are more," I order the guard and he begins to go, but I stop him. "We must tell Arthur. Send one of your men to his camp."

He turns and runs to the stables as I look around at the people walking about in the courtyard. A few are injured. I notice a Saxon lying on the ground, badly wounded in the leg and shoulder and trying to move. Anger begins to rise in me.

"Guard, quickly!" I shout.

Two young guards come running over to me and I walk right up to the Saxon and look down at him coldly, feeling no mercy for him.

"From where have you come?" I demand.

He remains silent for a moment, then laughs at me. He looks me up and down as he lies there, mocking me. Enraged, I determine to break him or kill him.

"Will you not speak, Saxon?"

He looks at me, remaining silent and I motion for the guards to pick him up. I stand close to him and look him coldly in the eyes.

"You mock me, Saxon," I say as the disgust boils in me.

I take my dagger in hand and stab the Saxon through

the heart, my body rigid with hate. He looks at me in disbelief as his mouth opens. Slumping as the guards hold him, he dies. I pull out my blade and motion for the guards to take him away.

"Rid this place of any Saxons. Burn their bodies. We wish no part of them or their spirits to remain here," I order.

I am determined to show the people of the fort that I am in control and capable of leading them. The guards look at me with surprise, then drag the body away.

As I turn around and see the fear and confusion everywhere, I feel uneasy and begin to tremble. Merewyn walks up to me and I look up at her and show her the knife.

"I just killed three men," I say blankly as a strange tingling overtakes me.

"You had to, they would have killed us," she replies as her voice recedes further and further away from me.

I look back at the knife. "Yes, I had to . . . My father would be proud of me," I say, although I feel dazed. "Then why do I tremble?" I ask, hoping for a wise answer from my friend.

"Because you are a creator of life, not a taker of life," she replies.

I sigh deeply at her words, wondering if they are true. Am I really a creator, I wonder? I look around the courtyard, then hand my knife to Merewyn.

"Take this. I am tired . . . I must sleep."

I turn and walk toward my room as Merewyn looks after me. As I find my way back to bed, I feel a rush of dizziness. I drift off to sleep but it is a restless and sweaty one.

21

The Error

THE NEXT MONTH COMES AND GOES QUICKLY FOR ME. I AM
still restless and longing to see Arthur. I decide to take
up sewing but find that my impatience rarely allows me
to produce anything of quality. I spend most of my time
visiting the outlying farms and speaking with the farmers,
trying to find out if they have seen any Scots nearby.

Farm life here is quite splendid compared to Northumbria. The farmland is rich and the crops are many.
The lands surrounding the fort are filled with many
animals and craftspeople. Merewyn and I spend many
days meandering through the various shops filled with
beautiful clothes, blankets, jewelry, and carved wood.

I decide to have a new dagger made for me by the
local ironworker. I inspect it and am very pleased with
its stiletto point and longer length. It is heavier than
my old one and I find it awkward at first, but as the
days pass and I practice with it, I find it much better.

One day I am sitting in my room as Merewyn braids my hair into two twists, when I hear loud footsteps and a knock at the door.

"Come," I call.

The door opens, and Lancirus enters, looking weary. His arm is wrapped in cloth and he is limping slightly as he holds his side.

"My Lady Gwynnefwar, I bring word from Arthur."

"You are wounded?" I ask with worry, then turn to Merewyn and plead, "Quickly, Merewyn, tend to him."

I look into his face, cupping it with my hands.

"What has happened? Have we lost the battle?" I implore.

He remains strong as Merewyn comes toward him and motions for him to take off his tunic.

"No, my lady, we are winning. Arthur, the others, they have killed many Angles and Saxons. I was ambushed on my way here."

"Remove your clothing, sir. I must clean the wounds. Come, by the bed," Merewyn says, motioning for him to move.

Merewyn and I each take an arm and lead him toward the bed, where we help him off with his clothes. He begins to drift as we tend to his wounds. He moves in and out of delirium and his body is on fire as Merewyn works through the night pouring herbal remedies down his throat and bathing him with cool water to break the fever.

The next day we move him to his own room and allow him to sleep and heal. Both Merewyn and I watch over him carefully. I enjoy caring for him, almost as though he belonged to me, like a child of sorts. Merewyn keeps telling me to get some sleep but I feel that I am finally needed, and I am not going to walk away from him. As I watch his gentle face, I wonder why he is a soldier.

After a few days of healing, he finally awakens and sees me watching him. His heart brimming with love, he looks longingly at me and sits up.

"How long have I slept?"

I reach for a platter of food and drink from the floor. "Three days," I answer. I place the platter on the bed and lift a cup to him. "Drink now, you need strength. Your wounds, do they hurt?"

He moves slightly, then smiles.

"I am very well. You are a gifted healer, my lady."

"Not I, Merewyn," I laugh, flattered that he should think me able to heal.

I rise and walk to the window, looking out at the hills, then turn back to him.

"Tell me of the battle now. I must know."

He picks up some food, eats and talks at the same time as I hang on his every word, thrilled to finally hear what is going on.

"There are many of the enemy. But they are on foot. They keep coming from across the sea in the east and from the north as you said. They are strong, but we are faster and more skilled than they."

I breathe in deeply, satisfied that I was right and hoping that Arthur will recognize it as well.

"We will defeat them, lady. Of that I am sure. I must hurry and return to them. I am needed."

I look at him and realize that I don't want him to leave. I have so enjoyed these last few days of caring for him. I don't want to be alone again with only Merewyn and the farmers to talk to. None of them understand the wars. I decide that I will try to keep him here for a while.

"Soon. You must rest a while longer here."

As he finishes the food his eyes catch mine and we stare for a long moment. I gently touch his stomach wound and run my finger up along his bare chest. He breathes more quickly and his eyes alight with love for me. I feel comforted by him as he takes my hand and pulls it to his mouth, kissing it lovingly.

"Lady, you fill my heart," he says softly, still looking at me.

I smile back but begin to feel a strange uneasiness building inside me. I can't seem to stop thinking about Arthur. Why is that? I try to forget him and think of this moment.

"You are so gentle, so sweet. I long to hold you in my womb, to care for you," I whisper tenderly.

I feel his excitement mounting and he moves closer to me and puts an arm around my waist, pulling me close and whispering, "To join my body with yours is to create heaven in my soul."

I close my eyes at his tender words and feel him kiss me on the shoulder. Oddly though, I do not feel that rush of energy that I feel with Arthur. I still feel strong and in control with him. As though I am his mother. He pushes my cloak down over my shoulders and brushes them with his lips.

"I worship you, my love," he moans.

He then lays me down on the bed beside him and slowly moves on top of me, kissing me. As he enters my body and gently makes love to me, I open my eyes. I feel odd inside, almost bored and though I feel him inside me, in a way, I still feel empty. How strange this act of sex is. He ejaculates quickly inside me, then rests his body on top of mine and whispers words of love to me.

"You have made me complete. Your softness and your love will remain with me always."

I look down at his head and smile to myself, still stroking his hair. "My dear Lancirus. You are so sweet."

I look up from his head toward the window and close my eyes as I try to push away thoughts of Arthur. Suddenly I am aware of a noise at the door. Turning, I see Morgana standing in the doorway, an evil look of triumph on her face. Dread and anger race through me as I push at Lancirus and try to get out of bed.

"MORGANA!!!" I scream as she runs from the room.

Lancirus, horrified, jumps from the bed, and I push him out of the way, grabbing my cloak and wrapping it around me as my head pulses with rage. I run out of the room and after Morgana as Lancirus, fearful, rubs his hands into his face and falls back on the bed in despair.

I chase Morgana into her room, where she stops and turns in time to see me slam the open door. Breathing hard, I walk slowly to her as she backs away to a table. My hands form fists and my jaw tightens as I try to think of how best to deal with her. My first thoughts are to choke her right here but sanity intervenes and I realize threats may work better.

"You will not speak of this, Morgana. Do you hear my words?" I threaten, knowing she is already afraid of me.

She remains defiantly silent. My anger is almost out of control.

"Do you hear me!" I yell at her, moving slightly closer to emphasize my words as she backs away to the wall.

"Yes . . . Yes, lady," she stutters.

I regain my composure and back away a few steps. She is weak and I could easily destroy her, but that isn't necessary. She needs to learn that I am stronger than she. I decide to leave her in this trembling state and walk out of the room, slamming the door. Morgana brings her hand up to her neck and rubs it, closing her eyes for a moment.

She looks to the door and starts to smile. "Arthur . . . Arthur . . . you will soon be mine," she whispers out loud to herself.

I make my way back to Lancirus's room, feeling confident that Morgana will remain silent, but also certain that I cannot have sex with him again. Something about it doesn't feel right. I feel old with him. I must focus on my country, not on taking care of Lancirus.

I return to the room to find Lancirus getting dressed. I walk over to him and touch his face and he takes my hand and kisses it. He really is a gentle soul.

"I am sorry, lady. I was wrong," he whispers.

He looks guilty as he kneels in front of me, like a boy asking his mother for forgiveness.

"No, Lancirus. Fear not . . . Morgana will not speak of this. I will take care of her," I assure him.

I pull away from him and run my hands up over my forehead and through my hair as I try to think. He comes up behind me and places his hands on my shoulders.

"My love, I cannot bear that I should bring you trouble. You are all I live for. Your spirit haunts my dreams, your beauty brings an ache to my heart."

I smile and laugh a little but worry fills my mind as I look out across the hills. I must be sure that Arthur never hears of this, yet in another way I want him to. Maybe he wouldn't spend so much time away then. I don't know what I want except that I must not weaken now. I turn to Lancirus and cup his face.

"You must return to Arthur," I say, trying to be kind.

His face fills with pain and he tries to protest, but I

cover his mouth with my fingers and shake my head. He turns silently from me and begins to gather his things.

I walk back to the map room, where I sit for a while pondering my recent actions. I admit to myself that I somehow enjoyed my time with Lancirus but I am not quite sure why. Is it like Merewyn said? Is he weak and therefore makes me feel stronger? I do know that I felt different with him than with Arthur. With Arthur I sometimes lose control and that terrifies me. With Lancirus I enjoy his lovely words and gentleness, but I know that he is not my equal.

I spend much of the next few weeks worrying and wondering about Morgana and Arthur and the other men whom I have bedded. I realize that in my frustration I needed them to make me feel powerful and wanted, and for that I am not ashamed. Besides, Celtic women often take lovers when they are alone.

22

❊

A Choice

The next few weeks pass uneventfully and on this radiant windy day, Merewyn and I decide to spend time outside, walking by the river. I feel more relaxed than I have in months.

"I am filled with the beauty all around me, Merewyn. How lovely this place is."

Merewyn looks at me with concern in her eyes. "Lady, you are very pink."

I feel my cheeks and confirm her words. "I do feel warm . . . It is the day."

Merewyn comes closer to me and looks me in the eyes. Her eyes widen and she grabs my wrist and feels my pulse, then puts her other hand on my belly.

"What is it?" I ask, becoming worried.

Merewyn steps back and lowers her eyes for a moment, then looks at me. "You carry a child, my lady," she whispers.

Horror rips through me immediately and I look down at my belly and grab at my clothes. I look back at Merewyn and plead, "No . . . it cannot be!" In shock, I say, "It must not be!"

"It is true, lady, I see the spirit of the child in your eyes."

I look around, feeling as though I need Father or someone to help me. Fear races through me as I wonder whose child I am carrying. What can I do? I cannot have this child. I turn back to Merewyn.

"You must help me, Merewyn. I must not have this child," I say in panic.

Merewyn just stands there and I insist.

"Merewyn, you must help me!!!" I yell. "NOW!"

She tries to calm me by placing her hands on my arms. "You are sure you wish me to rid you of this child, lady?" she says with sadness.

"Yes, I am sure," I reply, convinced that I have no choice.

She beckons me to follow her, and we make our way back to the fort and to her room. I find it difficult to stay calm as my mind races with horrible thoughts of spending my life like the other women here. All they do is raise children and become fat. Arthur would never allow me to stay his second in command if I were to have a child. All of my life's work would be for nothing. Father would never forgive me if I were to become weak and frail like my mother. My path is not like other women's, surely Merewyn must realize this.

We enter Merewyn's room and I sit on a stool, nervously waiting for her to end this pregnancy. She places a bowl full of herbs into a pot above her fire and turns to me. I rub my hand down the center of my body over my belly, drawing in a deep breath.

"I am not ready for a child, Merewyn. It is through

this body that I rule. I will not become like my mother. The child then becomes the treasure of the husband and the wife is no longer looked at. She had nothing in her life. It will not happen to me," I say, feeling as though Merewyn is judging me. "I do not ask for your blessing, only your medicine," I say in annoyance.

How could she understand my life? No one does, only Father. He would agree with my decision. Besides, if it is Lancirus's child, I could not carry the secret throughout my life. I cannot help but wonder if it is, but I would think that Merewyn would have seen something in her visions if it were Lancirus's child.

Merewyn dips a cup into the pot, then comes over to me and gives me the cup. "Drink ... It will make you unwell for a while," she says solemnly.

I take the cup and quickly drink it down. Standing, I give the cup back to Merewyn and walk out as she shakes her head. I make my way back to my room and lie down on my bed, waiting for the pregnancy to leave my body.

The next hours are very unpleasant for me. My body releases the pregnancy, but a fever arises in me as well as sickness throughout. I become weak and emotional as the day passes through to the next. My dreams are filled with Arthur and Lancirus standing over me and judging me. I fight for control but feel unable to find a sense of where I am or why I feel so many different emotions.

As morning comes, I writhe around in delirium while Merewyn sits beside me, wiping my forehead with a damp cloth as I moan aloud.

"Arthur ... Arthur, where are you? Arthur, I need you, where are you?"

Merewyn gets up and walks to the door, opening it. "Guard, guard ... quickly!" she calls.

A moment later as Merewyn walks back to the bed, a guard appears at the door. Merewyn says to him, "You must go to Lord Arthur. Lady Gwynnefwar is ill, she calls for him. Go quickly."

The guard turns and leaves, leaving the door open as Morgana comes closer. She hides just outside the door, listening. Merewyn returns to my side and strokes my face.

"I have sent for Lord Arthur," she whispers.

"I am sorry, Arthur. I have destroyed your child. Arthur, do not leave me ... Arthur ... ," I moan aloud, unaware of Morgana's presence.

My voice trails off as Merewyn tries to quiet me.

"Quiet now, shhhh, quiet. All will be well."

Morgana smiles excitedly then runs to her room. She slams her door and begins to dance around her table gleefully, singing aloud. "I have you now, Gwynnefwar. Destroying Arthur's child. He will never forgive you. You will soon be gone back to the North."

She sings and hums as she plays with a tiny doll she has made up to look like me. She tortures the doll with a knife, then pulls its hair out as she laughs maliciously.

Three days pass and the illness begins to leave as I wait for Arthur to come home. Although still weak, I am no longer delirious. Merewyn tends to me like a mother as Arthur walks in and rushes to my side. He touches my face as I look at him with tired eyes, glad to see his handsome face.

"What has happened. Why is she ill?" he questions Merewyn.

"I do not know, my lord," she says, hiding the truth.

I pull at his tunic and whisper, "Arthur, ... I knew you would come ... ," I say weakly.

He kisses my face and forehead tenderly. "I will always be by you, my love. I will not leave," he says tenderly.

"Can you make her well?" he asks Merewyn.

"Yes, my lord. She will be well in a few days."

He sighs, relieved, then turns back to me and strokes my hair. Merewyn, turning, says, "I will leave you, lord. She needs sleep now."

She walks out, closing the door and Arthur crawls onto the bed, taking my head into his arms and holding me close. I feel happy to be with his strength. How different he is from Lancirus. His arms are like Father's and I feel like a young girl again, cared for and wanted as I drift off to sleep.

After a while Arthur leaves me to sleep and enters the great hall, motioning for a young man to come over as Morgana walks coyly up to him.

"I know what ails Gwynnefwar," she says wickedly.

Arthur turns toward her, his eyes filling with anger. "Have you poisoned her again!" he says with his voice raised.

She pulls back slightly, defending herself. "No, my lord, not I."

Arthur takes a deep breath, then relaxes as the young man comes toward him. "Bring me food . . . and drink," he says to the boy.

The young man turns and rushes away as Arthur looks to Morgana, waiting.

"Well . . . speak."

"She has rid herself of your baby," she replies in a triumphant tone.

"What?" he replies, shocked.

"It is true. I heard them speak of it . . . her and Merewyn," she says like an excited child.

Arthur starts to fume. He brushes past her and out

of the hall and Morgana follows him as they make their way back to my room.

Arthur bursts into the room as Merewyn stands by my bed. His face is fired with rage as he stops and stares at Merewyn and me. "Is it true? Have you rid her of my child?" he says to her, his breathing controlled.

Merewyn backs away from the bed, speaking quietly. "It was her wish, lord."

Still weary, I am unable to find the strength to talk. Arthur looks at me with anger in his eyes, then storms out of the room, bumping into Morgana in the hallway.

He makes his way back to the great hall and proceeds to get drunk. A short while later Morgana joins him and tries to bring him comfort. Arthur turns and calls again to a young man for more ale, and in a quick movement Morgana takes out a small bottle and looks around her once, then pours the liquid into Arthur's ale on the table. She then laughs out loud as Arthur turns and sees her. She picks up his ale and hands it to him.

"More drink, my lord?" she says gaily.

"Yes, yes . . . more drink . . . ," he replies distractedly.

He takes the cup from her and drinks it down and Morgana smiles wryly. Arthur spends the next hour drinking heavily until Morgana finally has to help him back to the map room. She helps him to the corner bed and proceeds to climb in after him.

Arthur, drunk and intoxicated by the herbal mixture she made him, becomes both delirious and sexually aroused at the same time. Morgana is thrilled at finally being with the man she adores, and she begins to make love to him as he drifts in and out of sleep. Afterward, she slips out of the room and back to her own, where she picks up the doll fashioned after me. Turning to her oil pot, she lights the doll on fire and lets it burn in a plate as she watches it with a wickedness in her eyes.

As morning arrives, I feel much better and am anxious to get up and clean myself. Arthur enters my room looking quite disheveled as I stand combing my hair. Rigid with nervousness, I wait for him to speak, knowing full well how angry he is. He looks at me and walks around the table, trailing his fingers around its edge and looking down at it.

"Merewyn tells me you are better," he says, trying to control a shaking in his voice.

"Yes," I reply, careful not to anger him further.

"Why did you rid yourself of our child?" he asks, his voice cold and distant.

Nervously, I walk over to him. I need to touch him and make him understand. "Arthur . . . I am not ready for a child. I wish to be with you," I say, touching his arm and looking seductively at him, hoping he will again become enchanted with my body. "I wish you to love me."

I run my hand down my breast, hoping to seduce him so that he will forget about the child. "Look at me, Arthur, this is what you love in me," I plead. I take his hand and place it on my flat stomach as he looks painfully into my eyes. "This is why I rid myself of the child. So you could love me. We will have a child later, when we have loved much."

I take my other hand and push my cloak off of my shoulders, staring into his eyes seductively. "Love me, Arthur," I say as he looks lustfully at me.

"Oh, Gwynnefwar, you possess me," he says as he kisses me passionately on the breast and pulls my body close to his.

I knew this was what he wanted. I suddenly feel more justified in ridding myself of the child. I have to maintain this body so I can keep his attention. I will not be pushed into the background.

As we lie back on the bed, I again feel that powerful heat and longing rise in my body. Why is it so different with him? Why do I feel as though I am losing control? I must try to detach myself from him. But as usual his passion overtakes me, though I am aware only of a strange pain inside me. Then I realize that it is much too soon to make love after the abortion. I disguise the agony and let him take his pleasure.

Afterward, I get up and wash myself as he sleeps. I look carefully at my body in the polished metal on the wall. Looking down at my belly, I can't help but wonder for a moment what it would have been like to carry a child in my body. I quickly push that thought from me and begin to focus on the present. Arthur will be leaving again, and I will be back to my daily routine of frustration. I think I will ask him if I can take a small band of men to the West to scout for the Scots.

As I turn, I notice Arthur watching me. I stop, almost embarrassed that he may have seen me touching my belly. He smiles at me and rises. As he dresses, I tell him that I wish to bathe and that I will see him before he leaves.

I walk out of our room and sigh in relief, glad to be alone. As I approach the bath, I notice Morgana wandering outside. I watch her a moment, realizing that she has too much information about me. I must take greater care with her. She must be stripped of this power she thinks she has over me. I am sure she is the one who told Arthur about the child. Who else would be that cruel? She turns and sees me watching her. I continue to stare at her until, obviously worried, she rushes away.

I slip into the hot bath and allow the intoxicating

scents to carry me off into oblivion. As I linger, I begin to think again of Morgana. There must be a simple way to control her. After all, she has the mind of a child and surely is no match for me. I chide myself for worrying about her at all and begin instead to think of how to convince Arthur to allow me to patrol the West with some men.

After my bath, I make my way back to my room only to find it empty. I locate Arthur in the map room, studying my newest plans. He looks at me and then down slightly as he thinks.

"I know you want to come with me, but it cannot be," he says, reading my thoughts. "I have looked at your newest plans."

I turn to him hopefully.

"I will speak with my men about them," he says as he rolls them up.

I roll my eyes and turn my back to him in annoyance.

"I already know what *they* think," I say sarcastically. "Will you never allow me to be by your side?"

Bending to pick up his sword, he says, "We will speak of it when I return."

"Wait, I have another plan. I would like to take a patrol along the West to find the Scots for you. It will save you your men. I promise not to engage in battle, only to scout," I plead, begging for something to do.

He pauses a moment, thinking, then speaks.

"I know you have difficulty staying here, my wife, but unlike your father, I have many soldiers here. I will not risk your life in fighting. I would never forgive myself," he says pausing for a moment, then continuing. "I know you are skilled, but my soldiers will not follow a woman, it is not our way here," he says, looking pained, then turns and leaves.

I feel as though a spear went right through my stomach. The men will not follow a woman! I stand there dumbfounded and unable to think of what I can do next. What does this mean, that I will never be able to lead? How can I stay in a place where people will not follow me?

I wander out of my room and toward Merewyn's, finding her resting on her bed. She rises as I enter and asks me if I want a hot drink. I look at her in the hopes of finding answers.

"I do not understand these people, Merewyn. Arthur has told me that they will *never* follow a woman. I will never be able to lead these people as Father has taught me. I thought with time they would learn to trust me. To forget about their Christian beliefs of women." I look at her for an answer.

Merewyn shakes her head slightly as she speaks. "It is true. These people have different beliefs than ours. They do not honor women as we do."

"I do not understand, how can they not? They have tapestries of the Mother Mary everywhere. What sort of people are they?" I question angrily.

"Your father's people cherish women as equal to men. Our own people would not question your leadership. These people must learn that your power is real. This is part of your purpose here. To teach them of the Celtic ways. That a woman has the power of spirit and earth within her."

I look at her hopefully.

"How do I do that, Merewyn? How do I teach them?"

"It will not be easy. They are fixed in their ways. You must use your gifts of wisdom to show them your might. You cannot physically challenge them, you must use your mind and your heart to show them who you are."

She pauses and looks deeply into my eyes. "This is one of your greatest battles. To show these people that a woman has power and skill. You are wiser than most, but you have not yet learned how to use that wisdom. To balance the man and the woman in you."

"How long will it take me to do this?" I ask.

"This is your lifelong quest. When you balance the two selves inside you, then these people will understand you and give you their loyalty," she says gently.

I walk out of her room with my mind racing. A great part of me wants to return north to be with Father. There, I am accepted. But it is here that I am needed. The biggest battles are being fought here, not in the North. I could not return north now anyway. I would be a failure if I did. I must make Arthur and these people understand that I am a capable leader. That it doesn't matter if I am a woman or a man.

23

Realization of Power

THE NEXT DAY IS COLD AND WET AND THE RAIN PERMEATES my cloak as I ride toward the stone circle. I make my way through the mist and arrive at the circle in time for a burst of lightning and thunder. I secure my horse and find cover under the many trees until the storm passes. When it does, I sit in the center of the stone circle.

I stare up at the sky as Merewyn did, hoping for an answer to drop into my mind. I find myself speaking aloud to the universe.

"Why? Why was I born a woman? It would have been easier to be a man. Is there no one to answer me?" I plead. "Hear me, great goddess, Arianrod. Why could I have not been born a man? Am I being punished?"

What have I done to deserve this body? Was an ancient spell put upon me, that I must suffer so? If I were a man I could help this land be strong again. People would listen to me. I feel angry at Arthur suddenly, that he should be born a man and easily be accepted as a leader. I shout at the sky, "Who taught these people these things? Who is this God of theirs that does not allow women to rule? ANSWER ME!" I feel a rage building in me as I scream aloud to Arthur's Christian God.

"YOU SAY YOU ARE A GREAT GOD! THEN TELL ME WHY? WHY AM I NOT ALLOWED TO LEAD? I DARE YOU TO TELL ME. COME, FACE ME NOW IF YOU ARE SO GREAT . . . FACE ME!" I spin around in frustration and drop to my knees yelling, "AAARRGGHHH!!! I WILL SHOW YOU CHRISTIANS! YOU WILL NOT BEAT ME! I AM STRONGER THAN YOU AND YOUR GOD! I WILL SUMMON ALL OF THE POWER IN THE UNIVERSE AND ALL OF THE GODS AND GODDESSES AND SHOW YOUR ONE GOD WHO IS MIGHTIER! DO YOU HEAR ME, CHRISTIAN GOD?" I scream at the sky. Breathless from my tirade, I run to my horse, untying him and mounting up. I begin to ride through the rain and trees in a fury, racing as fast as I can until I finally come to a stop by a hillside. I notice a cave opening and, dismounting, pull my horse toward it. Once inside, I lie down on the cool earth and enjoy the smells all around me. I allow my horse to linger inside the large cave as I lie there thinking about Merewyn's words.

If it is my purpose to teach these people about my power, then that is what I will do. It doesn't matter how frustrating it is. I can do anything. I remember Father's words when I was small. He always taught me that I was as strong as he, and I will show Arthur and the others that. Even if it does take me a lifetime.

I linger in the cave until dusk, then make my way back to the fort. As I enter, one of the guards shows his concern at my having been gone so long. I smile to myself, realizing at last that he simply does not understand my nature. I turn to him.

"Where I have come from, women are taught to ride and care for themselves, just as men are here. I do not need a caretaker," I say firmly and he looks down away from my eyes.

24

Morgana's Mystery

THE NEXT SEVEN MONTHS PASS WITH GREATER EASE FOR ME. I am eighteen now and resign myself to the fact that it will take much work for me to win these people over to my ways. I fall into a daily routine of riding and planning as well as spending much time at the stone circle.

Merewyn and I decide to go for a walk on this winter day. As we walk down from the fort into the valley below we notice that many others have had the same idea. The valley is busy with people.

We notice Morgana walking amongst the people with her hands on her very pregnant belly. Seeing her, I wonder how she came to be in this way. I have never seen a man with her. Maybe once she has the child she will forget about annoying me.

Morgana turns to us, realizing that she has been watched, and waves, then rubs her belly, as though taunting me. I can't help but think briefly of the child I didn't have. I wonder what my life would be like now? No doubt filled with motherly duties. No, motherhood is not my purpose in life. I turn to Merewyn, noticing that she is watching me intently.

"Do you know who the man is that Morgana has bedded?" I ask.

"I do not. She came to me many moons ago asking for a potion to make her more desirable."

We both look at each other and laugh.

"This I understand," I say, sarcastically.

What man would want to bed Morgana? She hides behind her messy hair and never takes care of herself.

As Merewyn and I ponder the strange life of Morgana, I am suddenly overcome by a horribly empty feeling and a pain in my chest. I begin to gasp, trying to find my breath as my mind is flooded with images of my father, lying in bed with his eyes closed. Merewyn grabs my arms.

"Lady, what is it!" she begs.

"Father . . . my father," I say weakly, looking at Merewyn. "Merewyn, I must go to him," I say with urgency.

Merewyn nods in response to me and together we run back to the fort and my room. I begin to pack a sack quickly and ask Merewyn to get me some food and meet me at the stables.

"Lady, you must take some men with you. You will be riding through dangerous territory," she pleads, and I agree.

"Only one. Too many and we would be easily spotted," I say as I hurry with my sack. I grab my dagger and belt as well as my new breastplate and shield and run from my room toward the stables.

Seeing one of my favorite guards, I rush to him.

"Hurry, gather some things, we go north to my father's for a short while," I order and he responds with a surprised look at first, then turns and rushes away.

At the stables, I gather my horse as a young stable boy readies my guard's horse. I try to check over everything, making sure not to leave anything behind that I may need, when I see Merewyn coming toward me with a sack of food.

The guard quickly returns and we ride out of Salisbury Fort and head north to Northumbria.

25

A Journey of Grief

AS WE RIDE SWIFTLY THROUGH THE VALLEYS, I FIND IT DIFFI-
cult to focus on my surroundings. I feel glad to have
the company of my guard, for I am far too distracted
to keep a close watch for the enemy. The day seems a
long one as we make our way northeast. I want to race
the whole way home, but am reminded by my guard
that we must pace ourselves or our horses will not last.

A light rain starts to fall as evening comes over the
land. I find it reflects the feelings in my heart. We make
camp for the night in a thickly wooded area, sheltered
by a steep hill behind us. My mind is overflowing with
dreadful thoughts of losing Father. I pray that I am
wrong, but the look in Merewyn's eyes when I first felt
the pain confirmed my worst fears.

I have never thought of Father dying before. He has
always been so strong, I think I felt he would always
be with me. As we lie under the night sky with only a

simple tent, I am unable to find sleep. My mind questions my beliefs in spirit. I have been taught that spirit
lives on after death. That the spirit is renewed again in
some way. But how? I find myself wishing Merewyn
were here to help me understand.

I must speak with her again about death and spirits.
When Mother died I didn't really want to know more.
I never felt close to her and didn't feel the need to
know where she went or why, but Father is different.
I feel a sudden urgency to understand our spiritual
ways and regret not having listened to Merewyn more
when I was growing up.

Morning comes none too soon, and I realize that I
have not slept at all. Anxious to continue, I hurry and
pack my blankets and try to eat some bread and salted
meat but find water is all that my stomach will tolerate.

On this second day of travel, I find it more and more
difficult to focus. My head is swimming with thoughts
of Father and my body is weak and tired from the lack
of sleep and the dampness that permeates every bone
from this rainy winter weather.

We arrive at Father's fort early the next morning, and
I am barely able to dismount on my own. I hurry to
his room as my legs shake with a mixture of exhaustion
and worry. Before entering the building, I find Derwyn
standing there, looking tired and sad.

"Father?" I question as Derwyn shakes his head.

"It is a dreadful illness. Many in the village have
died," he says with an emptiness in his voice.

I walk into the room and feel my body go cold as I
see Father lying on his bed, his eyes closed. My heart
begins to beat wildly and my throat closes tightly as I
move closer. He opens his eyes and smiles, and I find
myself struggling for control. I must be strong for him.
I sit on the bed beside him and hold his hand next to

my heart, noticing how weak his breath is. He tugs at my hand and I move closer to him as he tries to speak.

"You are my greatest treasure ... I leave this earth in peace knowing you are well," he whispers.

My heart seems to miss a beat as I answer with a choked voice. "You must stay with me, Father. I will come back here and take care of you," I beg softly.

"No ... you must not. You belong with Arthur now ... Let us remember the joy we shared when you were a girl," he says, trying to force a smile as he coughs.

I touch his face, feeling the immense heat that pours from him. I take a cloth of cool water from the basin by his bed and tenderly wipe his face and neck. The fever in his body causes him to sweat profusely and I can't keep his face cool for long.

He looks at me with a loving gaze as he thinks back to my childhood, and he gently raises his hand and rubs the top of my head.

"Remember when you fell off your horse and grew so angry you kicked it?"

"I blamed the horse," I say, trying to laugh a little but finding it a great struggle as my heart begins to well up with pain.

"How I loved to watch your face when I first taught you how to fight. You were splendid," he whispers, his breathing becoming weaker.

I'm not certain I can even speak. My throat is closing tight with emotion.

"You were a great teacher," I manage as I wipe his forehead.

He reaches over and touches my face. "For you I would slay all the dragons on the earth," he says with love.

I fight to hold back tears and kiss his cheek. He closes his eyes and I watch him take his last breath. My heart is stabbed by a searing pain as I realize that I will never know love like this again. I whisper to him, "You are the greatest warrior, Father."

I sit for an endless period of time staring at him. He was the most magnificent man I would ever know. I am proud to be his daughter. I lay my head down on his belly for a long while and hold him. All in life feels lost to me.

As I finally stand and look at him, I become cold and empty. A great part of me has just left, but I must not show weakness now. He taught me to be strong and I will not let him down. I take many deep breaths and gather myself together. Clearing my throat, I make a commitment to myself to carry on his ways.

I walk from the room and look back at him one more time. Breathing deeply, I suppress a wave of emotion that tries to bubble up in me.

I walk into his main quarters, where I find Derwyn sitting and staring off into space. As I enter, Derwyn stands and comes to me. We look at each other a moment, finding it difficult to speak. I walk around the room a little, touching Father's things, and am glad to be here.

"You need rest, my lady. Shall I leave you?"

"No," I answer, not wanting to be alone now. "We must speak. I must decide if I am to remain here or return to Salisbury Fort."

Derwyn's eyes widen in surprise. "My lady, your father would want you to return. The real battle is in the South now. The Picts no longer invade here. They have learned of our skills."

"Yes, but Father is not here to lead you any longer. The Picts will hear of this and return. You need someone to lead you," I reply coldly. If I think of battle then I will not think of Father.

"Gwynnefwar, your father asked me to lead his men. I have been his second in command for your whole life. There is not much to do here now. The illness has taken many, and I am sure the Picts will not return. They make their way south to join with the Saxons.

"You will wither here, Gwynnefwar. There are no great battles to plan, only old memories to cause you pain. You must grow. Your father would want you to go back to your home with Arthur. He spoke to me many times of his pride in you."

"I am not accepted as a leader in Salisbury, Derwyn. Here I am. The people here honor me and will listen to me," I say as I stare at Father's table, running my fingers over his favorite blade.

Derwyn, seeing my confusion, tries to help. "You were not born to have ease, my lady. You were born to lead. You must show your worth to those southern peoples. We need you there so you can help push out the Saxons and others and form a greater union with Arthur's people. To stay here would be to hide."

His words sting me and I immediately turn to him. "I would never hide!" I retort.

He smiles. "I know, you are Lord Penryth's daughter. That is why you must be where you are truly needed."

I smile back at him and fall into Father's chair. "Yes. I understand," I whisper tiredly. "I must sleep now."

I rise from the chair and make my way back to my old room. It feels oddly small to me. I lie on the bed and slip easily into sleep.

When I awake, I am hungry and eager to go south again. I spend much of the day wandering about the fort and the surrounding area and feeling as though my time here has past. This place does not hold me, it was Father that did. Without him, I don't want to stay.

We burn Father's body and personal belongings in a

great ceremony the next day. One of the priestesses from a nearby village leads the people in calling the spirits to lift Father's body into the next journey. It is a grand ritual and the people feast afterward and each throws an offering of food into the great funeral pyre, which is kept burning all day and night. I watch the ceremony which a sense of detachment. I find it hard to believe that he has really left me.

After a few days of rest, my guard and I make our way back to Salisbury. Father's death has changed me in a way I find difficult to understand. I feel empty and alone. I know now that I cannot waste my life trying to convince people of who I am. My life is not like others. I know who I am. I am a leader and a strategist. I will do my job.

26

❖

A Job to Do

WHEN I RETURN TO SALISBURY, I AM SOMEHOW OLDER AND more alone. I sit with Merewyn in her room and drink some berry tea. We have exchanged few words since my return. Mostly because there isn't anything to say. Father is gone; I must move forward. Merewyn senses the change in me and hovers with a worried look on her face and tries to cheer me.

She keeps asking me how I feel. I don't feel, I tell her. Feeling makes me weak and confused. I decide to go for a walk down by the river and away from conversation.

The air is damp again this day, and a mist seems to hide everything. I wish it could hide me as well. I don't want people to read me so easily anymore. As I watch some children playing nearby, I decide to create a special school for young girls. It is time these girls learned to care for themselves.

Back at the fort, I summon one of my guards and instruct him to tell the community of my plans. Every girl from the age of eight is welcome to begin lessons with me starting two days hence. The guard purses his lips together in obvious dismay, but I do not care. I am going to do something worthwhile while Arthur is away.

I knock on Merewyn's door and she beckons me in. Excited by my new idea, I wait for her reply.

"Well. It is a grand plan. I am very pleased for you. It is wise for young ones to have many skills. I ask only one thing of you," she says, then hesitates.

"What is it?" I ask, not sure if I really want to hear.

"Do not teach them to hide their feelings. Only to awaken their strengths."

"I will teach only that which Father taught me," I say with annoyance in my voice. "Did he go wrong in his lessons?" I ask.

"No, he did not," Merewyn answers, knowing she is not wise to tell me my father was wrong but worried just the same at my increasing detachment from my emotions.

27

The Teacher

I AWAKEN THIS NEW DAY WITH A RENEWED ENERGY. THE thought of teaching my young female friends brings me great joy. I ready myself quickly and go to the kitchen for some food.

Finding it busy with cooks and wondrous smells, I am ravenous. I grab some freshly made bread and make my way to the great hall.

Few people are here at this time of the morning. Most of the people are working at their daily chores. I finish my food and walk out to the courtyard, where I stop in dismay when I see only six young girls there. I walk over to them and ask, "Where are the others? There must be more of you?"

"They are not allowed, my lady," Arius replies shyly. "Their parents say they must stay at home and cook and sew like other ladies."

Angered by this, I resign myself to teaching these six

girls. "Well then, you six will be the most powerful girls in the community. You will grow to be strong and wise and able to fight alongside any soldier if you choose," I say with pride. "How many of you can ride a horse?" I ask.

The girls all look at one another and then to me as no one replies. I realize that there is much to teach them, and I begin by taking them to the stables and introducing them to the horses. I notice that some of the women in the fort area are watching me carefully. Some smile as they watch, but most just stare, unsure of whether this is a good idea or not. It doesn't matter, as second in command to Arthur, I cannot be questioned.

I spend the next two months teaching the girls how to ready and mount a horse. Soon, two other girls join my lessons, as the word spreads out farther into the surrounding communities that I am teaching them.

When it rains I take them to my map room and show them how to read maps and plan basic battles. When the sun shines, I take them outside to learn how to ride or to fight with makeshift knives made of wood, just like Father did with me.

One day as we create a mock battle down in the valley, I notice Merewyn rushing toward us.

"My lady!" she yells as she comes closer. "My lady . . . Morgana has had her child. A boy."

A cold chill runs through me like a knife. I look around at the girls and find old feelings erupting in me again. I whisper to myself, "Everywhere there is birth."

Merewyn comes closer to me and touches my arm, as I sigh, suddenly tired.

"I am weary of this place," I say to myself, then I turn to the girls. "We have finished for this day."

The girls rush about excitedly and I watch them. I

feel a sudden urge to fight someone. I need to escape from here, it is like a prison sometimes. I turn to Merewyn.

"I do not belong here, Merewyn. I belong out there," I say pointing to the hills.

A long and lonely year passes, and I spend most of it thinking about Father and my role in life. Depression permeates my being on rainy days and I rarely hear word from Arthur, as he is kept busy in the East by the invaders. Once in a while, he sends a messenger to me with words of the war and of love. Little good it does me.

Merewyn and I wander about outside and notice Morgana and her boy playing by the little river nearby. I have watched Morgana often over this last year and find myself envying her sometimes. I wonder how my child would be if I had not rid him from me. No. I mustn't think this way. I am not a mother figure. It is not for me, this tenderness and nurturing. Still, my mind drifts often to thoughts of the child I could have had. I wonder if Arthur would stay home more if he had a child. Father certainly did. Oh well.

Both Merewyn and I turn as we hear a rider come. He dismounts in front of me and speaks anxiously.

"My lady, the Scots, they have made camp by the hill on the south bed of the Tribius River."

With a rush of excitement I recognize my wishes have been answered. This is my chance. Arthur is in the East and too far away to make it back in time. I must take some men and go. I order the rider.

"Have some men ready themselves. We must find them."

Merewyn shakes her head in worry. "Please, Arthur will be angry," she pleads.

I wave my hand in the air. I don't care what Arthur feels. I must protect the land. This is why I came here.

"It is my duty to defend this land. Arthur is busy fighting the Saxons and Angles. He cannot do it all alone."

We hurry back up to the fort and I change into my battle dress. I feel amazingly calm and assured as I ready myself. It is time for me now to show my skills.

I hear the commotion in the courtyard as I make my way down to it. The men and women there look at me with surprise in their faces, and it is difficult to tell that I am a woman now.

With my dagger on my hip, my breastplate and chain mail on and shield through my arm, I walk with assurance to my horse. I must gain their trust if I want them to follow me. I swiftly mount my horse and stand ready.

"Let us move forward. To the Scots," I order as I slowly leave the courtyard with six of Arthur's soldiers close behind.

The woods are quiet with little wind as we make our way southwest along the river. The men are close behind me and seem to feel assured of my leadership. We ride over the paths and Roman roads for two day's time before we come close to the old riverbed. I make my way to a clump of trees and stop. The others are close beside me.

Taking out my map, I show the men where the rider told me the camp was. I instruct them to surround the camp at dusk when the Scots settle and kill them before they have a chance to become organized. I realize that the Scot camp has many more men than we do and our skills must be superior. I order them to dismount for now and wait for dusk.

The waiting is difficult and time passes slowly. Finally, the light fades and we mount our horses and make our way to the Scot camp. Seeing their fires in the near distance, my heart begins to race. This is what I was trained for. I know I am able. I must be strong for my men or they will ride into the camp unsure of themselves. I motion for the men to prepare to invade the camp.

I wait with one other man beside me for the others to position themselves, and with sudden swiftness we charge into the campsite, spears and daggers at the ready. Suddenly, shouts fill the air as men and horses collide. I am easily pulled from my horse and onto the stomach of a Scot. I lash backward at him and fight to regain myself but he holds tight. All around me, my men fight for their lives and land against terrible odds. I see one of my men slain in front of me. I scramble to turn over and lash out at the Scot, who still holds me, with my blade, only slightly wounding his arm. Unarmed, he grabs my wrist, and I twist myself free. Realizing that he is too strong for me and will soon seize my blade, I bite at his face. Yelling, he rolls me over suddenly and I hit my head on a nearby rock, falling unconscious.

I awake sometime later to find one of my men wetting my face with cold water. Dazed, I sit up with great difficulty and try to focus on my surroundings. I see only bodies around me and two of our men left alive. Saddened by the loss, I raise myself with the help of my guard.

"Careful, lady. You bleed from the back of your head," he says as he steadies me with his arm. I look around at the dead Scots.

"Did you kill them all?" I ask.

"Yes. It was a difficult battle. They had more men and were good fighters. Better than the Saxons," he says with an emptiness in his voice.

I look at our dead men.

"We must take them home to their families," I say and motion for the two men to help me lift the bodies onto the horses.

"Rest, lady. We can lift them. You are wounded."

He beckons me to sit as he and the other guard lift our dead men onto their horses. After a short while we make our way slowly back home in silence.

Upon entering our fort in two days, we are greeted by cries of emotion from the dead men's families. The women look at me as though to blame me for their deaths. I understand. I blame myself. Was I wrong to go? Just as I think this, one of my remaining men says aloud to the others, "We were victorious! We slaughtered the whole camp. Twenty men to our loss of four. It is a victory over the Scots!" he yelled aloud, but the people don't cheer.

Merewyn comes rushing over to me, and seeing the blood, helps me to her room. Once there, she tells me to lie on her bed as she gathers some herbs for my wound.

After only a few moments though, I become restless again.

"I must go to Arthur's camp. I must tell him of the battle before he hears it from others," I say to Merewyn.

Merewyn just returns my look, almost as if she knows that it is pointless to try to stop me.

I go back to my room and change my clothes. After a quick bite of food in the kitchen, I leave the fort for the journey to Arthur's camp. I decide to go alone, as I feel the men need to rest.

I know the roadway well to Arthur's camp, for I have followed it many times on the maps. It feels good finally to see some of the country that I am fighting to save. I plan my journey slowly and carefully, not wanting to make any mistakes, as I have no one to help me.

When night falls I make a small camp by a creek, careful to keep my fire small. Alone in the wilderness I am aware of every sound in the night and the sweet smells that permeate the senses. This is where I love to be, not locked away in a moldy old fort. I need fresh air and the night silence to sleep under.

A wondrous peace runs through my body as I lie back on my blanket and stare up into the night sky. The stars are wonderful to gaze at. Looking at them makes me feel so tiny and unimportant. I think back on the day's events and question my leadership.

It was the first time I had been in command, and I had lost the lives of four men. That pains me greatly. I try to think of what Father would have done in that situation. I had to act immediately or the Scots would have made their way northeast, possibly to Arthur's camp, or more likely still, to Salisbury Fort. Action was essential. The Scots had to be stopped, and they were. It cost us some fine soldiers, but it was necessary. As I look into the sky I can feel Father's presence guiding me. A feeling of comfort comes over me and I hear his words in my mind telling me that I was right in my actions. No other leader could have done better with so few men against so many.

Feeling better, I allow myself to drift into a light sleep, my blade ready in my hand should I need it.

The next morning I awaken cold but otherwise content. I prepare myself a brief breakfast of bread and meat and watch the morning birds gathering seeds from neighboring trees. Life is so simple here, battle seems a vague memory.

I pack my belongings and mount my horse, anxious to see Arthur again after such a long separation. I wonder how he will react to my arrival. I wonder how I will feel about him.

I am almost at Arthur's camp when a scout comes up behind me. Surprised but impressed by the scout's silent approach, I ask him to lead me to my husband.

At the camp, many soldiers move about, sharpening blades and eating. They seem jovial and glad to be a part of Arthur's army. I move through them and they watch me with disapproving eyes as I follow the scout to a fire where Arthur sits.

My heart begins to race a little and I am suddenly nervous at the thought of his reaction to my news. He stands and looks at me with disbelief, then comes over to me and helps me dismount. He looks both happy and concerned.

"Gwynnefwar, why have you come?" he asks softly, then looks around to see Gulwain shaking his head in disapproval.

He takes my arm and leads me to his tent. Inside, he looks at me intently. "Now, speak."

"I heard the Scots were near. I took some men and went to find them. There were too many for us, we were outnumbered," I say hurriedly. I pause a moment and look around the tent, not wanting to be heard, then back to Arthur.

"We killed twenty of them but lost four of our men," I say with worry. Feeling the need to explain further, I continue. "I had no choice but to fight them. They were close to the fort and I knew that you had no men near. It was a successful battle. The men agree with me," I say, almost pleading for him to agree but watching his expression grow cold instead.

"Let me stay," I say. "I need to be a part of the victory."

He walks around the tent, his annoyance building, then looks at me with distaste. "You are foolish. I have scouts to tell me where the enemy is. Your place is at home," he says, then adds angrily, "why can you not listen?"

I turn away from him, angry myself. I should have known that he would not understand. Only Father could do that.

"I was not born to be a wife, Arthur. I was born to lead like you," I reply just as coldly.

"Then you should not have married me. I want a woman for my wife, not a man. A woman who will give me a child," he says, knowing that this remark would wound me.

I turn to him with my eyes glaring and my heart pounding.

"Then you do not want me!" I spit out at him.

We stare at each other in silence, breathing hard as we both wait for the other to speak. After a long pause, he draws a deep breath, remaining steely.

"I will be taking my men across the land to the north to fight. We will be gone for many moons, so you need not concern yourself with wifely duties any longer," he says sarcastically. "I will have one of my men follow you back to the far valley. From there you will find your own way. I will tell you once again. You are to stay at Salisbury Fort."

He brushes past me, refusing to look at me, and I kick a nearby bag of supplies in anger.

I storm out of his tent and see Gulwain standing nearby with a smirk on his face. Angered, I walk up to him and stare him in the eyes. "Do you wish to fight me too, Gulwain? I do not fear you nor any man."

He looks down at me a moment and we stare. I almost want him to say something so that I may lash out at someone, but he turns and walks away. Coward.

I mount my horse, not waiting for Arthur's scout to lead me back. I am fully able to find my way without any of them. I storm out of the camp, knowing that Arthur and his men are watching me.

I make my way through the woods and again find a place to camp for the night under some trees, where the ground is dry. Settling down, I still feel enraged. How could he, my own husband? He knows that I am skilled at leadership. He uses my plans in the field. How could he not understand? Was I wrong to marry him? I thought he understood my power, but now I wonder.

I pace around the campsite and yell aloud at Arthur and the others. Why can they not see me? I wrestle with myself most of the night and awaken tired and hungry the next morning.

I take my time going back to the fort, almost wanting to ride back to Northumbria and forget about these southerners, but I hear Father's voice in my mind and again I remember my duty. It is not for me to please Arthur or anyone else. The only thing that is important is ridding this land of the enemy. With this in mind I return to the fort, knowing that Arthur and these people will probably never accept me.

I take a few days to resettle myself into the routine of fort life and then walk past Morgana's room. I stop as I hear her talking to her son. The little boy, sitting on her table, looks at his mother as she washes his face. I am silently asking myself how Morgana could be a good mother when I hear her whispering the most horrendous words.

"My dear little one, you are truly blessed. One day Lord Arthur will claim you as his son. Then we will live very happily," she coos.

Shocked at her words, I storm into her room.

"You lie!" I shout, wanting to strangle her.

Morgana wavers a moment, taking her son down

from the table and putting him in his cot nearby. She then turns confidently toward me.

"I do not, lady. Lord Arthur came to me, that time when you rid yourself of his child. I have given him a son, not you," she says triumphantly.

Overwhelmed with confusion and fear, I try to remember the time when I aborted my child. Trying to focus, I walk out of Morgana's room and back to my own, where I fall down onto my bed in horror. Can it be true? Can Morgana have bedded Arthur? I am more angry at Arthur than Morgana. How *could* he? I jump out of bed and run to Merewyn's room to tell her the story.

Merewyn thinks to herself for a moment as I pace about her room nervously. "Yes, I understand. Remember I told you that long ago Morgana asked me for a potion to help her attract a man?" she says, looking to me for confirmation.

"Yes, I think so," I reply, unsure.

"She must have used that potion with Arthur! I remember when he came home to find you ill. He began to drink heavily. If Morgana gave him some of that potion with ale then it would make him delirious," she says, pausing for a moment to think.

Merewyn then goes to her table and begins to make some calculations on her astrological charts. Then nodding to me, she continues.

"Yes, the dates are correct, it was nine moons from the time we rid you of your child that Morgana gave birth to hers." She looks at me with wide eyes as I drop to her cot, astonished.

"Why did we not see it, Merewyn? Why did you give her the potion? Did you not foresee her trickery?" I plead.

Merewyn turns to me sadly.

"I have let you down, my lady. I did not foresee it. She covered her mind from me," she says as she then pleads to me. "Can you forgive me?"

"Of course. I do not mean to blame you, Merewyn. I blame only myself."

I stand and look around her room as I try to think of a plan.

"Morgana has become a dangerous enemy. I must stop her from ever telling Arthur. We must find some way to rid ourselves of her. Her only purpose in life is herself. She cares nothing for this country. I must find a way. She will know my wrath," I say coldly as I leave the room and walk toward Morgana's.

I find Morgana happily moving about her room with her child in her arms. I stop in her doorway and stare with an intensity that would frighten anyone. Morgana stops when she sees me and backs away as I stand there, looking at her and not saying a word. I notice her breath quickening and I smile at her, then walk away, assured that I have shaken her confidence.

When I return to my room I realize that it will not be so hard to undo Morgana's sanity. She is already half-mad, everyone knows that. I must simply push her over the edge. In fact, it will be a pleasure to torment her. I laugh as I walk to the baths and enjoy a long hot soak before bed.

28

Who Is Gwynnefwar?

MONTHS PASS INTO TWO YEARS AND MY ONLY ENJOYMENT IS in tormenting Morgana and teaching the girls. I have spent many hours following Morgana and have noticed much, especially that she often goes to the woods and meets a strange man.

On this particular afternoon, I follow her to the spot where she had buried the old box filled with Arthur's father's coins and papers. I wait behind some trees as she digs for the box but is unable to find it. Frantic, she begins to dig a wider and deeper hole when I decide to surprise her. I walk out from the trees and smile at her.

"Are you seeking something, Morgana?" I say as she jumps back, startled at seeing me.

"What is wrong, dear sister? Are you not glad to see me? What is in the hole?" I say as I move closer and peer into it. "Nothing I see. I wonder what it is you seek."

I rub my hand over my chin in a mock expression of concern as I taunt her. "Could you be seeking a box, Morgana?" I say, smiling again.

She fumbles for her digging tools and runs away from me in desperation while I laugh aloud.

The next month I again follow her out into the far valley at dusk. It is a quiet evening and a mist is falling gently, creating an eerie restlessness in me. I wait for a long time behind some large rocks until finally I see the strange man that she has been meeting walk swiftly up to her. Unable to hear their words, I wait patiently for them to finish and for Morgana to come past me along the path back to the fort.

"Why, Morgana, who was that strange man?" I say as I walk in front of her.

She stops, horrified, and begins to tremble as she stares wide-eyed at me.

"What is wrong, Morgana? Why do you tremble? Are you ashamed of that man? Shall I go after him and ask why he speaks with you so often?" I say sarcastically. "Speak, Morgana," I taunt her.

"I have done nothing wrong," she blurts.

"Then why do you meet him out here and not in the fort?" I ask inquisitively as I move around her.

She spins quickly as nervousness rises in her. "I may do as I wish," she replies and then begins to rush homeward with me quickly behind her.

"I am watching you, Morgana. You cannot hide from me," I laugh as she runs away.

I follow slowly and return to the fort in a euphoric mood. When I enter, I notice Merlin watching Morgana as she rushes about. I walk up to him and say hello and he turns to me.

"Are you tormenting Morgana, my lady?" he says with an eyebrow raised.

I smile and reply, "Yes, Merlin. I must have some fun in my day."

He shakes his head and smiles at me. "Will you walk with me?"

I nod and we walk outside of the fort and down the road that surrounds it. I always find comfort in his company. He is never in a rush and always has something interesting to say.

"You are not at home here yet, my lady," he states rather than questions. "I have watched you these years and sense your frustration in our ways. You do not spend much time trying to fit in with our people. Am I right?"

"You are," I reply with resignation.

We walk a ways farther in silence and notice an extraordinarily large eagle flying above us. It soars downward with such grace and lands in a nearby nest where its mate waits for it. Merlin motions to the birds as he speaks.

"You are like a great bird. But which one? The one that flies and comes home with food or the one that waits and guards the nest and family?" he questions to the sky, then looks right at me and waits.

"I want to be the one that flies and conquers the vast horizon. The one that soars freely and is not chained to a nest and chicks," I say with confidence.

Merlin beckons me to sit with him. Together we watch the glorious birds for a long while, then Merlin continues speaking.

"They are different, yet alike. The female has great strength. She alone creates a safe haven for families to be raised. He merely finds food."

"He also keeps the surroundings safe from other predators," I reply.

"As does she. He is often away foraging and she must protect the nest," he says smiling.

"Is that why I am here, Merlin? To keep predators away from Salisbury Fort while Arthur forages?" I smile in return as Merlin throws his head back and laughs.

"No, my lady. Both you and Arthur are fighting to save this great land. You were both given the same purpose, and you both forget that there will always be fighting, always be enemies. If you keep wasting time fighting each other, you will never find happiness."

"What is happiness? I am happiest when I am out there defending this land," I say stoicly.

"Then you and Arthur will never be content. You will not find pleasure in land, only in each other. Look at the birds now," he says as he points to the nest.

The birds preen each other and nuzzle the chicks.

"They have a greater understanding than you or Arthur. Sit and watch them. You will learn more from them than you ever would from a human," he says as he stands and walks back up the hill to the fort.

Why do I always feel mystified by Merlin's words? I think he purposefully tries to confuse me with riddles of happiness and birds.

Looking at the eagles, I do have to smile a little at their tenderness with each other. I am reminded of my first night with Arthur and him gently kissing my belly. Is that really what life is about? That is not what I was taught. I never saw Father being tender with anyone, especially my mother, and he was happy. Or was he happy because he was being tender with me?

As I sit there watching the birds, my young friend Arius comes walking toward me. She is growing quickly, and I love to see her change before my eyes.

She is so much like me at that age. I ask her to sit with me a moment.

"Are you well, my friend?" I ask.

"The boys would not allow me to play battle with them today, my lady," she says as she looks down at her hands, which are bloodied.

"What happened to your hands?" I query.

"I fought with one of the boys, my lady. Please, my lady, I am sorry. Please forgive me," she pleads.

I smile to myself in understanding and pull her close to me.

"I am not angry. I understand. You did well to fight him. He must learn that you are able to play the same games as he is. I am most proud of you," I say and hug her to me.

Holding her creates an odd feeling in me. As though I want to keep her with me, to protect her and teach her.

"We must gather the other girls when the sun rises next and continue your lessons," I say with renewed purpose.

We walk together up the hill to the fort, and her mother comes toward us, obviously upset. She calls her daughter angrily and Arius obeys, her head lowered. Pain floods my heart and I want to take Arius to stay with me. I know her mother punishes her often and it worries me. I must make sure that she learns to be wise and strong.

Back in the great hall, a large feast is being prepared, for word has come that Arthur has succeeded in overcoming a great many of the enemy in the Celidon forest in the North.

Rhianne and Olwy are quick to come to me with the exciting news. They both invite me to sit with them and celebrate the evening with dance and food. Life is so simple for these two women. They think only of beauty and love. I wonder how their minds work and am glad that mine is not like theirs. I see Merewyn nearby and decide to join her and share the evening in talk of spirits and goddesses and the power of ancient women.

29

Morgana's Banishment

THE NEXT THREE YEARS PASS SWIFTLY. A GREAT COLD SPELL engulfs the fort. Most of the people huddle by the blazing fires that burn all day. It is far too cold to venture outside, and I spend much of my time alone in my room. I wonder how Arthur and his men fare in this weather. I had expected them to come home, but then, battle does not wait for good weather. The news I hear is that the campaign is successful. Word comes occasionally from scouts and the odd soldier returning home that all is well and the enemies are being kept at bay, for now.

I can't help but wonder if these invaders will ever give up their quest. At this point, it does not seem likely to happen soon.

I am in my midtwenties now, and sorrow fills much of my days as I recognize there is only a very small chance I will ever be acknowledged by these people as a true leader or allowed to be at the front of the battle with Arthur. I often forget what his face looks like, as I have only seen him a few times in the past three years when he returns to resupply his troops.

I have noticed a young stable hand lately who watches me. He cares for my horse with extra attention and often asks me if he can assist me in any way. I see him today brushing my horse and notice the sweat pouring from his face as he works tirelessly. I enter the stable and say hello and notice him blush.

Bored and restless, I sit and watch him and find myself hungering for attention. He takes a cloth and wipes his sweaty forehead and neck and suddenly looks at me with a fierce intensity that causes a stir in my womanhood. I haven't felt that since the last time I had been with Arthur.

Confused by my body and longing for companionship, I pull him down to me and swiftly untie my breeches. With wild abandon, he overtakes me and I find my mind racing from thoughts of Arthur to thoughts of the brutal Pict who raped me.

It is soon over and I lie in the straw questioning my motives and choices. The young lad looks up at my face and tries to kiss me tenderly but I pull away. Tenderness and love are not what I seek. All I really want is a way out of my boredom, and he has succeeded in helping me a little.

I continue to watch Morgana. It amazes me to find that as time moves by, she becomes more and more erratic, continuously rubbing her hands together and frowning with anxiety. I know I am getting closer to discovering her secrets, but I can't help wondering if she is mad. She rarely speaks to anyone and has taken to eating alone with her son in her room. When I ask others about her, they know even less than I do.

I decide to spend this evening in the hot baths alone. I can hear the pounding of rain on the roof and am glad to be warm and soothed. As I become intoxicated by the wonderful smells of perfume in the hot water, I stare into the flames from the oil bowls and drift. Odd how time seems to pass differently in this place. I finally rise and dry myself and start back to my room. As I walk down the hall, I notice Morgana standing in her doorway watching me. I move closer and she steps back and closes her door.

I enter my room and am glad to find it warm and the pots lit. Olwy always remembers to care for my needs. I must remember to thank her, I always seem to be angered with her and Rhianne for their silliness, but I am glad they are here with me.

I notice some food on my table and take a bite of warm bread when I hear the creak of my door opening. I turn to find Morgana standing there stiffly, her jaw rigid and her hands nervously twitching. Annoyed by her intrusion into my peaceful evening, I speak harshly.

"Why do you follow me?"

She saunters in, suddenly self-assured.

"I know of the men you have bedded," she says coyly, trying to taunt me.

Bored with her antics, I reply, "Oh do you? What is it you *think* you know?"

Morgana squints her eyes, like a child playing a game. "I know Lancirus and others have bedded you."

Rage courses through me now, and I am no longer patient as I glare at her. "So. Just what do you plan to do with this secret of yours?" I ask sarcastically.

"I will tell Arthur! Then I will tell him that my child is his son. Then he will rid this place of you and take me for his wife," she says as her breathing quickens.

I throw my head back and laugh. Then I try to control

my laughter as I make my way close to her. My mind races with plots and I am barely able to contain myself.

"So, you are going to tell Arthur?" I mock her. "You think Arthur will send me away, do you?"

I walk closer to her and she backs away alongside the bed, wringing her hands nervously as she tries to remain strong.

"Yes. When he learns that I have his son, he will choose me."

I turn from her a moment, pretending not to care as I trace my finger along the edge of my bed. "You, Morgana, are his sister."

"It matters not. I have his child. Arthur longs for a child of his own. He will not deny me," she says rapidly, her eyes wide in fear.

I walk slowly up beside her, looking down at the floor and rubbing my chin with my finger as rage builds to a frenzy in my body and mind. My breathing quickens and I decide that I have had enough of this wicked brat.

In one swift movement, I grab Morgana by her hair and push her down onto the bed. Then I bring up my knee and press it into her chest as she gasps in shock. Swiftly, I take my dagger from where it lies tied to my calf and bring it to her throat. Anger burns in me and I twist the blade under her chin, enjoying her terror.

"You dare threaten me!!! I am Arthur's wife. I have Arthur's trust," I spit as Morgana winces. "You will never have him. He is mine, always."

I find myself almost unable to control my rage as my mind screams at me to kill her. "You dare tell Arthur, and I will have your head!!!" I say as I push down on her chest and move my face closer to hers.

"Do you hear me, Morgana ... You will never have him. You are weak, Morgana."

She pants for breath as I hold the blade at her throat.

"Do you fear me, Morgana? Do you fear death?" I say as she begins to shake in terror.

"It would give me great joy to kill you now. But I am merciful," I say as I twist the blade again, sure now of how to get rid of her. "You will take that child and leave this land. Do you hear me?"

Morgana, frozen, is unable to speak, and I scream into her face, "DO YOU HEAR ME?"

"Yes," she squeaks.

I take the dagger away and lift my knee, then I push her down onto the floor in disgust.

"LEAVE!"

She scrambles to her feet and runs out of the room. I turn back to my table as a guard walks into the room.

"I heard voices, lady. Is all well?"

"It is. Help Morgana pack! She leaves immediately. She is a traitor. Take her far away!" I order.

"Yes, my lady. It is done," he replies, then leaves.

I take my dagger and stab it into the bread on the table. So she thought she could threaten me? No one threatens me. I look at my blade as I remember the rape when I was young. How I wish I had had a knife with me then. I take it from the bread and restrap it to my calf, glad of my decision to have it always handy. I blow out some oil bowls and go to bed, where I lie thinking for a while.

I can't help but laugh now as I become calm again. Morgana must have been terrified. She had no idea who she was crossing. I think back on the events and find a strange shiver run through me as I recall my rage.

I yawn and settle into bed as I push away any more thoughts of my rage or of Morgana. I decide that I did what was necessary. Morgana betrayed me. It is done.

30

The Betrayal

At Arthur's camp a month later, the weather is wet and cold. The men slowly move about, eating and preparing themselves for the day as they warm themselves by blazing fires. Arthur sits by his tent looking at a map when a young rider comes up to him. Dismounting, the rider holds out a piece of paper to Arthur and speaks.

"From Morgana, my lord."

Arthur takes the note and reads it. His eyes widen as he learns of my bedding other men. He angrily storms over to Lancirus's tent. Bursting in, he stands fuming as Lancirus jumps from his bedroll. He then throws the note at him and Lancirus scrambles to read it.

Lancirus tilts his head back and sighs heavily as Arthur struggles with his confused mind. Arthur desperately hoped Lancirus would laugh at the note and toss it aside as one of Morgana's pranks, but as Arthur sees his guilty face, the anguish begins to overwhelm him. Lancirus lowers his eyes as Arthur speaks in disgust to his once friend, his voice shaky as he tries to control his pain.

"You have betrayed me."

"Forgive me, lord. It was only once, years ago. It was my doing, not hers. She sent me away," he begs.

Enraged, Arthur lunges at Lancirus and wrestles him out of the tent. Arthur pushes at him roughly and draws his sword.

"I should have seen this. The way you first looked at her. Draw your sword," he orders.

Lancirus looks at him but does not move or speak.

Arthur yells at him, "Draw your sword!"

Lancirus looks down a moment, then back to Arthur. "I am your servant, I cannot fight you. I am unworthy." He continues to look down as Arthur pokes at him with his sword, but Lancirus falls to the ground, his hands open beside him.

"I cannot. Kill me and end my torture," he begs.

Arthur, breathing heavily and still enraged, looks at him with disgust.

"You must suffer as I do. Leave this land, before my loathing changes to madness."

Arthur walks to a nearby tree. He looks up at the sky, then turns around in a circle, looking for some way to vent his rage. He holds his sword in both hands, then turning quickly, he slices his sword into the tree as he yells, "GYNNEFWAAAAAAAR!!!"

He drops to the ground in dismay and stares at the tree in front of him. "Why?" he whispers under his breath. "Why do you do this? Why must you anger me so?"

He makes his way back to his tent and fills a sack with supplies, then walks absentmindedly to his horse and prepares to leave the camp. Gulwain walks up and questions him.

"Where are you riding to?"

Arthur looks blankly at him and replies, with an emptiness in his voice, "I must return to Salisbury. I will not be gone long," he says as he stares into space.

"I will ride with you," Gulwain offers, but Arthur just rides forward. Gulwain quickly gathers a horse and follows him.

As they ride back to Salisbury Fort in silence Arthur is tormented as he tries to understand me and my actions. What will he do with me now? Gulwain follows close beside him, understanding that his best friend is in pain but not knowing what to do for him. He too thinks of me and wonders if I am to blame.

31

❖

Arthur's Wrath

MANY WEEKS HAVE PASSED SINCE I BANISHED MORGANA, and I feel wonderful as I dress for the day. Hearing riders, I run to my window and see Arthur and Gulwain coming near. Excitement pulses through me and I look around my room and run to my chest. I must ready myself for him. Where is my red dress? I open the chest, and finding it, I pull it on quickly. I rush to comb my hair and pretty myself to please Arthur as I hear his footsteps come closer. Nervously, I stand by the bed then quickly place my hair so that it lies across my shoulders.

Arthur enters the room and looks at me with fierce eyes and face. Realizing he is angry, I pull back in confusion, then move closer to him to try to show him tenderness.

"Arthur," I say softly.

He brushes past me and stands on the other side of

the table. "I will not have your womanly ways disrupt me, lady," he says icily.

"I do not understand. You have been away so long. Why are you still angry with me?" I plead.

"So, you have missed me?" he says with a sarcastic tone.

I interrupt him, standing very still and firm as I realize someone has told him something. But who? It couldn't have been Morgana. She had no way to get to him. The soldier took her southeast.

"What have you heard?"

"I have heard many words of wisdom," he says coldly.

"Will you not hear *my* words?" I ask defensively as I realize he must have heard about Morgana's child and that I have sent her away. That's it. Morgana must have told someone by now that he fathered her son.

"I will listen, speak," he says sharply as he stands straight and crosses his arms.

Trying to think, I stammer a little. "I sent Morgana away because of her lies. She spoke evil words . . . that her son was your child."

Arthur, shocked, looks gapingly at me.

"What? . . . *my* child?" he sputters.

A sick feeling comes over me as I realize I have said the wrong thing. I must cover myself somehow. If it's not my banishment of Morgana, then why is he angry?

"Is that not why you are angry, because I sent her away?" I plead softly.

He tries to regain himself and paces the room, still angry.

"No. I have heard words of your love with other men. You have brought Lancirus and others to your bed. You have betrayed me," he says coldly.

My mind goes blank as I try to find something to

say. How can I explain it to him? I didn't love them. Moving closer to him, I try to plead, but he keeps his distance.

"I have not betrayed you, you left me. You left me for years. I was empty. You would not let me be with you," I say. He backs away from me, disgusted.

"You are no longer my wife," he says blankly.

Terrified, I run to him and grab his arm as he tries to leave.

"Listen to me! I am your wife!" I say, almost screaming. "You cannot leave me!"

He turns and leaves, slamming the door, and I slam my fist down on the table, screaming. How dare he turn from me? He leaves me with nothing and expects me to honor him. Why doesn't he understand? I need to have the companionship of men. Not to love, but to be with, to talk to. I didn't want to bed them. I run my hands through my hair and pace the room in frustration. I start to shout at the closed door, "I did it because I was angry with you! You always leave me! You do not care! You do not want to be with me!"

Enraged, I throw some cups across the room until, tired, I slide down the wall and sit, waiting.

Hours pass and I wait in the same spot, thinking about what I will say to him. Why must he be so jealous anyway? He is never here to bed me. Why do men place so much emphasis on this lovemaking business? It isn't so fascinating. It is a game of power as I see it. I stare into the sky that pours through the open window and wonder about sex. I felt stronger when I bedded them, but not with Arthur. Why is that? Was Merewyn right? Are Lancirus and the other men weak? Is that why I felt good bedding them? With Arthur it was different. I felt out of control. Well then, if this means that he does not bed me anymore then that is fine and well. I do not have to fear being out of control with him. Maybe now we can just be partners.

Finally, I hear footsteps come closer. I stand, frozen as the door opens and am surprised to see two guards. Disappointed, I walk toward them.

"What is it?" I ask, looking for Arthur behind them, but not seeing him.

"We have orders from Lord Arthur. My Lady Gwynnefwar, you are not to leave this room," he says coldly.

"I do not understand?" I say, confused.

"You are imprisoned in this room! It is our Lord Arthur's command."

Enraged, I try to push past them but am unable to.

"I think not. Let me pass," I order.

They stop me and push me lightly back. They then walk out of the door and close it. I quickly try to open it but cannot. Working myself up into a frenzy, I pace the room, rubbing my face and walk toward the window. I look out and see Arthur riding out of the fort and away. Terror fills me and I start to scream at him, "ARTHUR!!! ARTHUR!!! COME BACK! NO!!! AR-THURRRRR! NOOOOO!!!"

I scream hysterically and turn and run to the door, trying with all my might to open it, then pounding on it, screaming, "LET ME OUT . . . LET ME OUT!!!"

Exhausting myself, I fall against the door and down to the floor. How could he? How could he imprison me? I am his wife, his partner. I look around as a trapped feeling overwhelms me and I scream aloud, pounding the door again.

"YOU HAVE NO RIGHT . . . I AM A LEADER . . . YOU HAVE NO RIGHT!"

I lean against the door, exhausted and angry. This can't be happening to me. I do not deserve this. What kind of man is he? This is not the end of it. I will show you Arthur, duke of the Britons. You will not be rid of me that easily.

I fall asleep on the floor as visions of showing Arthur and his men just how powerful I am drift through my mind.

32

Confinement

MORNING COMES ALL TOO SOON AND I FIND TO MY DISGUST that I am still locked in. I make my way to the window and look longingly out at the rainy winter day. A sense of betrayal fills me and I long desperately for Northumbria. Oh, Father, why did I come here? These people will never accept me. I am too different. I lean my head against the wall when I hear my door being unlocked. I look up anxiously, hoping for Arthur, but am disappointed when Merewyn enters with a plate of food and drink. She places them on the table and comes toward me, then squats beside me as we both hear the door being locked again from the outside. We stare at each other for a long moment.

"I am sorry, my lady ... It is not right that you be locked in here," she says softly as she looks at my lost face. "They are allowing me to stay with you for company," she smiles tenderly.

"How long, Merewyn? Do you know?" I plead quietly.

"A long time, my lady. Until Arthur changes his mind."

I lean my head back against the wall and sigh heavily, drained of energy.

"That may be forever . . ."

"No . . . trust me, I know it will not. He will come back, someday . . ."

I look at her and find comfort in her wisdom. She never lies.

"I do not understand why I must be *imprisoned*. In our land it was common that women bedded other men. The men do also. Is that not true?" I plead.

Merewyn nods.

"I only know that their ways are different here. It is not allowed for a woman to bed more than one man. It is sinful against their god," she says sadly, shaking her head.

"*Sinful* against their god!" I yell. "This god of theirs has only rules. Rules that fit well for men alone, not women."

How could I forget their precious god. But imprisonment. Why doesn't he have sex with another woman. Then all will be even.

"I want to go home, Merewyn. This place is not for us. I have tried to understand their ways. I have even read some of their Christian teachings, but I do not agree with them. I will never be one of them."

"Yes you will," she said hopefully. "You cannot leave. You will be shamed by our people if you do. You must remain and wait until Arthur comes back. You have a purpose, you must remember that," she pleads.

Resignation comes over me and I make my way to my bed.

"I shall sleep the time away," I say with no hope left in me.

I lie in bed for hours before blessed sleep finally comes and rescues me from my prison. I spend much of the next six months sleeping and pacing, as though exhausted from the simple act of breathing.

33

Despair

TWO YEARS PASS AND MEREWYN TRIES VERY HARD TO brighten my days. She fills the room with scented plants and herbs and shows me many rituals that were taught her by her mother.

I learn to sew and brew potions with her as we speak of the spirit world. She teaches me about the ancient women and their power and I long to be one of them. Free and honored in their villages, with the power to make changes. How wonderful it must have been for them!

My fantasy world grows ever more enchanting and helps to pass the days. We create games about other lands and how we would rule them, but still, a gnawing emptiness creeps further into my soul. I feel as though I am dying in some way. No matter how much Merewyn tries to cheer me, I slip further into despair with each passing day.

I wonder if he will ever come back. It has been two years now and I have not heard from him. Merewyn tells me that he is well and far away to the north.

As I sit by the window on a lovely spring day, I cannot help but think of him. I do care for him. I find the anger has passed and loneliness has set in. I miss him terribly. Merewyn comes to my side and touches my hair as we look out at the budding trees and the many birds flying about.

I walk toward my bed and pull out some maps that I have underneath. I find them oddly comforting. Merewyn smiles at me as I stare at them, wondering exactly where Arthur is at this time. One day I will prove to him that I am worthy. This life of mine cannot be meant to be spent this way forever.

34

Growing Old

ANOTHER YEAR PASSES AND IT BECOMES MORE AND MORE difficult to stay sane. I stare into the distance most of the time and I know Merewyn is worried about me. I can watch a bug on the wall for hours, talking to it in my head, then laughing at my madness. Am I going insane, I wonder? Does it even matter?

Merewyn comes into the room with food and drink and a great smile on her face. She rushes to my side.

"I have heard from Gulwain. He is here, we have spoken of Arthur," she says excitedly.

My heart seems to burst and my breath becomes short as I wait for her next words. Tears start to well in my eyes but I fight them back.

"Tell me of him, is he well? Where is he?" I plead.

"He is still in the North, but he is well, physically."

"What do you mean, physically?" I ask.

"Gulwain tells me that he is plagued by dreams of

you," she says smiling. "He says that Arthur is not the same. He will not take another woman, even though Gulwain has found him many. He spends most time alone and tormented. Gulwain is worried for him."

My mind races with many thoughts of him. Is it good that he is tormented like me? "But when is he coming back, Merewyn? Does Gulwain say?"

"No. But he thinks it will be soon. After their next journey. They go still farther north. He says they will be gone for a long while, there is much fighting between the local tribes."

I wonder. If he really dreams of me, then he must still love me. Could he, after such a long time? I feel a pain in my chest as sadness and hope war within me. Still, they will be gone for a long time. I may go mad by then.

35

A New Beginning

IT HAS BEEN FOUR YEARS NOW OF MY IMPRISONMENT AND THE
sun pours through the window, creating a lazy afternoon haze in the room. I am nearly thirty, and I sit by
the window watching the sky and holding a piece of
parchment and quill in my hand. I have taken to writing my thoughts and memories of Father. It brings me
some peace.

I often wonder about Lancirus. Where is he? Merewyn heard from Gulwain that Arthur sent him away.
I cannot help but feel badly for him. It was my fault. I
should have kept him at bay. Merewyn warned me.

Merewyn sits nearby on a chair, sewing, her hair
a little gray now. Bored and staring off into space, I
talk aloud, not caring if Merewyn listens or not
anymore.

''Every year it is the same. The flowers come, the
flowers go. Life is so simple from here. What shall

I write of today? Shall I write of the wind ... how it whispers in my ear of my days as a child . . . I was happy then. Life was a gift to me," I say, drifting off.

I scribble a little on my paper, then seeing my hand, I touch it with the other, noticing that it looks older.

"I grow old here, Merewyn. I feel I wish for death to come and free me from this place. The years pass so slowly. I fear Arthur will never return."

Merewyn looks up from her sewing. "He will come ... soon," she says, smiling.

Hope fills me as I remember Merewyn's gift of sight.

"Can you see him, Merewyn? Is he well?"

"I do. He is."

"What else do you see? Tell me of the future. Will Arthur and I regain this land?" I ask hopefully.

"It is not wise to see the future, it can only bring you pain."

"What does that mean? It can only bring pain?" I say disheartened.

"There is always pain in one's future. It is best not to know of it," she says, looking up from her sewing and straight into my eyes.

"I go mad, Merewyn. I see the flowers laugh at me," I say as I laugh at myself.

Rising, I walk to the window, pulling my cloak around me tightly. Suddenly, I cry out with joy as I see Arthur and his men riding toward the fort. Emotion sweeps through my body and I can hardly breathe. It has been so long! Finally, you come back. Oh, please, please, let it be to free me.

"Merewyn! Come quickly!" I cry.

Merewyn rushes to my side in time to see Arthur and his men riding toward the gate. I squint my eyes a little and fear fills me as I see Morgana riding beside him.

"Morgana! Morgana rides with him!"

I pull back from the window and pace the room worriedly as Merewyn continues to look out the window. Why has he come back? I must think ... think! "This cannot be ... The boy, Merewyn, what of the boy, her son?" I ask nervously as Merewyn continues to watch out the window.

"I do not see a boy."

"Help me, quickly. I must ready myself," I urge.

We start rummaging around in trunks of clothing and I pull out an old dress, the red one that Arthur loved me in. With shaking hands, I manage to put it on and with Merewyn's help, tidy myself as quickly as possible.

Moments later, we hear footsteps, and I steady myself against the table as weakness and fear overcome me.

The door opens and Arthur enters, older and tired. He must be near thirty-six now. He stops and stares at me, then nods to Merewyn. He walks close to me as I try to breathe and steady myself.

"My dear Gwynnefwar, you look well," he says taking my hands. "My wife, ... forgive me. I have wronged you," he says tenderly.

I weaken and lose my balance for a moment and he helps me. I have waited so long for those words. Over four years. With my heart beating wildly, I straighten myself, thrilled to hear him speak.

"I was wrong to judge you. I too have been untrue, as you know, with Morgana. I was wrong to leave you so long," he says, then pauses for a long moment and looks lovingly into my eyes. "Forgive me!" he says, and

I feel I could burst with joy, even as I fight the tears that threaten to pour.

I breathe a deep sigh of relief and fall into his arms.

"Oh, Arthur, yes. I forgive you."

He holds me tight for a moment and then I pull away from him.

"Why have you brought her back? She will try to destroy us again," I whisper.

"No, she will not. She is my sister. The time is now for peace, not anger."

I look down for a moment and then back to his eyes. "What of her son, did he not return with her?"

"No," he says, shaking his head. "She keeps him from me. She does not trust us. Let us walk outside. It has been too long that you have been locked in this room."

Excitement rises in me and I turn to Merewyn, whose eyes are filled with tears as we walk out together.

As we move into the courtyard and through the many people gathered to greet the men, I feel their eyes upon us and am proud that Arthur holds my arm. We make our way out of the fort and down into the valley below. I twirl around, inhaling the fresh air. Falling to my knees, I rub my hands in the dirt, laughing.

Arthur helps me up and we run and dance around on the grass together. I cannot remember feeling so full since I was a child with Father.

"Arthur, I am alive again. I am so happy. At last we will be together, partners. I will be always by your side," I promise.

His head droops slightly and a sad look comes over him. He walks a little, then sits on the ground as I come beside him. I withdraw as I wait for bad news that I know is to come.

"My dear, the enemy grows large and our army very small. They push closer to this land each day. Some of the Britons in the north have joined with the Scots, and Angles and Saxons have joined together as well. I must return again to battle to hold them back," he says sadly.

"When must you leave?" I say, disappointed.

He turns to me and touches my face, and I feel warm all over.

"I will stay until the moon is full."

"Arthur, take me this time. I will go mad in this place. We are partners," I plead softly, knowing that he will refuse me, but trying all the same.

He smiles sadly and shakes his head. "No, this will be a difficult battle. I cannot worry that you are safe. Do you understand?"

"Yes, I understand," I reply, just glad to be free again.

He pulls me close and looks intently at me. "I entrust the land here to your care. The Saxons may come from the south shore. I need you to lead the people here."

"I will not let you down, my lord," I reply, happy to have a job to do.

He kisses me passionately and pushes me back onto the ground and begins to kiss my stomach. Suddenly, my passion too begins to rise and my breathing quickens as he moves his lips down my body. My body moves into a frenzy and I tighten my face in fear as I feel myself becoming lost in waves of emotion. I gently push him away.

"No! I cannot," I plead.

I bring my hands up to my face and try to gain control of my shaking body. Arthur watches with concern and sadness.

"Why do you deny your passion?"

I bring down my hands and look at him with torment in my face. "I will lose myself," I barely whisper.

Arthur shakes his head and wraps his arms around me, holding me gently as I close my eyes. What is wrong with me? Why can I not allow myself to be free with him? Why does he scare me so? I want to, but I can't. How can I explain to him that I must remain in control?

We rest there for a long while and watch the evening settle into night, then make our way back to our room. Arthur leaves me for a while as I ready myself for bed.

He walks to Merlin's room and, finding him there, enters. Merlin rises and greets his old friend with a large hug, then settles himself in an old carved wooden chair as Arthur wanders about, pondering the many books.

"Arthur, . . . what troubles you?"

Arthur paces about the room, then stops and looks at Merlin.

"Help me understand my Gwynnefwar. Why does she turn from me? Why does she hide from my heart? Does she not love me?" he asks in a soft voice.

Merlin smiles as he pours himself and Arthur some ale and settles back again in his chair.

"It is not you, Arthur, who she runs from. She runs from herself . . . You see, Arthur, she fears the fire that you create in her. For it burns down the shield that surrounds her. It leaves her naked and open."

Merlin stands and looks directly at Arthur as Arthur rubs his beard in confusion.

"Think of your men, Arthur. What is their greatest fear in battle . . . to be naked, to be open, without a weapon, without a shield to protect them."

Arthur walks to the window, then turns to Merlin. "But I am not her enemy!" he sighs.

Merlin smiles again and places a hand on Arthur's shoulder.

"Ahh! But do you not see. All her life is a battle. There is no time of peace. War is everywhere. One must always be ready. She is always fighting, Arthur." He pauses a moment to take a drink, then continues. "When you touch her, she loses her shield and she loses herself. This is her greatest fear."

He sits back down on his chair, looking absentmindedly at his writings. "So you see, it is not you. Life without battle, without strength, is no life."

Arthur looks at Merlin sadly.

"I begin to understand. Thank you, my friend. I must return to her now," he says smiling and walks out of the room, leaving Merlin to shake his head in wonderment at the problems of life and love.

Merlin sits down in front of a fresh piece of paper and writes the word *love* in the center in large letters, then smiles to himself.

Back in my room, I pull my blankets close to my breast as I hear Arthur come closer to our room. He enters and the soft light from the bowls creates a wondrous glow across his face. He stands there for a long moment and I know he is thinking about this afternoon in the valley. I vow to myself to try to be more open with him this night and I pull back the covers to welcome him.

He smiles and undresses as I watch. I never really looked closely at him before tonight. His body is strong and powerful and I feel a warmth begin to flow rapidly through me. He stands before me in his nakedness and slowly enters the bed. As he settles

248

beside me, he cups my face with his strong hand for a long moment.

"I think I begin to understand you, my love," he says as he caresses my neck. "I am not your enemy. You need not be on guard with me."

His fingers wander to my breasts and linger there as a fire erupts in me. I gasp slightly and he pushes me back onto the bed and kisses me very softly. I realize suddenly that I have missed this terribly and I find myself struggling as my body clings to him but my mind tries to push him away.

I give in to my body as it erupts with hunger, and we join in a rhythmic dance that I have never known before and know that I will always want again.

Afterward, as we lie beside each other, I notice his smile and feel glad that we have joined in this way.

As I drift into sleep I once again remember that brutish Pict when I was sixteen. A coldness seeps through my veins and I recoil under my covers, no longer able to touch or be touched. Why does that memory always haunt me? Why won't it go away? Arthur, half-asleep, touches me, and I jump in surprise. Glad that he still sleeps, I rise and cloaking myself, make my way down to the bath room.

Finding no one there, I light an oil bowl and pour some scented oils into the heated water. I sink into it and find my thoughts melting away as the water surrounds me. I linger there, soothing my soul and finally, much later, I walk back to our room and settle in to sleep beside Arthur. His body is warm as I slip in close to him and drift to sleep.

The next week is one of joy for both Arthur and myself. We spend much time riding together and I take him to visit my sacred circle. As we pass through the woods, we come across Merewyn and Gulwain in an act of passion. Giggling, they jump and grab at their clothes, embarrassment burning in their faces.

Gulwain stands as quickly as possible and refuses to look at us, so we bid farewell and move onward, enjoying the moment and laughing together.

We enter my sacred circle and settle for some food and drink by a large stone while Arthur tells me stories of his childhood days. He tells me of when he and Gulwain used to ride together and when his father fought the enemy with a great army. He feeds me some meat and tells me of the Roman/Britons and their vision for this land, and how they had to return and defend their own against their enemies in Rome.

I enjoy his stories immensely and I find myself sharing tales of my childhood with him. Oddly, we never spoke much before this moment, I wonder why? I am enjoying him more and more.

Afternoon comes and we decide to make our way back soon. He turns to me as we begin to pack our food remains.

"You are a great leader, my wife. I know that now." He pauses and looks at me for a long moment. "I have been taught that women are mothers and lovers, not warriors . . . but . . . you are different. I see now."

My body feels warm as I hear his words. I have waited so long for his recognition and I relish hearing more as he continues.

"Forgive me for not seeing before . . . I remember in Northumbria when I first met you . . . you were so wise about battle, I could not believe it. I believe now," he says firmly and rises, lifting me with his hands.

"My wife, I honor you, as a leader and wise

woman. You are my true partner. We lead this land together now."

His words surround me with strength and I feel as though I could slay any enemy that came across my path. We embrace warmly and walk to our horses. Packing them and mounting, we ride back to the fort swiftly as rain begins to pelt down on us.

36

❖

Gwynnefwar, The Leader

THE NEXT MORNING ARRIVES EARLY AND FINDS ARTHUR AND his men readying themselves to leave again. The court-yard is bustling with people, and Arthur, resplendent in his battle gear, stands by his horse as I hand him his sacks. He takes my face and kisses me.

"The woman in you is awakening. Do not hide her so well. I love you," he says smiling and looking deeply into my eyes. He rides out of the courtyard and I find myself unable to speak.

I notice that the people are watching me. I decide then that I must immediately meet with the guards here and plan a scouting troop to patrol the nearby hills. I walk stiffly toward a nearby guard and ask him to gather the others for a meeting in the map room. He nods and leaves me and I make my way to the map room myself.

Thrilled to be amongst the maps again, I study them

carefully, noticing the vast differences in enemy movement since I last saw them over four years ago. Arthur
was right, this will be a difficult battle for him. The
Angles, Saxons, and Picts have made great advances,
as have the Scots. Some of the Briton tribes are also
fighting amongst themselves and are a great threat. For
the first time, I feel worried as to whether we can regain
this land.

The guards enter, one by one, and stand silently,
waiting for me to speak. When they all arrive, I motion
for them to surround the table and look at the map.

"Rest is over. We must plan a protective barrier
around the fort. Arthur tells me that the Saxons plan a
massive battle and may make their way here along the
southern coast. You will place scouts along the southern
farms and alert the farmers to watch for Saxons in disguise. You will also send a scouting party to the East
here and West," I say, pointing, "and to the North
here." I wait for a moment then lift my chin and look
at all of the men.

"Arthur has renewed his faith in me as second in
command. I expect your loyalty as well. You may
leave."

The men exit quietly and I realize that despite my
words I may not have their complete loyalty. I am hoping that they all saw how Arthur has treated me during
these last weeks and will not question my orders.

The next few days are quiet and lovely and I notice
Morgana walking out in the valley nearby. What shall
I do about her now? I cannot banish her, but she has
nothing to hold over me now, so she will surely stay
out of my way. She turns and notices me from my
window. Yes, Morgana, I am watching you, very carefully now. You betrayed me once, it will not happen
again.

37

❀

Merewyn

A BEAUTIFUL NEW DAY FINDS MEREWYN KNEELING IN A patch of soft grass in the center of the stone circle. In front of her burns a small fire. She has also placed a bowl of water and various herbs on the ground. She prepares some herbs in a bunch while humming softly.

Nearby, Merlin walks quietly through the trees toward her. He stops behind a tree and watches her with fascination.

She stands and pours some crushed herbs in a circle. Stepping into the middle of it, she raises her hands and throws the remaining herbs in the air. Merlin edges a little closer, his curiosity peaking. Merewyn throws her head back and begins to sing.

"Arianrod, Goddess of the Earth, come. Awaken me. Awaken my power of healing."

She picks up the bowl of water and dipping her fingertips to it, shakes droplets into the air. Humming, she then picks up a small bag and begins to bury it in the center of the circle. Merlin steps out from behind the tree and surprises her. She turns and looks wide-eyed at him, disturbed at having been watched. They stare a moment, then Merewyn stands defensively.

"Why do you watch me?"

"Your ceremony is most unusual. Where did you learn it?"

"It is an ancient ceremony of blessing. It was given to me by my teacher."

Merlin circles Merewyn, looking curiously at the spot behind her where the bag is buried.

"What have you buried?" he asks with a smile.

"A gift to the earth," she returns, calmly.

"You are a wise woman, Merewyn. I have watched you often. You know many secrets. Will you share them with me?"

They stare at each other for a long moment as Merewyn searches her mind for a greater understanding of this man. She realizes he is genuinely interested and offers to show him some of her rituals.

"I will share with you, Merlin. Some of my secrets at least," she says with a gentle smile and he comes closer as they sit together and talk the day away.

The next month passes with little excitement. I spend most of my time riding and relaxing at the circle of stones. The simplest of pleasures fills me with delight after my long imprisonment.

Morgana also seems to spend little time at the fort. I often see her in the far valley to the south wandering about, as though she waits for someone. What a mystery she is. I am glad that she is away from me so often, but I cannot help but wonder why she did not bring back her son with her. I wonder if he died. I must remember to ask Merewyn if she sees anything of him.

Arius is grown now. I meet her again in the community of craftspeople in the west village as I wander about. She is selling clothes at a booth amidst the other vendors. I beckon for her to join me and we walk amongst the many people shopping on this lovely day. She is tall now and plain, and somehow she seems sad.

"Are you well?" I ask.

She nods but has difficulty looking into my eyes. I can't help but feel that something is wrong in her life.

"Tell me, what fills your life now? It has been so long since I taught you of battle and strategy."

We walk beyond the village and she motions toward a small timber hut nearby and we walk to it.

"Here. It is my home, now," she says shyly. "Will you come, my lady? Will you drink with me?" she asks.

I nod and follow her into the tiny house. In one corner, a large woman sits feeding a baby. The rest of the house is filled with three cots and a table and chairs. A fire burns in the stone corner and a pot of steaming liquid simmers.

Arius shows me to a chair and hurriedly gathers a cup with some liquid for me and herself. She sits beside me and we both look at the baby and woman. I turn to Arius and plan to speak but she speaks first.

"Yes, my lady. The boy is mine. This is my husband's mother," she says, and the elder woman nods to me.

"Your child!" I reply in shock. "Arius, you have married?"

"Yes, my lady. It was arranged by my mother," she says solemnly, looking down at her cup of brew.

Sadness fills me as I remember the dreams she used to have when she was younger. She looks up at me and I smile.

"I understand, Arius. It was necessary. Your husband, where is he now?"

"He is in the fields. He is a farmer, my lady," she says, almost embarrassed that he is not a soldier.

The woman in the corner rises and carries the baby to Arius. Arius takes the boy, and the woman walks out of the house.

Glad to be alone, I notice Arius smile as she holds her child.

"Are you happy?" I ask delicately.

"When I am with my son, I am," she beams. "He is my only joy now." She looks at me and hesitates for a moment. "Are you disappointed in me, my lady?"

"No," I say, shaking my head. "No, Arius. It is the way of your people. I know."

We sit and finish our drinks, then I rise and say good-bye. As I walk away from her house and through the village, I notice more and more young women holding babies. What happened to those young girls whom I taught? Was it all a waste? Sorrow fills me as I realize that it was.

I walk back to the fort and into Merewyn's room. Aromas drift about, overwhelming my senses. I adore her room, there is so much mystery here. She stands by her table, looking resplendent in a crown of flowers and a beautiful vibrant green robe.

"Why are you dressed this way?" I inquire with surprise.

She whirls about as she sees me, a large smile on her face. "It is the solstice! The moon is also full! It is time to celebrate and create! Will you come to the circle with me? We will dance and wake up the earth!" she exclaims with a huge smile.

Thrilled at the chance for some fun, I nod.

"Yes! Yes! I will gather some horses and wait for you

at the stable!" I hurry out of the room and rush to the stable.

Soon after we arrive at the stone circle in the evening, Merewyn places a crown of flowers on my head and a veil of beautiful red silk cloth around me. We then surround the inside of the circle with bunches of dried plants and berries.

Soon, we notice the beautiful orb of the moon, and we begin to chant and swirl about, creating a mood of sacredness around us. As we sing and twirl around, arms outreached to the moon, my body and head begin to surge with a tingling sensation.

We then lie on the ground, and I feel as though I am melting into the earth. My heart beats wildly and it is as though I am being pulled upward, toward the moon itself as a dizziness comes over me. I sit up quickly and place my fingers firmly on the earth. Looking beside me, I notice Merewyn lying as though dead. Her face serene and still, she seems to be a goddess as her eyes, open, look unearthly in their beauty.

Afraid to move or disturb her, I lie back down and stare off into the night sky. Somehow, lying on the earth brings me a wonderful feeling of comfort. As though I am being held in a womb again. I want to stay forever in this place.

A short while later, I turn to look at Merewyn, who lies with a lovely smile on her face. I envy her sometimes. She is wiser than most and always seems to be at peace. It is as though she were from a different time, a more ancient civilization.

Suddenly, as though reading my thoughts again, she turns and looks at me. Smiling, she sits up. "It is time to return. My power is renewed," she says softly as she rises.

"What power?" I inquire.

"The goddess inside my belly," she says with a smile.

I know I will never fully understand her, but I am glad that she is my friend. We gather our things and make our way slowly home by the light of the moon. We ride in silence, enjoying the breeze through the trees. It is as though we are guided by the moon herself, and I am again entranced by the giant orb as she hovers above us. There is so much of this earth I do not as yet understand.

38

Morgana's Undoing

A FEW WEEKS LATER I AM SUDDENLY AWAKENED IN THE
early dawn by the smell of smoke and the sound of
screams. I jump out of bed and run to the window and
am shocked by the sight of Saxons moving about in the
valley below. Then just as I am about to turn and run
out of the room, I catch sight of something out of the
corner of my eye. Looking again toward a tree nearby,
I notice Morgana talking to two Saxons and pointing
to my room.

Enraged, I quickly search for and find my dagger and
a cloak, then run out. Once in the hallway, I realize
that smoke is everywhere. I race down to the courtyard
and am stunned to find the guards engaged in battle
with some Saxons on horseback. Buildings burn and
people scream and run about in terror. I step over a
dead body and see one of the Saxons retreat as the
guards overcome the remaining two, pulling them from

their horses and killing them. I run over to them, saying, "Quickly, bring Morgana to me. She has betrayed us. She waits outside by the path near my room with another two Saxons!"

Two guards turn quickly and jump on the Saxons' horses, then ride out. I look around in dismay, then run to the stables and grab some blankets to help beat out the fires with the other people. The smoke almost overwhelms us but everyone helps and soon the fires are extinguished.

Out of breath and with my heart pounding wildly in my chest, I try to understand what just happened. The guards then return with Morgana across one horse. They let her down and call to me.

I rush over to them as the two guards, now dismounted, hold Morgana. I realize now that she has been plotting this for a long while. She brought the Saxons here! She even paid them! That is why she did not bring her son back with her.

I walk right up to her and spit at her feet, my blood boiling with rage.

"Well, well, my dear sister. You have betrayed *Arthur* this time!" I spit again.

"You cannot harm me. Arthur will never forgive you," she says, feebly, trying to look forceful.

I push her roughly backward. "Arthur will bless me. *I* am the ruler here. You brought the Saxons here, to harm our people. There is no forgiveness in my heart for you," I growl.

I turn to the guard. "I want her head," I order with a satisfaction in my voice.

Morgana, terrified, falters, and the guards hold her up.

"No! My son! I have a son!" she pleads.

Inflamed, I point at her. "Your son! Your son that you

got through trickery! I care not for your pain! Your end is now!"

I look at the guard and nod, then watch with satisfaction as the guard takes out his sword and chops off her head.

"Take her body from here," I say to the guard.

I turn toward the other people and notice that the fires are out. I soon see a young boy of seven lying on the ground dying as blood pours from his belly. Horrified, I rush over to him and drop to my knees. I lift him close to me and touch his face. My throat feels as though I am being choked and tears well up in me as I hold him.

"No ... No ... You are so young," I plead softly, wanting him to live.

He opens his eyes and smiles. "I was a good warrior, was I not ... , my lady?" he whispers.

I hold back my tears and touch his face tenderly with my fingers.

"You are a mighty warrior indeed ..."

He dies in my arms and I pull his body up against my breast and rock him, closing my eyes as a searing pain pierces me. Why? Why such a young child? I sit there for a long while and rock him. My mind races with thoughts of the child I never bore.

Suddenly his mother comes screaming toward me. "My son!! My son!!" She drops to the ground and pulls him from me and cries out, "Nooooo!! Noooo!"

I watch as the woman holds her dead son. I want to hold him too. Why does this hurt me so much? Some other women come to help and take them away. I watch them go, and a hollow feeling grows inside me. A guard helps me up. I falter slightly and tremble as I regain my composure.

"The Saxons, have they left us? Are there more?" I ask.

"No, my lady. They surprised us but we were fast. The damage is small."

"We must post guards farther out into the hills," I say sternly. "This must not happen again!"

He nods and I walk past him and back to my room. I fall onto my bed as the vision of the young boy fills my mind. The world seems so empty suddenly. A child's laughter is missing.

Why are we so brutal? Why do we kill so easily? I sit up and look at my dagger in my hand. I killed Morgana today and a Saxon killed a young boy. My hands begin to tremble terribly and my breathing becomes heavy as outrage takes over.

"What is wrong with us all?" I cry as I throw my dagger viciously into the wall. "Why does this hurt me so?" I ask as I look around for an answer. "Father, you never warned me."

I stare at the blade stuck in the wall and lie back in bed, my body void of all emotion now as a coldness seeps into my veins.

39

Battle of the Warriors

AT ARTHUR'S CAMPSITE BY THE RIVER, THE MIST DRIFTS through the chilly morning air and Arthur and his men begin to rise. Suddenly a young man comes running through the camp, yelling, "The enemy!! The enemy!! Arm yourselves!"

Arthur and his men run out of their tents and grab their weapons, but the enemy are already jumping out of the bushes, armed and raging. Arthur tries to grab his sword but is hit in the back by a heavy club. He falls to the ground as Gulwain and the others fight with all of their strength. The element of surprise has helped the enemy immeasurably, and Arthur's men are being cut down left and right.

Rising with his sword, Arthur begins to fight back, stabbing one man through the heart. Still weak, he turns to face another but is stabbed from behind by a third soldier. He falls to his knees, then drags himself to a tree as the others continue fighting. He looks around him and all he sees are dying friends.

As the battle comes to an end, Gulwain finds Arthur leaning against the tree. Arthur grabs Gulwain's shirt.

"I cannot breathe," he gasps. "Take my sword to Gwynnefwar. Don't give up . . . Gwynnefwar, she can do it . . ."

Gulwain tries to check his wound but Arthur stops him and holds out his sword.

"Take it," he says and gives the sword to Gulwain. "Tell Gwynnefwar . . . I wish her to continue the fight. She must stop them . . . Promise me, Gulwain . . . you will follow her," he begs.

Gulwain looks down, not wanting to acknowledge Arthur's words. He cannot bear the thought of his best friend dying or of me being in command.

"Promise me . . . You can do it . . . together," Arthur pleads. He winces and slumps a little, struggling to continue as Gulwain stares at him.

"Arthur, no . . . you must live. I cannot follow her . . . ," he pleads as he begins to weep softly.

Arthur stares at him and gasps, "You must . . . Promise me . . . together . . . push back the enemy . . . Promise . . ."

Gulwain looks down at the ground as he fights with his emotions. He cannot imagine life without Arthur, but he must respect his friend's dying wish. He looks up and notices that Arthur is gone before he has said he would promise to follow me.

He looks down at the sword and then to Arthur again and, sobbing, takes Arthur's body into his arms. "How can I follow her," he mutters softly through his tears. "You are the only true leader, my friend. Without you there is no army."

He lies against the tree for a long while, holding Arthur's body close to his own.

40

※

Gulwain's Betrayal

It's a misty day outside and I am sitting at a table eating when the doors opens and Merewyn walks in with a hesitant step. She is followed by Gulwain, looking beaten and wounded. My heart seems to skip a beat when I see their sorrowful faces.

"What is it?" I ask, then louder. "WHAT IS IT?"

Gulwain comes closer to me and lifts a sword that he carries in his hand. He holds it out to me. I look at it confusedly, then freeze as I recognize Arthur's sword. Stunned, I back away a step and gasp for air, bringing my hand to my throat. I cannot think! I cannot breathe! I open my mouth and try to speak, but nothing happens for a moment.

"Arthur . . . where is Arthur?" I beg as I fight the pain that begins to fill me.

"My lady, . . . our Arthur . . . is dead!" Gulwain says, fighting back tears and choking on his words.

He holds out the sword to me again and I take it from him and hold it in my shaking hand. This cannot be.

"Where does he lie?"

"By the river Camglann, lady. There was a surprise attack. There were too many for us," he says apologetically.

I look up at Gulwain and try hard to focus as I feel a tightening around my heart. "The other men, what of them?"

Gulwain shakes his head sadly. "Most are lost, only a few are left."

I turn away for a moment, trying desperately to remain calm. I look back to Gulwain and Merewyn. "Leave me, now," I plead. I cannot stand to have them here.

"There is not time, lady. We must flee this place. There are many more of the enemy and they come this way quickly," Gulwain warns.

I look at him with disbelief. "Leave? No! I cannot speak of this now."

Reluctantly, he nods and says. "Lady ... Arthur ... was ..."

I nod my head slowly as I try to remain composed. "Yes ... yes," I quiver.

Gulwain turns and leaves and Merewyn starts to come closer to me, but I put out my hand to stop her.

"NO! Leave me," I insist. "Please!"

Merewyn, her eyes full of tears, walks out, closing the door behind her. I stand their and hold the sword to my breast as my body begins to shake terribly and I begin to weep softly.

"Arthur ... Arthur ... Come back to me ... Arthur please ... I need you now." I weaken and fall to the floor, holding the sword, and continue to struggle with my emotions as my world falls apart.

"Arthur . . . It hurts so . . . Arthur . . ."

I try to regain myself as I talk aloud to him. "I must be strong . . . They need me now." I stand and walk to the window and look out at the sky. Oh, it hurts so much.

"I will be strong for you, Arthur. I will not let you down. I will prove my worthiness to you," I whisper to the sky.

I take a deep breath and look at the rising sun as I fight to control the pain in my heart. "Oh, Arthur, the sun is so bright. How can there be sun when there is darkness in my soul."

I squeeze the sword to my breast as I look around the room for an answer. I swallow hard and compose myself a little. As I begin to pace about, rubbing my face with my hands, I try to think.

"Gulwain . . . yes . . ."

I walk to my wooden chest, open it, and find my waist belt. I place Arthur's sword through the silver ring and touch it gently, then rub my eyes and face and walk to the door and open it. Merewyn stands there weeping.

"No, Merewyn . . . We shall not weep this day. We must be strong. We must gather the people. Find me Gulwain," I say stoically. I must stay in control. I must.

Merewyn turns and leaves and I go to take a drink of water from a jug on the table. My whole body shakes as I try to lift the cup to my mouth. Unable to hold the cup with one hand, I use two to steady it.

"Father . . . Father . . . I need you now," I whisper with a choking feeling in my throat. "I need your strength. Arthur, I need you with me. I ask you—"

I am interrupted by a knock at the door. "Come," I choke.

Gulwain enters followed by two of Arthur's men. They look at me with sadness in their eyes and I say to Gulwain, "How many of you are there?"

He shakes his head hopelessly. "Few lady. We are weary and beaten."

"We must gather our strength. We must fight back!" I say as I begin to pace around the room. I need to hold on now. I need to hold on for Arthur. Gulwain looks at me with astonishment.

"No lady, there are too many of them."

I pound my fists on the table in fury. "NO! There cannot *be* too many. We must fight . . . We must. Are you with me?" I ask. I walk up to Gulwain and look him straight in the eyes, daring him to defy me.

"No, lady," he says firmly.

Wincing, I remain strong, staring him down. "Then you are a traitor. To Arthur and to his people," I growl.

"I am no traitor, lady," he says angrily. "There are too many of the enemy and too few of us. The men do not trust you!"

My eyes grow wide and I step back, stunned. "Do not trust me? Why? I am second in command!"

Gulwain looks coldly at me now. "There have been many stories these last years. Arthur's time spent away from you spoke many words to his men. They will not follow you."

I look at him with an air of authority. So this is how it comes to be! You and me, Gulwain. I know he never trusted me. Now he proves to be my enemy. I must bring him over to my side.

"Gulwain, if you follow me . . . they will follow me. I must have your loyalty."

"No, lady. There are too many. We must leave this

place. The men prepare with their families to go west now," he says with finality.

I turn and pound my fist on the table, yelling, "NO! I WILL NOT LOSE ARTHUR'S LAND!"

Gulwain takes my arm and turns me roughly to face him. "Lady, it is lost! Arthur is dead."

I glare at him and shout, "I AM ALIVE! I WILL NOT LET ARTHUR'S LAND BE TAKEN!"

Gulwain backs away from me wearily, toward the door. He looks at me as he starts to turn and leave, and I notice his body beginning to shake uncontrollably as grief begins to overwhelm him.

He sighs heavily as a sense of hopelessness seeps through him. He stares at me for a long moment, remembering Arthur's last words to follow me, but confusion and sadness cause him to turn away from me and ignore Arthur's dying words.

"We depart in the morn. We will guide you and your ladies north a short way."

He leaves and closes the door, leaning his heavy body against it as tears pour from his weary eyes. He walks down the hallway and outside into the courtyard, where people are busily packing to leave the fort. He looks up to the sky as the tears pour down his cheeks and whispers aloud, "I am sorry, my friend. Without you, I cannot continue the fight. I fought for you alone." He brings his hands up to his face as he walks out of the courtyard.

Back in my room, I feel frustrated with Gulwain's rebellion and pace the room as Merewyn enters, looking flustered.

"Lady, we must hurry and gather our things. They will leave without us."

I stand by the window, looking at the sky. "Arthur, help me. It cannot end this way," I plead, then look to

Merewyn. "Can you not see the future? Is there nothing we can do?" I beg as Merewyn shakes her head.

"It is time to leave, lady. All is lost."

I straighten at those words with a resurgence of my old strength. "All is not lost! We will leave. We will gather our strength. And then we will return," I announce confidently.

41

✦

Deserted

MORNING COMES QUICKLY AND WE PACK OUR BELONGINGS onto the many carts in the courtyard. Gulwain sits mounted on his horse at the head of the caravan and I am filled with loathing at the sight of him. How dare he cross me and Arthur? He is a coward.

Merewyn, Rhianne, and Olwy climb onto a cart and I ride beside them on my horse as we make our way out of the fort and down the road. Fury seethes through my veins as we leave and I vow to return with or without Gulwain. I will never let Saxons live here! I will fight to the death first to defend this land. Gulwain is no leader, of that I am sure. We could easily gather enough men to fend off the enemy.

Merewyn, noticing my torment, tries to comfort me. "All will be well, lady. Please do not be so angry."

How could she possibly understand? We are deserting all that Arthur and Father stood for. All is *not* well.

As the day progresses, we make our way through the nearby hills. I stop and look back toward the fort and my heart sinks as I see smoke rising high in the air. The enemy is at Salisbury Fort. I turn to Gulwain and notice that he too sees the smoke.

I stare at him, and he knows that I will never forgive him for this as he turns away from me and continues on. I stay for a long moment looking at the smoke and promising Arthur in my heart to return and reclaim this land in his name.

That evening, the people sit around campfires, tired and heartsick. I sit in front of a fire, trying to forget the last few days as Gulwain walks toward me, his shadow crossing my face.

"Lady, we must speak. The men have decided to go west from here, across the sea," he says coldly.

Looking up at him, I stand. "No, Gulwain. I need them now. We must heal and go back. We can gather more men from the northern high kings. We must regain Arthur's lands."

Gulwain adds another stick to the fire, causing sparks to fly up and briefly illuminate his face. "Lady, we are weary. The men have families. We have chosen to leave come morning. Will you come with us?"

I stare angrily at him. "With traitors!" I spit. "No! I will not leave this land. Go! I need you not. I am still Arthur's second in command. I will not desert his land!"

Gulwain turns and walks silently away as I sit back down and stare into the fire. He comes upon Merewyn standing alone by a tree and looks tenderly at her.

"We leave for the West in the morning. Will you come with me?"

Merewyn looks past him at me, her heart torn. Then sadness fills her eyes as she turns to Gulwain. "I cannot leave her now. She needs me more than you do," she whispers.

He looks down, resigned, then back to her. "I am sorry."

He turns and walks away and Merewyn's eyes fill with tears.

Morning comes and I notice that most everyone has left except for Merewyn, Olwy, Rhianne, and a few guards. I sit quietly by a creek, dipping my hands in and scooping up some water to splash on my face. I stand up as one of the few remaining men rides up on his horse. Dismounting, he says urgently, "Lady, there is an old monastery near, to the north. We will take you there. We have chosen to follow the others west."

"I see," I say, resigned to my destiny. "Very well, let us go."

We turn and walk to the camp to gather our meager belongings together. For most of the day we ride northwest until we come upon an old monastery, in obvious ruins. As we move closer, I notice one of our guards coming out of the front gate with a woman dressed in long brown tattered robes. We ride into the courtyard and are greeted by the elderly woman.

"Welcome, Lady Gwynnefwar, to the home of the Christian Mothers. I am Mother Anne, head of this house. We have prepared rooms for you and your ladies. We hope you will find peace here," she says softly.

Peace. Ha! That is not a possibility. We dismount and are helped by some men who tend the grounds.

As Mother Anne leads us inside, a cold chill runs through my bones, and I look at Merewyn as we both rub our arms. "It is the stone," Merewyn says in answer to my thoughts.

We are led through the long stone hallways to some

rooms with ready fires. A young sister named Merys helps me unpack as Mother Anne leads Merewyn and the others to their quarters nearby.

The room is sparse, a cot, table, and two chairs. Certainly not homelike. One of the keepers drags in my chests and I eagerly open them and take out my maps. Merys watches with curiosity as I place them on the table and stare at them.

42

Isolation

MONTHS PASS SLOWLY IN THIS PLACE. I SIT AT THE TABLE BY
the fire looking at two large maps. With my head leaning on my hand, I look closely at them, tapping a quill
on the map unconsciously. The door opens and Merys
enters, carrying food. She carries it to the table and
places it on top of the maps. Horrified, I bark at her to
remove it immediately. Terrified by my outburst, Merys
moves to the fire and adds more wood, then carefully
comes to the table and looks at the maps.

"What is it you do with these drawings?" she asks
softly, trying to befriend me.

"They are not drawings, they are maps," I say in a
tired voice. "One day I will gather Arthur's men, those
who are left, and we will regain the land that we lost."

I stab my quill into the map viciously, and the
woman looks aghast at me. She pauses a moment, then
tries to look interested.

"Lady, there are no men," she states.

I look up at her defiantly. "There are *always* men!" I retort.

She pulls back and quietly leaves me alone. No men. Ha!

Looking carefully at the maps, I realize that along the northwest shore there is a large contingent of Celtic/ Britons that may be willing to join me. I hurriedly prepare messages to be sent to these and other Celtic/ Briton tribes, including the remains of my father's, in the hopes that they will see the wisdom in joining together and pushing southward again.

I find some young men in a nearby village who are willing to make the journeys and take my messages to the various tribes. Afterward, I return to my stone fortress and wait.

Months pass and no word comes from the tribes. Disappointment is ever in my heart as I come to realize that no one is willing to fight our ever-growing enemies.

One damp, cold autumn day, I finally receive a message from Northumbria and my heart races with excitement. I take the note close to my fire and open it. It is in our Celtic language of drawings and is sent from Derwyn's son, Maelwych. It tells me that the tribe has scattered widely in these last years because of disease and fighting. They are in small groups now and unable to send any men for battle.

It also tells me that Father's old fort has been abandoned, and they have moved above the great wall in the North, where they have settled in some mountains. Food is scarce and they rely heavily on wild meat alone for their diet. He does not mention Derwyn, so I presume that he has died.

Father's fort abandoned! How can this be? We had so many men and such a great community. I have heard of other tribes struck by disease, but I had never thought Father's people would be vulnerable to it.

I toss the message into the fire and watch it burn away into nothing. Our people seem to be dissolving away into nothing as well. How can all of the Britons and Celts be driven from this land? Will no one fight anymore?

I watch the fire for a long while as resentment toward Gulwain and the rest of Arthur's men fills me. If they had stayed with me, then others would have joined us. Now, no one will join a lone woman.

I continue to send messages to other Briton and Celt villages that I hear of, but no word ever comes back.

43

※

A Loss of Purpose

I STARE OUT OF MY WINDOW AT THE COLD DRIZZLE OUTSIDE and hear the soft footsteps of Merewyn coming into my room.

My thirty-third birthday has just passed. We have been here for three years now, and still I am no closer to regaining Arthur's land. I hear from passing travelers that our enemies have overtaken most of the land. We who once were so mighty! I hear there is fighting everywhere. No one really leads.

Merewyn beckons me to walk with her. Winter is coming, and soon it will be too cold to get out much. We walk past the stables and I notice a few horses there. I rarely ride now. I seem to have little interest in anything. We stop and watch the trees dropping the last of their leaves onto the ground and Merewyn pulls my arm close to her.

"Try to find peace, Gwynnefwar. Life continues. The fighting is over for us," she says, trying to comfort me.

But little comforts me these days. Something still burns in my belly. I often think of Arthur and have to push the ache away. I want to be strong again. I had a purpose once.

We rest a little and Merewyn falls asleep against me. How peaceful she looks, she always did.

Back at the house, Rhianne and Olwy have grown accustomed to their surroundings these last years. Olwy has married one of the keepers and they seem to be happy. I am glad for her. Rhianne as well seems content. She has taken to organizing the house, as Mother Anne passed away last year. I do admit she has done well in beautifying it. She roused the keepers and restored much of the crumbling walls as well as finding old carpets in the nearby villages for our rooms. It is much warmer here now. This winter will not be as cold as the last ones.

It is a windy and wet day when I hear heavy footsteps on the stone outside of my room. I am sitting by the fire and thinking about Father and Arthur when a knock on my door rouses me back to the present.

"Come," I say.

The door creaks open and I see a haggard-looking man in his early forties. He is wearing a heavy dark cloak over brown woollen breeches. His unruly red hair covers much of his forehead, and as he enters he brushes it aside.

Through the messy hair and beard something familiar seems to awaken me and my pulse races as I recognize my old friend Lancirus. He smiles broadly and I stand with outreached arms to him.

"Lancirus, is it really you?"

"It is," he replies in a hoarse voice.

He moves into my arms and we hold each other for

a long while then move to sit in front of the fire. I stare at him for a long moment and remember the past.

"How well you look! Where have you been all these years?" I ask.

"I have been across the sea in Gaul. I have made a life for myself there. It is quite comfortable," he says as he looks into the fire for a long moment then into my eyes. We spend much of the afternoon speaking of his new life as a farmer and of how things have changed since we last saw each other.

"I heard of Arthur's death only last year. I tried to stay away, but I needed to see you again. To see your lovely face."

I smile at his tender words. I had forgotten how charming he could be. "I am so glad you are here. I have been in need of company," I say, then hesitate for a moment before I add, "I must ask for your forgiveness. It was my fault that Arthur sent you away—"

Lancirus shakes his head and interrupts as he takes my hands. "No. No. Please. Let us forget the past. I have come for a reason," he says and pauses to stare into my eyes as I wonder what he could mean.

"I have come to ask you to return to Gaul with me. To be my wife?" he asks shyly.

I am overwhelmed with surprise and find myself once again feeling a gentle mothering love for him as I look into his eyes for a long moment. I realize that I do love this man, but not as a wife loves a husband.

"My dear Lancirus, I have come to understand much these last years of myself. I cannot go with you to be your wife. I thank you for your love and gentleness. For a moment, I had hopes that you had come to help me form a new army," I say with a smile.

I stand up and walk to the window and stare out for

a long moment as Lancirus comes up behind me and places a hand on my shoulder.

"I understand. You will never belong to any man," he says tenderly and kisses me gently on the cheek. I tighten my body as tears fill my eyes. I do belong with one man. Arthur. I turn to him and touch his face. I want to speak, but I cannot find the words to express my torment and need to remain here in Britain. He smiles and walks away, closing the door behind him. There is nothing that can take away this ache I feel in my heart.

44

❖

Emptiness

WITH ANOTHER WINTER HOWLING AT THE WINDOWS, MERE-wyn and I sit by the table of maps. Boredom fills me. She tries to sew but coughs and wheezes and pulls a cloak around her. I worry about her, she coughs so much now. She sips a hot herbal drink while she continues to sew. Merys enters the room with a platter of food and places it on the floor beside us, and I smile, remembering when she was younger and placed it on top of the maps. She says nothing and leaves as Merewyn's cough worsens.

"How do you fare this day?" I ask with concern.

"It is almost time for me to leave this world," she wheezes. "I have seen much. Much that I did not wish to see. I long now for the skies, for peace. To be one with the wind." She smiles and looks lovingly at me, noticing my sadness at hearing her words.

What will I do without her? She has been with me since my birth.

"Do not be sad for me. My real journey begins now," she says with hope.

She takes another sip of her brew and coughs again while I look at the maps a moment, then stand as a sense of dread comes over me.

"It is over!" I grab the maps and tear them up angrily, then throw them into the fire. "I have lost! I have lost! Oh, Arthur, I let you down!" I whisper with resignation.

I look around as I hear a thud and see that Merewyn has fallen forward, her head on the table. Horrified, I rush to her side and touch her. She doesn't move. I turn her head to the side and place my hand in front of her nose to find her breath, but it isn't there. As I realize she is gone, I close my eyes and fight the tears and searing pain that flood my heart and soul.

"All is lost . . ."

45

Gwynnefwar, The Woman

OVER THE NEXT TWO YEARS A SENSE OF DESPAIR PERMEATES me. There is no one now in my life. I spend my days walking and remembering the past. Was it all in vain? If I had only had my child, I would have something of worth.

Spring has finally arrived and I walk through the budding trees around the monastery, watching the birds singing nearby. I am thirty-six now and tired from the long winter. I find it difficult to rouse any energy for anything these days and even walking seems a chore. I lean against a tree for a moment, then squint a little as I notice a man in flowing robes walking toward me.

The sun is in my eyes and I bring my hand up to shield them and try to see the man more clearly. As he moves closer to me, my heart leaps with joy and I laugh aloud at the wondrous sight of Merlin. Older, but still looking the same, he walks to me with a broad grin on his face.

"Merlin, my friend, from where did you come?" I say joyfully.

He smiles and greets me, taking my hands and looking deeply into my eyes for a long while.

"From the East. It has been a long journey."

"I am so happy you have come. I thought you had left us like the others."

"Soon . . . my work here is not yet finished," he says, then becomes serious. "I have seen Lancirus on the eastern coast. We spoke of you and the past. You are troubled, lady?"

I laugh and turn from him. Just like Merewyn, he could always sense my inner feelings. "Troubled!" I laugh ruefully. "Yes, I have fought so long, Merlin. I have failed."

He walks with me, holding my arm close in his. It feels so good to be near him again. He was so close to Arthur and he always understood me. We walk amongst the trees and enjoy each other immensely. I feel so comfortable again.

"Ah, no. You have won, Gwynnefwar, though you do not know it," he says as he stops and looks close into my eyes.

"Won!" I say with shock. "How can you say this. I failed Arthur, I failed my father. I lost our land!"

He pulls me to face him and looks down into my eyes. "But *you* have won."

"I do not understand you, Merlin," I say, shaking my head.

"You do not understand yourself yet. The time is now, my dear Gwynnefwar, to face the truth. Many years ago I told you that your power lay not in the skin of a man but in the skin—"

"Yes, I remember."

"You have lived in fear for many years."

Surprised by his words, I become defensive. "In fear! I have no fear!"

"Lady, it is time to face the woman that you are," he says softly.

I turn sideways, not wanting to look at him as he continues, knowing he speaks the truth, again.

"You try so hard not to weep. You try so hard to be strong. Look at yourself. There is nothing left to fight for. The battle is over."

I start to feel my emotions erupting and I clench my jaw.

"Your greatest fear was of just being a woman. You have feared your body for many years. You have feared your emotions your whole life. Arthur sought to find the woman in you. Gwynnefwar, my lady, allow it to happen. Allow yourself to love."

He waves his arms around me as I fight my emotions, wanting desperately to weep. "Look around you. All is flowering, all will die. Now is the time to face the pain of life."

I stand there and my eyes start to water.

"Gwynnefwar, face the love that you miss. The love that you never allowed yourself to feel. Feel it now and you will win. You will be free to find peace," he says and cups my face.

"Merlin, you speak wise words. I am so tired." I sigh, and he comes close to me and holds me in his arms.

"You are tired of fighting yourself."

I close my eyes and sigh heavily, then look up at him with tears in my eyes and he kisses me on the forehead. It feels so good to let go, finally. We walk back to the house together and I take him to the kitchen for some food.

We spend the evening talking of Arthur and times past. I ask him about himself and what he has been doing these last years.

"I went away for a long while and have been writing my words for future people to read." He takes his sack and pulls out a large volume bound in string.

"Where do you go from here? Will you stay?" I say hopefully.

"No. I go north. There is a special place for me. A place where I will bury this book and know it will be kept safe for many years."

We look at each other for a long moment and I feel such a longing for the past. "Will I see you again?"

"When we are free from this heaviness," he says smiling. "Merewyn taught me much of the spirit world. Is she here?"

I shake my head sadly. "No. She died," I say, feeling choked again.

"She is happy. Of that I am sure," he says with confidence.

We both smile, and he finishes his food and stands.

"I must move on. I have much ground to cover and little time. Walk a ways with me, will you?" I nod and we walk back outside and enjoy the spring loveliness all around us.

I walk with him to the creek nearby and he pulls me close into his arms. Then, releasing me, he touches my heart with his hand and smiles. As he walks away, tears flood down my cheeks.

I walk for hours after he leaves, pondering my life, and realize that I have not finished with Salisbury yet. I always felt that I had to return, and now I know that I must. I hurry back to the house and change into my riding clothes. I search my chest for my dagger, which

I have not worn since Merewyn died, and tie it to my calf. It feels strange there.

I make my way to the stable and ask one of the keepers to help me ready a horse for my journey south. Rhianne, seeing me leave, comes running toward me.

"My lady, where are you going?" she cries.

"Back to Salisbury. I promised Arthur I would return, and I must see if it is still there and if the enemy occupies it," I say with determination.

I turn to her with a serious look on my face. "Do not fear for me. I will be well."

46

Going Home

WITH THE SUN SHINING BRIGHTLY ON THIS SPRING DAY, I RIDE southward with a feeling of purpose and strength. It is wonderful to ride again! The land hasn't changed much in the six years since I have ridden this way, and I relish the warm feelings that fill me as I make my way closer and closer to our old lands.

I stay as far away from villages and farms as I can, for fear that they may be inhabited by Saxons now, and keep to the higher hills and dense forests. I spend the night camped under some trees on a hill, careful not to have a fire or anything that might attract attention.

Come morning, I ready myself and am quickly moving again. It isn't long before I am riding up the hillside that looks over the fort. As I come to the top, I look for a place free of trees and find the same plateau that I used to go to.

I stop, frozen, and look to the adjacent hill. I gasp

and quickly dismount as I see the few remains of our fort.

Ruins, it is in ruins! Waves of emotion and tears begin to flood to the surface as I see what is left of that most beautiful place.

I start to weep uncontrollably and gasp for breath as I look from the sky to the fort and back to the sky, hugging myself tightly.

"Arthur . . . Arthur . . . It's gone."

I drop to the ground and sob. Then I look around me quickly, as I feel sure I have heard his voice.

"Arthur, can you hear me. Where are you?" I plead through my tears, wanting to hear him more than anything. "Arthur . . . you did find me. You did touch me. I do love you." I cough a little as I sob, my breath quickening.

"I am . . . sorry . . . please hear me . . . ," I plead as all the emotion that I have held through my life bursts out. "I was too afraid of you . . . I need you . . . Please . . . I am sorry I did not tell you . . . I love you . . ."

I look around again, hoping to hear his voice. "Arthur? Arthur? Are you here. Forgive me. I wanted to show you . . ."

I lean back a little, the tears flowing, and look over at the ruined fort, my body tired and weak.

"I love you, Arthur . . . we are one soul . . . one spirit . . . please . . . come for me . . . ," I plead, looking at the sky. "I just want to be with you again."

"I'm ready . . . ," I whisper as a sense of calm comes over me. I know he is waiting for me. I feel him here. I feel his love. I am ready now. I want to go home.

I look to my calf and calmly take my dagger out from its harness. Breathing hard, I hold the dagger in front of me. With tears pouring from my eyes, I stare at the fort and smile.

"I am ready to be with you, Arthur, and to be your wife."

I thrust the dagger into my stomach and my body jerks. Staring forward, I put one hand down to brace myself and lie down, the other hand still holding the dagger as I die, happy at last to be free. My spirit floats higher and higher and I look down to see my body lying peacefully on the land that I so loved.

Epilogue

The Healing

WHEN I CAME OUT OF THE REGRESSION AND OPENED MY EYES, the world seemed altogether different and I knew my life would never be the same again. I stood and looked into the mirror and stared for a long while. I understood Guinevere now and began to love her. After all, she was a part of me.

My body was ill and I wept for days as the suppressed pain from Guinevere's life swept through me. I felt naked and vulnerable and unable to cope with anything around me. She was everywhere, and it felt good finally to feel her suffering and release it.

I began to write. It helped to purge the pain. It was quite amazing how the writing flowed, as though the words were crying out to be written. Although I had never written anything in my life, the words poured out of me with the greatest of ease. It was as though it was time for the truth to be told and Guinevere's spirit would not rest until the story was complete.

After two weeks of intense writing, I felt exhausted and relieved. I believed that my healing was complete. I was wrong.

As people read what I had written, they were mesmerized and excited about Guinevere's story. Suddenly I realized that this was only the beginning of something greater. Seeing how touched others were by Guinevere's life, I began to understand that it was part of my path in this life to teach people about Guinevere's struggle with her inner power. The central truth of Guinevere's life is that you must honor your inner self and your emotions. This will ultimately lead you to peace. If you are enchanted by outer, conquering power, it will only cause loneliness and frustration.

As I began to understand Guinevere more and more, my own healing began to unfold. At first, I felt a terrible heartache. I also began to feel a constant longing for love, something I had never felt I needed before. I was in a relationship but had never allowed myself to open fully to love. Through my whole life I had experienced only superficial short-term relationships with men, and yet now a burning desire for real love kept pushing at me.

Eventually, I decided I needed to go back to Salisbury in southern England to try to understand Guinevere's pain even more and, hopefully, heal my ache.

Home Again

On a clear and cold day I arrived in England and made my way southwest to Glastonbury with my friends Terence and Charlie. The ruins at Glastonbury are reputed to be the site of Arthur's grave. I was excited and a little nervous as we drove westward. Emotions began to stir in me again, but I did my best to hide them. I had few expectations. After all, Glastonbury was only rumored to be where Arthur's grave is, and I had by this time realized that most of the rumors about Guinevere and Arthur were untrue.

We made our way to the ruins of Glastonbury Abbey, which is a beautiful place, with ancient stone walls that give off an aura of sacredness and sadness. As we walked through the ruins, something changed in me. I felt a heaviness in my heart and a pulling, as though an invisible force was calling me to come outside of the abbey and onto the side lawns. My pulse began to race and I couldn't help myself. I had to answer.

I left Terence and Charlie and made my way out through the side door with Terence calling after me to come back—that the grave was the other way. As I looked out on the lawn, I saw a tiny plaque sticking out of the ground a ways in front of me. A wave of sadness filled me as I walked toward it. I knew inside, I don't know how, but I knew. This was it! This was where Guinevere was buried. I walked right up to it and froze. My body began to tremble as I stared at that tiny plaque, which stated that this had been the original grave of both Arthur and Guinevere.

I cannot easily explain what it feels like to stand on your own grave. Grief overwhelmed me and I began to sob and shake. Terence came up to me and held me for a moment, then allowed me some time to myself.

I stood there for a long while and wept for her, for lost love, for words that were never spoken. It felt terrible and wonderful at the same time.

I wanted so much to place a proper gravestone there, to honor her properly. It hurt terribly to see such a tiny plaque on a stick marking their graves. I vowed to my-self that I would make sure to honor her, that I would someday place a proper gravestone there.

As the day passed, we decided to drive south, to the reputed location of Cadbury Hill, thought to be the site of an ancient Dark Age fort. We drove closer and watched carefully on the map when I saw it in the distance. I knew it was the hill, and I told Terence and Charlie to go that way. I was right.

We climbed up the hill and a surge of joy swept through me. I raced around in circles and ran to the center, leaving Terence and Charlie behind. Home! I was home! A strange energy filled me, and I felt stronger than I ever had before. I wanted to stay for-ever. This was where I belonged! I wished that I could camp there and never leave. I wanted to rest and be alone with my feelings, and I walked and walked. As I stared into the sun, something wonderful happened. I felt as though Arthur's presence was there with me, and I kept receiving the same words over and over in my mind.

"You have not lost it. It is still here. I do not blame you. Look around."

I felt confused as I tried to understand the words. What did it mean? "You have not lost it. It is still here." I tried to think, and after a short while it all became clear.

I had until that point thought that to heal Guinevere, I needed to express my love to Arthur somehow, but that wasn't it at all. It was the land. Emotion surged in me again as understanding filled my mind. I had felt that I had lost Arthur's land, and somehow his spirit was trying to tell me now that I hadn't lost it. As I looked around, I realized he was right. It was still there.

I never lost it after all. No one lives there now. It will always be Arthur's land.

I sat on the ground as a sense of forgiveness filled my heart. He never blamed me, because I never let him down. The guilt that I had carried all this time was that I had let Arthur and my father down, but I hadn't.

I looked around me with joy and pressed my hands to the earth. It's still the same here as it was then. I closed my eyes and realized something else. I had been waiting, waiting all my life for forgiveness. So much so that I had never allowed myself to have a long-term relationship. I was waiting for Arthur, so he could forgive me.

I didn't have to wait any longer. I knew then that I could at last have a full and loving relationship. The ache was gone. I also felt so powerful inside. As I sat there and thought to myself, I began to understand that I had also never allowed myself to be truly powerful or creative. It was as though some part of me was afraid that I would again focus my power outwardly, as Guinevere had done, and fail everyone.

Through understanding Guinevere and the other previous lives that I have remembered, I have realized that my path in this life is to teach people, especially women, about inner power and also about reincarnation. We have so often been taught in our society to suppress our emotions, taught that they are not acceptable if we want to be taken seriously. I believe that in order to be true to ourselves, we must express our emotions freely. Only then can our creative power awaken and grow.

I learned from Guinevere a most valuable lesson: "Suppression creates separateness. Expression creates oneness."

I have also begun to teach people about the goddess

energy. I became fascinated with Merewyn's understanding of spirituality and her connection with the earth and feminine power and have since taught many goddess workshops to women who had forgotten their inner strengths and connection to the earth. By teaching others I have awakened my own feminine power of creativity and love.

I have a new appreciation of life and feel a deep and sincere longing to build some healing centers around the world that will help people through various types of healing techniques, including regression and workshops to awaken inner power.

I have also created a loving and wonderful marriage to an Irishman named Colm Weldon, whom I met just three months after my day on the hillside in southern England.